Assessing Through the Lens of Social and Emotional Learning

Dedication

Cynthia dedicates this work to all who have inspired her to pursue academic knowledge (dissertation committee members) and to the many colleagues who love making assessment work. She would also like to thank her mother and father, who have instilled in her an SEL mindset and a "can do" attitude, and her partner for always being her biggest cheerleader!

Dee dedicates this work to the MA SEL students who transform into SEL change agents. You are the future of SEL. And to her support team: Jim, Zekee, and Ric.

Assessing Through the Lens of Social and Emotional Learning

Tools and Strategies

Cynthia Sistek
Dee L. Fabry

Foreword by Nick Yoder

FOR INFORMATION:

Corwin
A Sage Company
2455 Teller Road
Thousand Oaks, California 91320
(800) 233-9936
www.corwin.com

Sage Publications Ltd.
1 Oliver's Yard
55 City Road
London EC1Y 1SP
United Kingdom

Sage Publications India Pvt. Ltd.
Unit No 323-333, Third Floor, F-Block
International Trade Tower Nehru Place
New Delhi 110 019
India

Sage Publications Asia-Pacific Pte. Ltd.
18 Cross Street #10-10/11/12
China Square Central
Singapore 048423

Vice President and Editorial Director:
Monica Eckman

Publisher: Jessica Allan

Content Development Editor:
Mia Rodriguez

Editorial Intern: Lex Nunez

Production Editor: Melanie Birdsall

Copy Editor: Heather Kerrigan

Typesetter: Exeter Premedia Services

Proofreader: Lawrence W. Baker

Cover Designer: Scott Van Atta

Marketing Manager: Olivia Bartlett

Copyright © 2024 by Corwin Press, Inc.

All rights reserved. Except as permitted by U.S. copyright law, no part of this work may be reproduced or distributed in any form or by any means, or stored in a database or retrieval system, without permission in writing from the publisher.

When forms and sample documents appearing in this work are intended for reproduction, they will be marked as such. Reproduction of their use is authorized for educational use by educators, local school sites, and/or noncommercial or nonprofit entities that have purchased the book.

All third-party trademarks referenced or depicted herein are included solely for the purpose of illustration and are the property of their respective owners. Reference to these trademarks in no way indicates any relationship with, or endorsement by, the trademark owner.

Wondering icons courtesy of iStock.com/Aleksandr Kharitonov, iStock.com/amtitus, iStock.com/rambo182. Chapter 10 divider artwork courtesy of iStock.com/EllenM

Printed in Canada

Library of Congress Cataloging-in-Publication Data

Names: Sistek, Cynthia, author. | Fabry, Dee L., author.
Title: Assessing through the lens of social and emotional learning : tools and strategies / Cynthia Sistek, Dee L. Fabry.
Description: Thousand Oaks, California : Corwin, [2024] | Includes bibliographical references and index.
Identifiers: LCCN 2023047101 (print) | LCCN 2023047102 (ebook) | ISBN 9781071907412 (paperback : acid-free paper) | ISBN 9781071907443 (ebook)
Subjects: LCSH: Affective education. | Educational tests and measurements. | Action research in education.
Classification: LCC LB1072 .S537 2024 (print) | LCC LB1072 (ebook) | DDC 370.15/34--dc23/eng/20231019
LC record available at https://lccn.loc.gov/2023047101
LC ebook record available at https://lccn.loc.gov/2023047102

This book is printed on acid-free paper.

24 25 26 27 28 10 9 8 7 6 5 4 3 2 1

DISCLAIMER: This book may direct you to access third-party content via web links, QR codes, or other scannable technologies, which are provided for your reference by the author(s). Corwin makes no guarantee that such third-party content will be available for your use and encourages you to review the terms and conditions of such third-party content. Corwin takes no responsibility and assumes no liability for your use of any third-party content, nor does Corwin approve, sponsor, endorse, verify, or certify such third-party content.

Contents

FOREWORD BY NICHOLAS YODER	xi
ABOUT THE AUTHORS	xv
ACKNOWLEDGMENTS	xvii
INTRODUCTION	1

1 ASSESSMENT THROUGH THE LENS OF SOCIAL AND EMOTIONAL LEARNING — 5

Why Apply SEL to Assessing Practices?	6
Social and Emotional Literacy Timeline	8
The Evolution of Social Emotional Learning	9
The Whole Child Emphasis: Historical and Contemporary SEL	11
Research Supporting Social Emotional Development	13
Responsive Teaching and Learning Through SE SEL Assessing	14

2 THE TEACHER ROLE AND THE STUDENT ROLE IN EVERYDAY SEL PRACTICE — 16

Setting the Stage—The Role of the Teacher in SEL Through Everyday Assessment	17
The Power of Effective Daily SEL Assessment	18
Shifting Your Mindset	18
What Is "Assessment" and What Are the Traits of an Assessment Literate Person?	19
How Do I Know What the SEL Learning Competencies Are?	20
The Role of the Student in Integrating SEL Through Everyday Assessment	21
Setting the Stage—The Role of the Student in SEL Through Everyday Assessment	22
Dream or Reality?	23

3 DEVELOPING A CULTURE OF SEL ASSESSMENT — 26

Your Role—Knowing What You Know and What You Need to Learn	27
Students at the Center	29

What Exactly Does SEL Assessing Look Like?	32
"Doing" SE SEL Assessing	33
Cultivating a Culture of SE SEL Assessing	36

4 ASSESSING AND ASSESSMENTS FOR RACIAL AND CULTURAL RELEVANCE 38

Co-Authored With L. Erika Saito

All Means All	39
Racism in Assessment: A Brief History	40
Measurement by Group	41
Examining Race in Grading Practices	41
Examining Language Bias in Providing Student Feedback	42
Gender Equity in Assessment	43
Shifting Toward Inclusive Grading	44
Culturally Sustaining Social and Emotional Assessment Practices	44
Centering Growth and Mastery	46
Teacher Education and Instructional Practice	49
Best Practices: Strategies for Assessing Without Bias	50
New Grading Mindset	52
Equity in Data Collection and Analysis: The Bigger Picture	52
The Issue With Current Racist Assessment Practices	53
Validity in Teacher-Developed Assessments	56
Looking Ahead	58

5 ASSESSMENT PEDAGOGY AND DESIGN 60

Universal Design for Learning and Social and Emotional Learning	61
Differentiation of SEL Tools: Diversity and Learner Variability	63
Differentiated Assessments for Inclusion: National Center on Educational Outcomes	63
The Case for Formative Assessment	64
Resources for Checking for Understanding (CFU)	65
Assessment Tools That Support SEL Skills and Competencies	69

6 ASSESSMENT TOOLS AND STRATEGIES 70

Begin With Learner Identity	70
Math Anxiety	71
Flexible and Growth Mindset Applied Toward Learning	72

Goal Setting as a Planning and Assessing Strategy	77
Check-Ins as an Assessment Strategy	79
Emotional Check-Ins and Emotional Labeling	79
Entry Tickets and Exit Tickets	82
"I" Statements and Self-Efficacy	84
Sentence Frames	85
Writing Frames	86
Close/Cloze	87
Student Self-Assessment	88
Student Self-Reflection	90
Journaling	90
Emotional Self-Assessment = Compassion	92
Putting Student Assessing Into Practice	93
Final Thoughts	94

7 ASSESSMENT, ASSESSING STRATEGIES, AND DIGITAL TOOLS — 96

Machine Learning vs. Human Learning	97
Assessment and Accountability Systems	98
Types of Assessments in the Digital Age	99
Rubrics and Rubric Creation: Learner-Centered Assessing Through Rubrics and Rubric Creation	103
A Look at Simulations	104
Intelligent Tutoring Systems	108
Emerging/Emergent Assessing Practices	108
Culturally Responsive Assessing	109

8 PRACTITIONER REFLECTION — 111

Teacher Inquiry	112
Teacher Self-Assessment	113
Developing a Practitioner Reflective Practice	114
Teacher Action Research—Connecting Reflection to Action	116
The Power of Peer Review for Assessing Practice	120
The SEL Self-Assessment	121
Extending Your Practice to Include Peer Observations as Teacher Assessment	123

9 DEVELOPING A PRACTICAL SEL ASSESSMENT PLAN THAT SUPPORTS TEACHING AND LEARNING 125

Developing an SEL Assessment Plan	126
A Note on the Progression of SEL	130
One Way to Consider Assessing SEL Competencies: A Learning Progressions Model	130
Unpacking the Learning Progressions Model	133
Student Efficacy in Assessing	137
Create Your Own Assessment Plan	137

10 EVIDENCE-BASED SEL ASSESSMENT 141

Assessment Tools, SEL, and Development	142
Case Studies in Action Research in TK Through Grade 12 Classrooms	142
Assessing SEL Through Action Research in Early Childhood Education	144
Transitioning From Preschool, Daycare, or Home to Kindergarten in the United States	148
Elementary Education Tools and Assessments	150
Summary of Action Research Strategies, SEL Skills, and Competencies Assessed	155
Teacher Assessment and Teacher Effectiveness	156

11 SEL INTERSECTIONS: CONNECTING TO CONTENT, CURRICULUM, STANDARDS, AND FRAMEWORKS 161

What Is a Framework?	162
Frameworks Are Developmental	163
Frameworks All Around Us	163
Common Core State Standards	164
Content Standards and Frameworks	164
Unpacking the History–Social Science Framework	165
Examining the SEL Intersections in Next Generation Science Standards	171
Health, Wellness, and Physical Education Curriculum + SEL	173
Health and Wellness: Connections to SEL and Academics	174
Positive Behavior Interventions and Supports + SEL	175
Coalition to Advance Future Student Success (CAFS Framework)	175

Behavioral, Emotional, and Social Skills Inventory (BESSI)	176
Career Technical Education	176
Exploring the Interconnectedness of Frameworks With EASEL	178
Where Is SEL in the Educational Workplace?	179
Assessment of Professional Ethics for Teaching: The Interstate Teacher Assessment and Support Consortium	180
National Education Association Code of Ethics + SEL	182
SEL Outside of the Educational Workplace	182
Assessing SEL	184
How to Get Started	184
APPENDIX: RESOURCES, TOOLS, TEMPLATES, AND ANCILLARIES	187
GLOSSARY OF TERMS	225
REFERENCES AND FURTHER READINGS	229
INDEX	245

Visit the companion website at
https://resources.corwin.com/AssessingThroughtheLensofSEL
for downloadable resources.

Note From the Publisher: The authors have provided video and web content throughout the book that is available to you through QR (quick response) codes. To read a QR code, you must have a smartphone or tablet with a camera. We recommend that you download a QR code reader app that is made specifically for your phone or tablet brand.

Foreword

Having taught when school closures were commonplace in one of the largest districts in the country made it clear to me the importance of centering relationships and attuning to my students' emotions. Each year, a nearby school closed and its community would join our school community. My "new" first-grade students would come to school on their first day frustrated, anxious, and unsure of who they would know. There was also a level of uncertainty with the students who had been part of our school community, wondering whether our school would be next. Our school was also in the process of becoming the first International Baccalaureate Primary Years Programme in the city. This was a lot to handle for first-grade students (and their teacher), making it incredibly important to pay close attention to their relationships and how they were feeling and processing those emotions so that all students could excel—socially, emotionally, and academically in my classroom.

These years transformed the way that I view teaching and learning and led me to the field of social and emotional learning (SEL). Most of my own research, professional learning, coaching, and tool development has focused on strategies to embed SEL within common teaching practices, for instance, the ten educator practices that promote social, emotional, and academic development (Yoder, 2021). In my work on SEL, I have also thought a lot about SEL assessment—putting on both my researcher and practitioner hats to determine what SEL assessment means for teachers, students, and leaders. The first set of questions to ask is, "How do we define SEL assessment—the SEL practices educators and schools implement and/or the social and emotional competence outcomes we are hoping to see as a result of implementing high-quality, evidence-based SEL programs and practices? How do we plan to use the assessment results? Are we ready to use SEL assessments?" To support educators and researchers in answering these questions, my colleagues at the American Institutes for Research developed a tool, *Ready to Assess* (AIR, 2019), to think about the conditions needed for researchers, practitioners, and policymakers to consider prior to using student social and emotional competency assessment.

When Cynthia Sistek and Dee L. Fabry approached me about writing the foreword for their book, *Assessing Through the Lens of Social and Emotional Learning*, I was excited to hear about this practitioner-friendly resource and that they were the ones writing it. Their insights provide a timely exploration of how SEL can transform an educator's approach to assessment. Cynthia and Dee invite us to embrace new perspectives on assessment, reframing our use of assessments to nurture the knowledge, skills, and mindsets we want to see for students as we prepare them to thrive in an interconnected and dynamic world. As you engage with this book, you will infuse principles from both SEL and formative assessment to better thread together the intellectual, emotional, and social fabric of teaching and learning.

I met Cynthia several years ago when we worked together at National University, with her focus on preservice and in-service educators, and mine on developing an SEL program—Harmony—to use in pre-K to Grade 6 classrooms. I was immediately impressed with Cynthia's dedication to her students, particularly since she was overseeing the first master's degree in SEL in the United States. Bringing in her expertise in curriculum, instruction, and virtual learning, she knew how to support educators to rethink the teaching and learning experiences they offer their students and help extend ways to use practices in support of student social and emotional development. Although I do not know Dee as well as Cynthia, I have been impressed with her depth and breadth of assessment experience and expertise—including her formative assessing systems and implementing feedback and feed forward for her own struggling seventh-grade students in Colorado, along with her decades in higher education with program annual reviews, accreditation processes, and service as the associate provost at National University. In 2015, Dee was appointed to the Northwest Education Association National Assessment (NWEA) Task Force where she served with Dr. Rick Stiggins for three years. Dee is a strong advocate for assessing student learning as a process of growth.

Cynthia and Dee are a perfect pair to help transform our thinking about how to assess through a lens of SEL and assess the "SEL Way." Through this approach, the primary goal is to uplift the social and emotional assets that students bring with them to their schools and classrooms as a foundational and critical element of academic achievement. When thinking about assessing the SEL Way, they help us recognize the multiple places that students use their social and emotional skills, encourage us to think of SEL and assessment as a path toward continued reflection and growth, and identify strategies to use SEL assessment as a way to build relationships with students. The SEL Way of assessment also helps teachers reflect on their own practice and the way that social and emotional skills show up in everyday interactions and instructional practices used in the classroom, inclusive of their engagement in formative assessments.

The pages that follow provide us with critical questions that must guide our use of SEL assessment and have us reflect on our own assumptions about what SEL means for ourselves and for our students. They specifically ask us to reflect on some critical questions, including:

- How do we take into account the contextual nature of social and emotional development? Specifically, how do we assess SEL when all individuals, including students, may use their social and emotional skills differently depending on who they are with, the activities or tasks they are engaged in, and the types of support they receive?

- How do we ensure that SEL assessment is reflective of the student and family cultures and backgrounds that we serve? How do we be mindful of any potential unintended consequences of using SEL assessment?

- How do we take into account the nonlinear nature of social and emotional development, in which we learn, relearn, and enhance our social and emotional competencies based on our culture, context, and practices (instructional and formative) we engage in?

- How do we ensure that SEL assessment is strengths-based and uplifts the personal and cultural assets that students can use across multiple domains of life (e.g., academics, career, and civic and community engagement)?

- How does SEL assessment fit within larger data efforts, particularly, how do they align with universal and targeted screeners for mental health supports?

The authors further guide us in reflecting on how to infuse the principles of SEL and formative assessment by providing us with rich content to explore, reflection questions that guide our thinking, practical insights, real-world examples, and innovative field-tested activities that we can readily implement. They offer formative assessment strategies that help students become more self-aware and connected, while also identifying assessment strategies that promote resilience and create inclusive spaces for all students. In other words, the authors help us conceptualize how formative assessments can nurture student social and emotional growth.

As you engage with the learning throughout the book, make sure to take time to think about your own social and emotional competencies and how you leverage them as you nurture your students' emotional and social experiences within the classroom. Bring your inquisitive spirit and be ready to identify steps you already take in understanding your student social and emotional learning and how you can be more intentional in empowering students, nurturing whole child development, celebrating student uniqueness, and setting students up to have the knowledge, skills, and mindsets that enable them to thrive now and into the future.

—**Nick Yoder**
Researcher, Author, Educator
Associate Vice President, Center on Whole Human Education and Research with Harmony Academy at National University
Former Principal Policy and Technical Assistance Consultant in the Youth, Family, and Community Development Program at the American Institutes of Research (AIR)
Former Director of Policy and Practice for the Collaborative for Academic, Social and Emotional Learning (CASEL)

About the Authors

Cynthia Sistek, EdD, (Dr. C) is a professor in the Sanford College of Education at National University in La Jolla, California. Currently, she serves as the academic program director for the Master of Arts in Social and Emotional Learning degree program. In 2020, Cynthia co-developed MA SEL. In addition, she designed and edited the ten playbooks in social and emotional learning (https://selplaybook.org). For the 2022–2023 year, she served as the chair of the SEL Special Interest Group for the American Education Research Association.

Cynthia is a recognized leader in educational technology, who in 2020 was awarded EdTech Digest's Higher Education Technology Leader of the Year. In 2019, she earned both the prestigious ISTE and CUE Award for *Making IT Happen* and a Gold and Platinum Disk from CUE for her lifetime achievements and service to the educational technology community.

Cynthia is a pioneer in online learning, having designed and taught online courses since 1999. Her ongoing research focuses on the efficacy of online learning in higher education, the intersections of SEL in online environments, and how synchronous methods of online communication enhance teaching and learning. Her book, *Exploring Online Learning Through Synchronous and Asynchronous Methods*, was published by IGI Global in April 2020 and showcased many studies and practices that support online learning.

Dee L. Fabry, PhD, is professor emeritus in the Sanford College of Education at National University in La Jolla, California. She serves as adjunct faculty for the Master of Arts in Social and Emotional Learning degree program, teaching graduate level research courses and assessing for learning to impact both teaching and learning.

Dee served National University as the associate provost, Academic Assessment Committee chair, Sanford College of Education coordinator of assessment services, department chair, and teacher education and program lead for the Master of Science in Advanced Teaching Practices degree program.

Dee previously served as vice president at Plato Learning, where she led the test development department, and she was also the project manager for Kaplan Learning in creating criterion-referenced tests. Dee was appointed to the National Assessment in Education Task Force where she contributed regularly to the blogs on effective formative assessment.

Her most recent publication is *Clarifying Learning Targets in Assessment Education: Bridging Research, Theory, and Practice to Promote Equity and Student Learning* (with M. L. Peterson, Rowman & Littlefield, 2020).

ABOUT THE CONTRIBUTOR

L. Erika Saito, PhD, is the director of strategic partnerships, P–12 education at UMass Global. She previously served as the director of curriculum and instruction at Teach Us, Versidi Inc., as assistant professor and academic program director of the Master of Education in Inspired Teaching and Learning (Single-Subject) degree program, and as a course lead in social and emotional learning at National University. She is a California credentialed teacher with more than fifteen years in K–12 public and private schools. Erika is actively involved in the educational community, serving on school site councils for both an elementary and middle school, and working with local and international organizations in training and supporting classroom teachers in how to teach social and emotional learning with English learners and, separately, Asian American studies in K–12.

Acknowledgments

PUBLISHER'S ACKNOWLEDGMENTS

Corwin gratefully acknowledges the contributions of the following reviewers:

Darilyn Gorton
ELA/Business/Middle School Teacher
Warwick Public Schools
Warwick, Rhode Island

Louis Lim
Principal
Bur Oak Secondary School
Markham, Ontario, Canada

Neil MacNeill, PhD, EdD
Author, Educational Analyst
Perth, Australia

Tanna Nicely
Executive Principal
South Knoxville Elementary/Knox County Schools
Knoxville, Tennessee

Derek Peil
Teacher
Fremont County School District #1
Lander, Wyoming

Jay Posick
Retired Principal
Merton Intermediate School
Merton, Wisconsin

Terri Serey
Teacher
Hacienda La Puente Unified School District
City of Industry, California

Patricia Long Tucker
Retired Regional Superintendent
District of Columbia Public Schools
Washington, DC

Crystal Wash
Researcher
Consortium for Educational Research and Advancement
Chicago, Illinois

Introduction

The authors of this book are both educators and researchers in a large college of education at a private, nonprofit institution. Our book's focus stems from our work as and with practitioners. What are we seeing? Wrong question. What are we *not* seeing? We are not seeing content that aligns to the needs of classroom teachers and their students. We see SEL being taught for twenty minutes a day in a morning meeting and then not included for the rest of the school day. We see thousands upon thousands of dollars being spent on SEL programs without adequate professional development or classroom/schoolwide implementation. We want to see SEL every minute, every day, everywhere, and ongoing.

Our passion for assessment does not come from working at an assessment company or as a psychometrician, although we have both run statistical data in our careers. While we love data, we primarily love qualitative data that tells a story; the numbers help show relevance. We have been drawn to using rubrics for our work in higher ed. As former practitioners in elementary, middle, and high school, we have embraced other forms of assessment, other than standards-based, norm-referenced, bubble tests (no offense Scantrons). As a writing project fellow (of an affiliate of the National Writing Project), Cynthia discovered the power of writing as a means of expression and art, and as an award-winning educator in the field of technology, she has taught others how to integrate technology tools to facilitate learning and to support knowledge building through constructing podcasts, videos, and multimedia presentations.

In our thirty-five-plus years of being in education, we have seen thousands of commercially created assessments. In our master of arts in SEL program, our students analyze a variety of assessment assignments, which are focused on *assessment for accountability*. The self-reports, observational checklists, and teacher, student, and parent surveys are all created for the purpose of *collecting data* for accountability. While that information is needed by a specific audience, practitioners tell us that what they need are student-empowered SEL formative assessments. When the student is at the center of the learning and at the center of the assessing, this provides a true SEL experience.

WHAT DOES THIS MEAN FOR THE CLASSROOM TEACHER AND STUDENTS?

So, why should you care? Why do we care? As the research on the effect of SEL deepens, there are many resources developed for assessing SEL programs, skills, and competencies. However, the literature is notably absent on assessment practices themselves that support learners with practices aligned *with* social and emotional learning. Assessment needs to be owned by the students as a developmental aspect of the process of learning progressions.

While data collected for accountability may be needed at the school, district, or state level, practitioners tell us that what they need are the "whys" and "hows" in using SEL formative assessment for daily and weekly information to impact student SEL knowledge and skill acquisition.

This book blends assessment strategies commonly used in any classroom worldwide and contextualizes these tools and practices through the lens of SEL. We have compiled these assessing/assessment strategies, which are primarily formative assessment tools, some paper-based, some templates (from our companion website), and some have harnessed the power of digital tools to construct your own formative assessments. We have also included other forms of assessment, alternative assessments, authentic assessment, and portfolio-based assessment. Our master's level adult learners have been using ePortfolio for the past few decades to demonstrate competency and knowledge in various forms. They have come to understand that portfolios lead to self-assessment and reflection in their personal and professional growth—a highly effective SEL assessment tool.

You will find that you are already using some of these strategies, and through these chapters, you will learn why these tools work for assessing learning and how using the tools elicits an SEL skill or disposition. We sprinkle in solid research to justify why we need to be using formative assessment in all classrooms with all learners. Some focus on writing through reflection, others are performance-based checklists, and others are traditional quizzes and tests implemented in untraditional ways; we recommend ungraded *tests* for mastery. Applying everyday assessment strategies to measure improvement and learning is our primary objective.

Our goals for this book include learning how to think about assessing the "SEL Way," how to use SEL assessing to provide feed-up, feedback, and feed forward to increase SEL competencies, and how to use SEL assessing *for* student learning to inform more effective SEL teaching. And that's a lot of SEL! By assessing through the lens of SEL, we have embedded intentional SEL that appeals to everyone.

As educators, we have embedded SEL into our practice, honoring the brilliance of all learners. SEL assessing will make learners feel more self-aware, more self-managed, more socially aware, and create learners who make intentional decisions as individuals and other times to build relationships with others.

The world organization for the promotion of SEL, Karanga, sums up our belief in SEL:

> In a complex, fast-moving world, it is imperative that we equip all learners for new challenges and opportunities. Evidence shows multiple long-term benefits from embedding Social and Emotional Learning (SEL) opportunities in education in both formal and non-formal contexts. SEL can contribute to more inclusive, dynamic and productive schools, communities and workplaces, and can in the long term save governments money and accelerate productivity. (Salzburg Global Seminar, 2018, p. 1)

And by the way, Karanga also says, "SEL is *life skills*." We should not politicize SEL. Social and emotional teaching and learning is a human right.

CHAPTER 1

Assessment Through the Lens of Social and Emotional Learning

. . . powerful road blocks to learning can arise from the very process of assessing and evaluating the performance of the learner, depending on how the learner interprets what is happening to him or her.

—Rick Stiggins (2014)

LEARNING OUTCOMES

Colleagues on the assessing journey will be able to

- Provide a brief overview of social and emotional learning (SEL)
- Examine how assessment practices are connected to SEL
- Understand that assessing practices measure learning
- Identify how SEL assessing is possible through daily practice
- Discover how SEL assessing is a relationship builder

Welcome, colleagues. We hope you are intrigued by the title of this book and this chapter, and are wondering what this is all about. Perhaps you are asking yourself, "Why 'assessing' and not 'assessment of'?" Maybe you are saying,

"How can the practice of assessing be done through a social emotional learning (SEL) lens? Don't we already have enough testing in our schools?" Or, it could be that you are wondering, "What do they mean by *this* version of assessing?"

WHY APPLY SEL TO ASSESSING PRACTICES?

First, we are happy that you are curious about how assessing can be applied through the lens of SEL. The need for SEL in schools and communities has never been greater. Students, teachers, parents, and our communities have been impacted by the global COVID-19 pandemic, social justice events in the United States such as Black Lives Matter and #MeToo, and other sociopolitical movements around the globe, including Russia's invasion of Ukraine. As a society, we are experiencing many emotional reactions, including confusion, frustration, exhaustion, and, above all, the loss of socialization, emotional disconnection, and isolation. However, the news is not all glum. These challenges are helping us to question long-held assumptions about our learners and learning. Some of us are reflecting and resetting priorities. We are feeling the need for more meaningful and deeper social connections—to be more compassionate, empathetic, kind, and humanistic.

The ever-increasing movement toward more purposeful inclusion of social emotional learning in our schools is a beacon of hope and inspiration. And, if you are involved in this positive movement forward, we are here to support you. This book is about you and your students. It is about making those deeper connections to self and others. It's about making assessment of learning more attainable, more formative than summative, more student-centered, and more in line with SEL skills and competencies. We want to humanize the assessing process to counteract the four-letter word T-E-S-T.

Our foundational principle is that **all** teaching and learning intersect with social emotional learning.

All teaching and learning intersect with social emotional learning.

In their book *All Learning Is Social and Emotional Learning* (2019), Frey and colleagues state, "We are teaching SEL even if we don't think we are doing so" (p. 3). Learning is emotional. Listen to the giggles of children reading *The Cat in the Hat*. Watch the brightened faces of young people as they suddenly "get" a concept. Learning is, indeed, emotional. The process of assessing is emotional and often associated with fear, anxiety, and failure. These feelings are the antithesis of attaining positive SEL.

Social and emotional learning is everywhere; it is in everything we do, in the way we deliver instruction, and the numerous ways we assess student learning. Social and emotional learning is inextricably intertwined with daily classroom and instructional practices. When we teach with SEL we involve students in the assessment process and practices. The chapter's opening quote from Dr. Rick Stiggins reminds us that we need to carefully provide feedback to our students about their social and emotional competencies so it will influence their acquisition of the knowledge, skills, and dispositions that are integral to their academic and life success. Assessment practices through the lens of SEL continuously support learning.

SEL assessing, therefore, needs to be in alignment with the intention of SEL competencies. Social and emotional learning assessing is about gently guiding each student toward deeper levels of self-awareness, social awareness, self-regulation and self-management, relationship building, and decision-making. SEL assessing is *not* about testing. SEL assessing is *not* about using commercially prepared materials that are not aligned to the SEL needs of the students in your classroom. SEL assessing is *not* about using data in any punitive or harmful manner. SEL assessing is about honoring and respecting the voice and mind of each child to support their journey toward reaching their fullest potential.

To do this we need to consider a different model of assessing. If we only continue to use the same long-standing mindset about assessing to understand student academic progress, we will undermine the intention of SEL. We do not simply use an end-of-unit summative quiz or a one-time test to determine progress toward SEL growth, but rather we provide meaningful ongoing "feedback" and "feed forward" aligned to the SEL competencies *with* the learner's complete engagement in the process. Assessing is not something done *to* the learner to get data. Assessing is a partnership—a relationship builder that provides essential information for growth.

To move toward a new model for SEL assessing, we need to consider what we understand about SEL and know about assessing, where we have been, and how we got to where we are now. The following brief history of SEL, along with a cursory look at SEL research, provide the context for this timely guide that explains why it is essential to conduct formative assessment *with* students and how to better create assessing practices that promote SEL skill acquisition. The end goal is to ensure the acquisition of SEL competencies and skills for student growth and to create a student SEL learning environment *with* the learners that honors and respects their voices.

SOCIAL AND EMOTIONAL LITERACY TIMELINE

375 BCE	Plato's *The Republic*, Greek philosophy, and social justice
BCE–17th Century	Ancient civilizations and founding of religious principles
1800	Character Education Movement and moral development (Europe)
1830	Horace Mann nineteenth-century champion of common schools (advocate for moral education)
1844	YMCA: Young Men's Christian Association (England)
1852	YMCA: Young Men's Christian Association (USA)
1906	Marie Montessori, Casa dei Bambini, scientific developmental pedagogy, teachers, young children, and doctors
1910	Boy Scouts of America (BSA)
1912	Girl Scouts of America (GSA)
1920–1930s	Lev Vygotsky (sociocultural theory)
1968	James Comer School Development Program (educating low-income children)
1970s	Claude Steiner and Paul Perry, emotional literacy, emotional interactivity
1989	Stephen R. Covey's *The 7 Habits of Highly Effective People*, SEL, and leadership
1990	Emotional intelligence (EQ), Yale University, Peter Salovey and John D. Mayer
1996	Daniel Goleman's four characteristics of emotional intelligence

THE EVOLUTION OF SOCIAL EMOTIONAL LEARNING

As educators, it is important to recognize how the field of SEL has evolved and how social and emotional skills and competencies are embedded in everything we do. Social and emotional learning is experiencing a resurgence in the US educational system and is now considered essential knowledge for fostering student success both in school and in life. While it may have a new name, SEL is not new. Social and emotional tenets were included in Plato's *The Republic* (375 BCE), where he described an integrated curriculum that included mathematics, languages, science, character development, and moral judgment. Interesting that as early as the 1800s, a parallel approach to social and emotional learning, the Character Education Movement, was founded for children as a way of living and behaving. Aligning with religious practices, morality, ethics, and civility, the movement began in Europe and was later recognized in the United States. In more contemporary settings, character education has been applied in both formal and informal learning. Organizations such as the Young Men's Christian Association (YMCA), Boy Scouts of America, and Girl Scouts of America integrated the principles of character education in their practices.

In 1830, Horace Mann, the father of the Common Schools Movement, advocated for universal education for all children, a concept quite radical for the time. In 1897, Howard Crummel called for the "cultivation of genius" (defined as the brilliance, intellect, ability, cleverness, and artistry of the mind and heart), which is vital to the success of all children. Some ten years later, in Italy, Maria Montessori founded schools that had a child-centered approach. The focus was and is on developing the whole child cognitively, socially, emotionally, and physically. Then as many of us know, John Dewey (1916/1966), noted as the father of public education, introduced the idea of "social responsibility," which included improving the quality of life for workers and their families. Did you know that Vygotsky's sociocultural theory is also grounded in SEL? Vygotsky (1978) argued that social interaction comes before cognition.

Did you know that Vygotsky's sociocultural theory is also grounded in SEL? Vygotsky (1978) argued that social interaction comes before cognition.

Another historical marker in the SEL evolution was the focus on emotional literacy. In the 1970s, the term *emotional literacy* (EL) was coined by clinical psychologist Claude Steiner, who defined EL as "the ability to understand your emotions, feelings, the ability to listen to others and empathize with their emotions, and the ability to express emotions productively" (Steiner

& Perry, 1997, p. 11). Steiner's framework also addressed the facilitation of relationships, including using dialogue and self-control to avoid negative arguments. The ability to be aware of and to read other people's feelings enables one to interact with them effectively, so that powerful emotional situations can be handled in a skillful way. Steiner calls this "emotional interactivity" (Tudor, 2020).

In 1990, two psychology professors at Yale, Peter Salovey and John D. Mayer, coined the term *emotional intelligence* (EQ), describing it as the ability to "assimilate emotion in thought, understand and reason with emotion, and regulate emotion in the self and others" (Mayer et al., 2002, p. 396; Salovey & Mayer, 1990). They also describe EQ as a form of social intelligence that involves the ability to perceive and express emotion, the ability to monitor one's own and others' feelings and emotions, to discriminate among them, and to use this information to guide one's thinking and actions.

Later that year, Daniel Goleman, a researcher specializing in the brain and its impact on behavior, worked with David McClelland from Harvard University and a group of other researchers who were studying cognitive intelligence. Goleman (1996) argued that in a business context, it was "not cognitive intelligence that guaranteed business success but emotional intelligence" (p. 23). Goleman described emotionally intelligent people as possessing four characteristics:

1. They are good at understanding their own emotions (self-awareness).
2. They are good at managing their emotions (self-management).
3. They are empathetic to the emotional drives of other people (social awareness).
4. They are good at handling other people's emotions (social skills). (Goleman, 1996, p. 23)

In our opinion, emotional intelligence implies cognitive abilities as opposed to SEL competencies. In fact, EQ as well as intelligence quotient (IQ) tests fail to address the whole child, their potential, and human capacity for learning. Instead of EQ, we prefer Steiner's term, *emotional literacy*, and apply the steps of EL to the process of assessing.

In 1994, the Collaborative for Academic, Social, and Emotional Learning (CASEL) was formed to focus on social emotional learning research initiatives (see Figure 1.1). This agency looked at how SEL impacts academic and personal success. Fast forward more than thirty years, and CASEL, together with the Aspen Institute and other agencies, have standardized the field of SEL into five competencies (see Appendix 1.)

FIGURE 1.1 • CASEL Framework

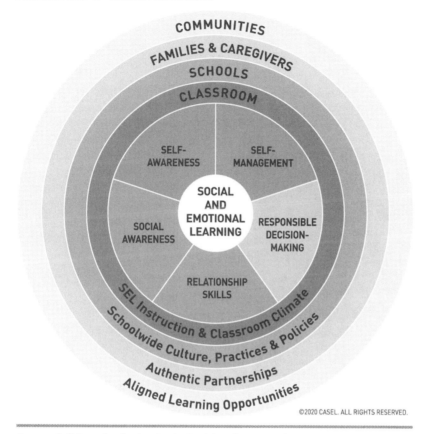

bit.ly/3NOaLDm

Source: Collaborative for Academic, Social, and Emotional Learning (CASEL). Reprinted with permission.

To read a QR code, you must have a smartphone or tablet with a camera. We recommend that you download a QR code reader app that is made specifically for your phone or tablet brand.

Over the decades, SEL has had many names such as "character education" and "values education." It was often viewed as an add-on and a soft skills curriculum—meaning it wasn't really important to academic development. That is changing. Research results show an undeniable connection between social emotional competencies and academic success (Durlak et al., 2011; Hawkins et al., 2004). For another reference to the history of SEL, a QR code is provided.

THE WHOLE CHILD EMPHASIS: HISTORICAL AND CONTEMPORARY SEL

The School Development Program, led by Yale researcher James Comer, focused on educating the "whole child." At the time, this was a new approach that relied on a system that deeply embedded social skills and social services and addressed the entire school community, including students, teachers, staff, and parents.

FIGURE 1.2 • Whole School, Whole Community, Whole Child Framework

Source: Centers for Disease Control and Prevention.

bit.ly/3K3UBVA

Educating the whole child focused on an integrated approach of academics and social emotional learning (Comer, 1980). According to Beaty (2018), the School Development Program in New Haven Schools continued as the "hub of SEL research from 1987–1992" (p. 68). Today, the emphasis on the whole child is included in the Whole School, Whole Community, Whole Child (WSCC) framework, an all-encompassing approach developed by the Centers for Disease Control and Prevention (CDC) to meet educational needs, public health needs, and school health. The WSCC is a collaboration between education leaders and health sectors to improve each child's cognitive, physical, social, and emotional development. What is unique about the WSCC model—and why we include it as an important framework—is that it is student-centered and also recognizes the connections between health and academic achievement, and the importance of evidence-based school policies and practices (see QR code and Figure 1.2).

The WSCC model has ten components:

1. Physical education and physical activity
2. Nutrition environment and services
3. Health education
4. Social and emotional climate
5. Physical environment
6. Health services
7. Counseling, psychological, and social services
8. Employee wellness
9. Community involvement
10. Family engagement

A QR code is provided for a virtual tour of a healthy school (interactive).

bit.ly/3OfULvw

RESEARCH SUPPORTING SOCIAL EMOTIONAL DEVELOPMENT

As the exigency for social emotional learning continues to grow, the research supporting its integration validates this need. CASEL is at the forefront in making evidence-based research available to support SEL in schools and beyond. Among its many initiatives, CASEL is reexamining the definition of SEL, which is critical to effective policymaking and classroom implementation. CASEL works with practitioners, researchers, and policymakers to deepen our knowledge base about SEL and what works for educators and students.

The research is clear. Dr. Kirabo Jackson and his colleagues studied more than 150,000 ninth-grade students who attended Chicago Public Schools between 2011 and 2017 and found the schools that scored high on metrics of social well-being and work habits were also the most effective at supporting long-term student success. Participants in the schools where social emotional learning was integrated into the school learning environment had fewer absences, more graduations, and higher college acceptance rates. Jackson's work was further explored by Terada (2021) in his essay on what constitutes a "good" school:

> Although all students benefit from attending high-performing schools, it's the schools that provide a well-rounded education that drove the differences that Jackson and his colleagues observed. They discovered

that a school's impact on the noncognitive dimensions of learning—healthy relationships and a growth mindset, for example—were much more predictive of long-term success than a school's impact on test scores. (p. 2)

RESPONSIVE TEACHING AND LEARNING THROUGH SE SEL ASSESSING

So, why do we care? Why should you care? As more and more states, districts, and schools include social emotional learning in their programs, SEL-focused curricula appear most often as a separate subject and not a daily practice. Many resources created for the commercial market have been developed to provide a standardized SEL curriculum paired with standardized testing tools. However, assessing practices that support learners with needs-based strategies aligned to social and emotional learning competencies are notably absent from these programs. For SEL assessing to be responsive to the needs of a classroom, SEL must be owned by the students as a developmental aspect of the process of learning progressions.

We use the term *SE SEL*, which is *student empowered social and emotional learning*. According to Brown and colleagues (2022), "Traditional approaches to social-emotional learning (SEL) often use standardized curricular materials to promote the development of personal and relational competencies and skills that students are assumed to lack. Such SEL curricula tend to be teacher-centered and, in some cases, even used as behavioral management or disciplinary tools. SE SEL, in contrast, encompasses practices that affirm what students bring to the classroom by encouraging students to identify and choose activities they love or value, to experience what it feels like to positively engage with and positively influence others, and in many cases, to share their expertise with classmates and teachers. These practices offer students a too-infrequent sense of control over their learning, connectedness to others, and sense that they matter in their school environment."

Our goals for you include learning how to think about assessing as a relationship building tool, how to use SEL assessing to provide effective, encouraging feedback as a process to increase SEL competencies, and how to use SEL assessing to inform more effective student-empowered SEL teaching.

Practitioner "Wondering" Reflection

Time to Start Your SEL Reflection Journal

Select a hard copy journal or create a digital journal with your wonderings. Be sure to include a date in your wonderings and wonder more than once!

As you read about SEL and assessing, what are your impressions of the intersections? What concepts or ideas strongly resonated with you? What did you immediately want to change in your thinking and in your practice? What do you want to know more about?

Takeaway to Practice

What is the one takeaway from this chapter you want to put into action? **Name it. Create your action plan.**

CHAPTER 2

The Teacher Role and the Student Role in Everyday SEL Practice

The most valuable metrics we can use to understand a student's academic progress will always remain the ones that are collected by educators and schools on a regular basis in the classrooms—even virtual ones—where individual relationships with students are fostered and strategies for support can be designed in real-time.

—Tony Thurmond, California State Superintendent of Schools (2021)

LEARNING OUTCOMES

Colleagues on the assessing journey will be able to

- Identify and explain the teacher's role in assessing SEL competencies
- Understand that they already "do" SEL assessing everyday
- Describe the feedback/feed forward assessment process
- Implement ongoing effective feedback/feed forward to set clear learning outcomes, provide ongoing information about learning progress, and support SEL growth
- Explain the student's role in increasing SEL dispositions, knowledge, and performance

SETTING THE STAGE—THE ROLE OF THE TEACHER IN SEL THROUGH EVERYDAY ASSESSMENT

Social emotional learning is about *the learner.* Assessment of SEL skills is a daily and ongoing process. Gathering data to provide feedback about SEL growth is intended to be used *for* helping students acquire SEL knowledge, skills, and competencies. It is not about collecting data for reporting, grading, or compliance. It is not about testing. That is why the role of the teacher is critical in creating an effective student-focused SEL learning environment.

What dispositions, knowledge, and performance skills are needed for a teacher to successfully integrate SEL through everyday assessment? Let's explore each of those areas.

DISPOSITIONS

Dispositions are defined as what one believes. Teachers who successfully use formative ongoing assessment practices to provide evidence of growth believe that students have an integral role in the assessment process. They believe that student voice is essential to student learning. Teachers believe that their ongoing formative assessment practices inform both teaching and learning. They include students in learning how to use assessment results through providing timely meaningful feedback for student success. They thoughtfully create a safe learning environment for students to practice becoming more SEL competent.

KNOWLEDGE

Knowledge is what you know. Teachers who integrate SEL through everyday assessment know that there are different purposes for assessment. They know that the purpose of SEL assessing is to provide clear feedback about student SEL knowledge and skills. They know that feedback needs to be immediate, meaningful, and given with sensitivity. Adults with strong SEL skills themselves understand that how feedback is delivered can be the difference between motivation to do better or demotivation to stop learning. Finally, teachers know how to engage students in using their own assessment results for personal reflection and goal setting. This teacher knowledge base creates a safe learning environment where students know that they will be encouraged to try and will be supported in their SEL journey.

Chapter 2 • The Teacher Role and the Student Role in Everyday SEL Practice   17

PERFORMANCE

A performance is when you apply something; it is your action, it is what you do. SEL educators use a variety of assessment tools and strategies to gather information about student progress. They use assessments that are developmentally and culturally appropriate. They apply the principles of Universal Design for Learning in their assessments. That means they create multiple ways for students to show what they have learned. They set clear learning targets that students understand. They use assessment results to make decisions about what comes next. They provide timely, meaningful, and descriptive feedback and feed forward to students. They teach students how to use this information to reflect, to set new goals, and to improve attitudes, dispositions, and achievement.

THE POWER OF EFFECTIVE DAILY SEL ASSESSMENT

Connecting SEL assessment and the learner contextualizes the ongoing challenge of providing clear feedback that *encourages learning* instead of impeding it. Punitive assessments in the form of summative tests, with high-stakes summative assessments being the norm, have dominated public education to the detriment of both learning and teaching for decades. Assessing through daily practice requires a major shift in understanding the difference between and the purposes of assessing versus testing. For some, "test" is a four-letter word that elicits fear and anxiety. Integrating SEL daily is presented here as the antidote to our overfocused attention on testing for ranking, reporting, and compliance. Teachers who believe that students should be active partners in learning, teach their students to use assessment feedback to improve their learning.

SHIFTING YOUR MINDSET

To understand and create a new SEL assessment system in the classroom, let's begin by talking about some assumptions we believe are true. The first one is that you, the reader, do not "buy into" either the educational assessment system as it is currently structured or the extensive reports and statistics that show by design that learners are in a constant state of "failing." Second, we would like to assume that you are an "assessment literate educator." Third, you know in your heart that students are struggling and that educators are struggling to apply methods of assessing that are more humane and more socially, emotionally, developmentally, and culturally relevant. Students are struggling with the aftermath of a pandemic that has disrupted the educational system as it was. Educators are struggling to help students gain self-awareness, self-management, social awareness, decision-making, and relationship competencies needed to be successful in school, the community, and beyond. And finally, we hope you believe there is a solution to these challenges.

WHAT IS "ASSESSMENT" AND WHAT ARE THE TRAITS OF AN ASSESSMENT LITERATE PERSON?

Assessing is not testing. Assessment is the process of gathering information in an ongoing manner to offer feedback by providing insight (how did I do?) and feed forward by planning (what do I need to do next?) for the purpose of supporting learning. Teachers assess all day, every day. Think about the hundreds of "assessments" you automatically do. You scan each student as you greet them, checking how they are feeling. You provide feedback—"Allison, are you feeling okay today?" You note when someone is distracted—"Jon, I would like for you to focus, please." We most likely do not even consider these thoughts as assessments, but they are. Ongoing formative assessment is an art and a science. SEL assessment is a daily process we are already using. We need to acknowledge this and create a system that works for student SEL growth.

In order to do assessing right and to do it well, we need some prerequisite knowledge and skills.

> Assessment is the process of gathering information about student learning to inform education-related decisions. One becomes assessment literate by mastering basic principles of sound assessment practice, coming to believe strongly in their consistent, high-quality application in order to meet the diverse needs of all students, and acting assertively based on those values. (NWEA, 2016)

The role of the teacher is to deeply embrace the SEL competencies for the purpose of creating and developing engaging learning opportunities so that students can acquire SEL knowledge and skills, and to confidently assess social and emotional competencies for the purpose of motivating and encouraging ongoing SEL growth.

In this book, we assume that the reader is assessment literate. When we integrate SEL through everyday assessment, by assessing using the feedback (how did I do?) and feed forward (what do I need to do next?) loop, we assess in a systematic manner that results in students gaining the social and emotional

Chapter 2 • The Teacher Role and the Student Role in Everyday SEL Practice   19 competencies necessary to be more successful in academics and life. And SEL assessment is not done *to* the learner. It is not simply implementing a learning activity and determining how that activity increased a specific SEL competency. It is done *with* the learner. The learner has had both choice and voice about the activity and understands how to show their understanding of the competency. This distinction is key to SEL success. We will provide details on how to accomplish this in later chapters.

HOW DO I KNOW WHAT THE SEL LEARNING COMPETENCIES ARE?

The broad list of SEL standards, also called competencies, is well known to those who practice and teach SEL competencies in their classrooms. In this text we have adapted the CASEL 5: self-awareness, social awareness, self-regulation/self-management, relationship skills, and responsible decision-making. States and school districts have adopted and adapted these core five SEL competencies, and many TK–12 institutions use them in the implementation of their SEL programs.

The next step for those who implement social emotional learning is to understand that students' social, emotional, and cognitive growth is neither linear nor even. Piaget's cognitive theory of implication assumes that all children go through the same sequence of development, but they do so at different rates. Educators must make a special effort to provide classroom activities and assessments for individuals and small groups, rather than for the total class group. There are not thirty children acquiring SEL self-regulation skills at the same time with the same degree of accomplishment. Assessment should be based on individual progress, rather than on the normal standards of peers of the same age. Individuals construct their own knowledge during the course of the interaction with the environment.

This bears repeating: The process of developing SEL knowledge and skills is not a linear one. There are a variety of factors that impact the acquisition of SEL competencies, just as there are many factors affecting cognitive growth. Family cultural norms, trauma, disasters and environmental events such as Hurricane Irma, and other factors disrupt the acquisition of SEL competencies. Knowing this allows the teacher to create learning opportunities that are aligned to the needs of students in a specific learning environment.

A framework brief presented by CASEL titled *Keeping SEL Developmental: The Importance of a Developmental Lens for Fostering and Assessing SEL Competencies* explains that SEL is developmental.

. . . certain SEL competencies "pull for" specific types of assessment, and particularly, perhaps, at specific ages. For example, aspects of early childhood and primary grades SEL (e.g., emotion knowledge, responsible decision-making) might require direct assessment for best results; competencies that refer to knowledge may always be best assessed directly. Behavioral skills are easily rated, but as children move into middle and high school, the question of who should do the rating becomes an issue. (Denham, 2018, p. 11)

The message is this—the role of the teacher in integrating SEL through everyday assessment is key to the effective acquisition of SEL competencies. Your SEL assessment dispositions, knowledge, and performances have the potential to create a safe, respectful learning environment that supports SEL learning.

THE ROLE OF THE STUDENT IN INTEGRATING SEL THROUGH EVERYDAY ASSESSMENT

An assessment literate educator knows that **student growth** is accomplished by engaging learners in learner-centric assessing practices, thus actively engaging them in their own learning.

In a learner-centric environment, learners understand:

- why their learning is being assessed in each context,
- what learning target they are trying to master,
- how they will receive accurate information about their learning progress,
- their individual learning progress is being assessed to help them develop,
- that they can ask for and receive the information they need to help them learn and grow in SEL competencies, and
- that they have an important role in promoting their own success.

SEL assessing is, therefore, a partnership with the learner. It is a carefully planned systematic practice that assesses *for* student learning. It provides practitioners with the standards, competencies, essential knowledge, performances, and critical dispositions that learners at each level need to know to move forward. It includes rubrics that are used to create intimate conversations with learners, in order to provide meaningful feedback to guide the learning. Every step of the way, learners know the answers to the following questions: What am I expected to know? How am I doing? What do I need to do next? Every element of the SEL assessment is designed to increase student learning in a safe and respectful environment and to give learners choice and voice.

SETTING THE STAGE—THE ROLE OF THE STUDENT IN SEL THROUGH EVERYDAY ASSESSMENT

In US public education today, students usually are passive recipients in the assessment process. They take tests. The results are given to their teachers and parents. Very little is explained about the purpose of the tests, let alone what the results mean. If data is collected, it is rarely shared with the learner. As Stiggins (2017, p. xi) has advocated for more than four decades, when educators are assessment literate, this abuse and misuse of testing in our schools, which leads too many students to conclude that they're not smart or capable enough and that school success is hopelessly out of their reach, stops. When ongoing formative assessment replaces testing, a shift occurs from using data about learning to make judgments to using data and information for learning.

The role of the student in the SEL journey changes in this learning environment. Let's identify the dispositions, knowledge, and performance standards that are embedded in an SEL manner when assessing is a practice integrated every day.

STUDENT DISPOSITIONS (WHAT STUDENTS BELIEVE)

Students and their families who understand the power of assessment for learning believe that students learn best when they are provided with clear expectations and learning targets. They receive regular feedback about their efforts and guidance about their next steps for gaining knowledge and skills. They engage with their teachers in conversations about their progress. They take responsibility for their own learning because it is very clear what SEL is and why it is essential to personal and academic development. Students expect to succeed in this learning environment. Their voice is included in their own learning process.

STUDENT KNOWLEDGE (WHAT STUDENTS KNOW)

Students in learning environments where learning outcomes are clearly explained, who engage in feedback and feed forward conversations with teachers, and whose voices are heard know that there are different types of assessments. They understand there are different purposes for different kinds of assessments. Sometimes assessments are used for accountability and other times for grading. Sometimes assessments are not graded but are used to determine progress toward gaining knowledge. In a classroom where the teacher provides ongoing formative assessment for learning—whether aligned to SEL competencies or academic standards—students know the results of assessments can help them to learn and set goals. They are knowledgeable about tools for self-assessment, such as reflection and journaling. They know that rubrics help them to understand what is expected, what the criteria are for learning, and how they are progressing. There are no surprises in a learning environment where formative ongoing assessments are integrated to support gaining new knowledge and skills. Both the teacher and the student openly discuss progress in a way that the student understands what they have accomplished and what is next.

STUDENT PERFORMANCE (WHAT STUDENTS DO)

Ongoing SEL assessment that is formative offers a variety of ways for students to represent their knowledge. The assessment literate educator knows that just as students learn in a variety of ways, they show what they have learned through different avenues. Sometimes retelling a story shows comprehension, while other times creating a timeline of events works. In SEL assessing, a student may share a story to show how a character made a decision and the impact of that decision on others. The next time the student might act out different scenarios.

In classrooms where SEL is integrated daily as a lived experience, it is normal to see students using rubrics to determine how they are progressing. They might be comparing their work to an exemplar or watching a video of students engaged in social interactions and talking to peers about what is appropriate or not. When receiving teacher input, students use feedback and feed forward to improve their learning. They can explain what the feedback means and how they use it. Students take responsibility for their own learning and track their progress over time.

DREAM OR REALITY?

Integrating SEL through everyday assessment is not a dream. You already do it. Every day in classrooms across the United States, caring, dedicated teachers advocate for their students. They show their passion for their calling through the hundreds of decisions they make, the care they take, the questions they ask, and the support they give. However, if social emotional learning is to succeed, it deserves to be an integrated practice that is recognized for what it does.

Chapter 2 • The Teacher Role and the Student Role in Everyday SEL Practice

Research on SEL clearly shows that its competencies impact student learning, behavior, self-management, and more. A significant meta-analysis that included research with more than 270,000 students revealed that compared to students who did not engage, SEL treatments targeting the five core competencies improved students' academic achievement by 11 percentile points. Additionally, students who took part in SEL programs had improved conduct in the classroom, an enhanced capacity for handling stress and despair, and improved attitudes about themselves, other people, and education. Further meta-analyses confirmed the same results. Consistency across independent study teams provides compelling evidence that successfully implemented SEL programs are advantageous (CASEL, 2023).

We believe that integrating social emotional learning via content and assessments every day is the most effective strategy for increasing both adult and student SEL competencies. We know that teachers already do this. However, in order for SEL to flourish, SEL integration needs to be a systematic process that is intentional (see Figure 2.1). Gathering evidence of SEL success provides stakeholders with real data. SEL works!

FIGURE 2.1 ● Learner Centered Assessment

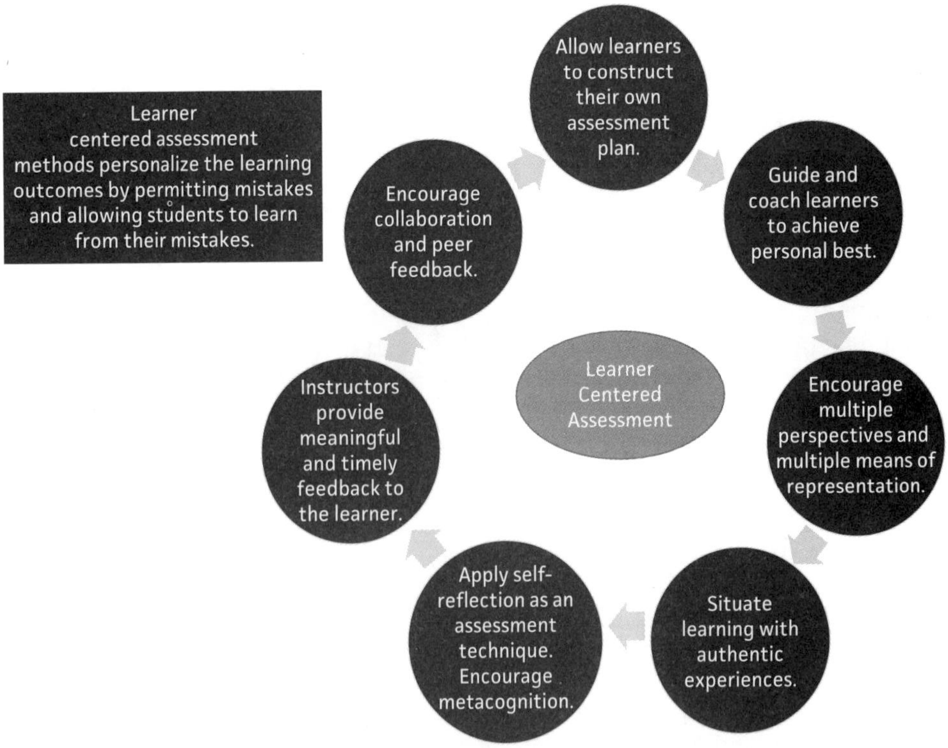

Modeled to Support: Cross, K. P., & Angelo, T. A. (1993). *Classroom assessment techniques: A handbook for college teachers*. Ann Arbor, MI: National Center for Research to Improve Postsecondary Teaching and Learning, University of Michigan.

Practitioner "Wondering" Reflection

Time for Your SEL Reflection Journal

In your SEL journal, reflect on what you have learned in this chapter. Consider these prompts:

- My biggest "aha" in this chapter was . . .
- One strategy, idea, or activity I will immediately implement is . . .
- One thing I am not quite clear on is . . .
- What I am curious about is . . .

Takeaway to Practice

What is the one takeaway from this chapter you want to put into action? **Name it. Add it to your action plan.**

CHAPTER 3

Developing a Culture of SEL Assessment

*In order to create a culture of excellence in assessment we will need to address the assessment culture—**the social** and educational environment—within which we will carry out new reconsidered assessment strategies and tactics. In other words, **we must assess well within the context of our social and educational aspirations, values, and beliefs** so as to promote a **universal opportunity for learner success, regardless of the learner's social or economic background**.*

—Rick Stiggins, *The Perfect Assessment System* (2017)

LEARNING OUTCOMES

Colleagues on the assessing journey will be able to

- Understand the connection between assessment beliefs and the need for developing a positive SEL assessment culture

- Explain the concept of an SEL learning environment where assessment feedback informs teacher planning and student growth

- Develop a cohesive plan for assessing SEL competencies that is inclusive of student feedback

- Develop goals about how to change the assessment culture beginning in their own learning environment—using their newfound knowledge, skills, and motivation

YOUR ROLE—KNOWING WHAT YOU KNOW AND WHAT YOU NEED TO LEARN

Words have great power. It was a challenge to choose the right words for the title of this chapter. While "cultivating" was selected, other words considered were "creating," "developing," and "nurturing." All are what this chapter is about—embracing the idea that how you assess (*not* test!) through the lens of social emotional learning will determine whether social emotional learning flourishes or not in your learning environment.

The quote from Stiggins, one of the preeminent leaders in formative assessment, was also a thoughtful choice. Go back and reread it, especially the part that notes, "we must assess well within the context of our social and educational aspirations, values, and beliefs" for the purpose of learner success. That is a total change from the culture of testing our public schools have been shrouded in throughout the No Child Left Behind and Every Student Succeeds federal legislation years.

We have lived in a *culture of testing* now for decades. As James Popham states in the foreword of Dr. Stiggins's book *The Perfect Assessment System* (2017), "The many misuses of educational tests are now suffocating us to such a degree that it's time to start over" (p. ix). Despite the research and the seminal leaders in formative assessment telling us that formative assessment *for* learning has the potential to transform teaching and learning, we continue to implement harmful testing practices in our schools and classrooms (Stiggins, 2017, p. ix). This chapter is about changing that mindset. Proliferating classroom environments that embrace and integrate the formative ongoing assessing of social emotional competencies is foundational to the success of social emotional learning in our schools. Where do we start to create this culture? With you.

Testing is done *to* learners. They have absolutely no choice or control about testing. It is a federal and state mandate. Both teachers and learners are subjected to the emotional chaos created by this culture. Assessing, however, is done *with* the learner. Assessing—done right—provides the teacher and the learner with information about progress toward the acquisition of the learning target or outcome. Assessing gently leads the learner in the growth process. Assessing allows the learner agency over learning. Assessing gives the learner a voice in their own learning. Assessing empowers student learning. Once again we ask, how do we create and nurture this learning ecology that fosters student voice and empowers well-being and positive learning?

Let's start with a visioning activity. Take time and deliberation with this. It is important. Gather your materials—drawing or sketch paper, a variety of colored pencils or pens, glue stick, stickers, magazines, your tablet, or whatever you need to create a portrait. No, not that kind of portrait. You are creating a portrait of a highly effective SEL learning environment.

Jot down a few words or phrases that describe your ideal highly effective SEL environment, the teacher, and the students. Find some photos, pictures, and visuals that help you to create this portrait of SEL in action. What does the classroom feel like? What does it look like? What kinds of visuals do you see on the walls? What is the teacher doing? What are the students doing? What knowledge, performance, and dispositions do the teacher and the students have? How are they different from other teachers and students who may not possess their SEL knowledge? Why? Keep adding elements until you have a very clear portrait of this SEL environment.

Here is a think-aloud (well, without the sound). Focus on the second paragraph from the CASEL explanation of what SEL is. The bolded italics are ours.

MY IDEAL SEL INCLUSIVE LEARNING ENVIRONMENT

Social and emotional learning (SEL) is an integral part of education and human development. *SEL is the process through which all young people and adults acquire and apply the knowledge, skills, and attitudes to develop healthy identities, manage emotions and achieve personal and collective goals, feel and show empathy for others, establish and maintain supportive relationships, and make responsible and caring decisions.*

SEL advances educational equity and excellence through authentic school-family-community partnerships to establish learning environments and experiences that feature trusting and collaborative relationships, rigorous and meaningful curriculum and instruction, and ongoing evaluation. SEL can help address various forms of inequity and empower young people and adults to co-create thriving schools and contribute to safe, healthy, and just communities. (www.CASEL.org)

Essential Questions

What does the teacher know and do?

What do the students know and do?

What do the parents/guardians/families know and do?

What does the community know and do?

---

28 Assessing Through the Lens of Social and Emotional Learning

STUDENTS AT THE CENTER

This vision of an ideal SEL learning environment answers the questions posed earlier as it is represented by a bullseye target (see Figure 3.1). The student is at the center of an ideal SEL learning environment. Everything we think, say, or do aligns back to what, how, and when we are integrating SEL competencies in order to increase student voice and enable "empowerment" for students. Student empowered (SE SEL) growth and development is an ongoing process of learning the essential SEL knowledge, performances, and dispositions (described in detail in the SEL Student Learning Progressions). SE SEL is a process and, as such, each person enters with a variety of competencies and a need for developing and increasing them. This even applies to adults—especially the adults supporting the acquisition of SEL competencies.

> The term *SE SEL* is introduced by Brown and colleagues (2022b) in *Letting Student Voice Lead the Way*. In the ASCD article/blog (see QR code), they present the concepts of "Some Days" and "Micro Adventures" that promote student empowered social emotional learning. Some Days are ideas elicited from students about what activity they would like to see implemented in the school day. For example, Some Day I would like to have reading class outside. Micro Adventures are mini field trips that are conceptualized by the students. As explained in the article, SE SEL "encompasses practices that affirm what students bring to the classroom by encouraging students to identify and choose activities they love or value, to experience what it feels like to positively engage with and positively influence others, and in many cases, to share their expertise with classmates and teachers."

bit.ly/3OlbFck

In the ideal SEL learning environment, that developmental process is recognized and respected. The teacher, who is the facilitator in guiding learners in the acquisition of SEL competencies, knows the SEL competencies and learning progressions; has self-assessed and has an action plan for increasing personal SEL competencies; and knows how to integrate SEL learning throughout the period, day, week, and year across all subject disciplines and extracurricular activities—always with the student at the center. The teacher is assessment (not testing!) literate and knows that SEL assessing is an ongoing process that provides formative assessment via feed up (answers the question What am I expected to learn?), feedback (How am I progressing?) and feed forward (What do I need to do next to keep increasing my SEL competencies?).

The teacher knows how to create an SEL learning environment that invites and supports the acquisition of SEL competencies. It is visually engaging. The SEL framework wheel is the first thing anyone entering the classroom sees. The students have created

FIGURE 3.1 • Ideal SEL Learning Environment

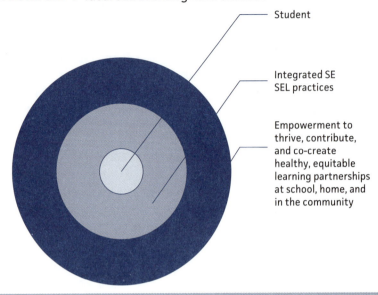

this stunning representation of the five core SEL competencies using a mixed media approach. The entire wall is filled with evidence of their SEL activities and growth. It also has resources that are student centric and that the students have selected. The teacher is at the door each period welcoming each student. As the students get settled, the morning/beginning of class circle starts the day. This ritual sends a clear message—I am so glad you are here. What do we need to focus on learning today? Let's effectively engage in our growth work, both academic and SEL.

What are the students doing in this ideal SEL classroom? They are engaged in learning. They are empowered because they feel competent, connected, and heard. They are effectively working on today's academic and SEL learning outcomes, which are clearly explained in the morning/beginning of class routine. Both the academic and SEL learning expectations guide the student work of learning.

Because they know the SEL competencies and the expectations of self-awareness, social awareness, self-management, relationship skills, and responsible decision-making, they work toward increasing those competencies. Whether they are pursuing the learning outcomes individually, in teams, or as a whole class, they collaborate to ensure the SEL and academic learning environment is safe and engaging for all learners. When expectations are not met, there is a clear process and pathway for dealing with issues.

Student self-assessment and reflection is a part of the positive assessing culture for the class. Students' journals/agendas help them to think about what they accomplished, what they need to do next, and what challenged them. They freely let the teacher know what kind of help they need to move forward—whether SEL or academically. They own their progress.

Parents, guardians, families, and the community are partners in understanding, knowing, and supporting the SEL learning environment. They know they play essential roles in the continuing SE SEL growth of all family and community members. They help plan, lead, attend, and participate in developing community-based SEL events—seminars, workshops, and learning opportunities. The family integrates many of the SEL routines and rituals at home. The family knows they have allies to support their children. The family participates in ongoing feedback and feed forward, via surveys and informal and formal meetings for a continuous improvement cycle.

In the ideal SEL learning environment, all roles—student, teacher, family, community—are interconnected. The educators do not "give" voice to anyone; they honor the many voices in their community. When all members of the community feel their voices are heard and honored, it has a significant impact on the cultivation of the SEL culture. For example, first responders are known and visit the school for various activities and events. Social services support is readily available inside the school and in the community. And all aspects of SEL growth are known, respected, and supported—whether it is at the grocery store, the gas station, the doctor's office, or the community library. Learning, then, does not just take place within the walls of the school; the entire community embraces helping youth to learn and grow.

Your role in cultivating an SEL culture of assessing is to first and foremost become assessment literate. You must know the SEL standards and competencies—the knowledge, skills, and performances—that guide learners toward growth. Second, you need to be well-versed on how to effectively assess SEL competencies. You need to know the difference between student self-reports, observations, and the variety of assessment tools available—whether commercially prepared and purchased or teacher made. You need to be cautious in how commercially prepared and purchased SEL programs are implemented and how that data is used. Making the same mistakes we have made in implementing standardized testing and in the use of standardized data is a cautionary tale. Using SEL data for punitive purposes—for ranking, for placement, for decision-making—destroys the efficacy of all SEL implementations. Knowing how to effectively create or select (if beneficial) an SEL program, implement it with fidelity to the principles of SEL growth, and use the data for formative ongoing growth are keys to the success of social emotional learning.

Chapter 3 • Developing a Culture of SEL Assessment   **31**

WHAT EXACTLY DOES SEL ASSESSING LOOK LIKE?

It is time to transition from our visions to the "how." How do we move from a culture of testing to cultivating a culture of assessing? Fortunately, we have a deep understanding and a wealth of resources from the seminal leaders in formative assessment. Unfortunately, the majority of teachers in the classroom today have not been introduced to the power of formative assessment to inform and transform both teaching and learning. If you are one of those educators, take heart. Now is the time to change your classroom, grade level, or school from a culture of testing to a culture of assessing *for* learning. Assessing *for* learning is essential for both cultivating a culture of assessing and cultivating an SEL learning environment.

The content experts in assessing *for* learning recognize that assessing is a moving picture. The assessing information (a snapshot) provided to you about a student's progress last week is out of date this week. Effective formative assessing is ongoing. It is continuous. It is a collaboration between you—the teacher—and the learner. It is a process of setting clear expectations for what is being learned (feed up), receiving feedback about what was done well, and having a conversation about what needs to be done next (feed forward) (Frey & Fisher, 2011). Stiggins (2017) describes a game-changing vision of assessment. In his description of re-creating assessment values and beliefs, he states the keys to changing our assessment culture.

Here is an abbreviated selection from his list that is highly aligned to our discussion:

1. "We must move beyond the long-standing belief that standardized achievement tests can pave the way to better schools" (p. 96). We know they do not, have not, and will not.

2. "We must shift the spotlight, resources, and locus of assessment control from federal and state departments of education to local school districts" (p. 96). This is where your knowledge of the characteristics of an assessment literate educator impacts the change from testing to assessing. Student learning success can be aggregated from the systemic ongoing formative assessing practices in your classroom.

3. "We must embrace a new role for students" (p. 97). Testing is something adults do *to* students. Assessing is done *with* students. We already know that students self-evaluate constantly. Unfortunately, the feedback they receive from high-stakes testing sends them the wrong information. Testing feedback stops learning. Formative assessment supports learning.

As Stiggins (2017) states, "Grades and test scores may serve summative accountability purposes, but they fail us in formative contexts, where instructional decision makers need detail about student strengths and weaknesses to inform decisions about what comes next in the student's learning" (p. 7). Formative assessment, unlike high-stakes testing or benchmark assessments, has been proven to impact student achievement. In the realm of SEL skill acquisition, formative assessment is essential for students to understand what is expected and how they are progressing.

So, hopefully you are getting the message: To assess the SEL way, the teacher is assessment (not testing!) literate and knows that SEL assessing is an ongoing process. This process, a partnership between the teacher and the learner, provides information that supports learning.

Back to the essential questions of this section:

1. How do I do SEL assessing?
2. How do I cultivate a culture of SE SEL assessing in my environment?

"DOING" SE SEL ASSESSING

To do SE SEL assessing right and well, you begin with a series of questions:

1. WHY AM I ASSESSING SEL COMPETENCIES?

This sounds pretty straightforward. You are assessing SEL competencies to determine where each learner is on the progression of acquiring specific SEL knowledge, skills, and performances. If you are assessing for any other reason, you need to ask why. Who is requiring this assessment (or testing)? How will the data be used? If it is for any reason other than to get feedback on where students are in their progression of SEL learning, then you really need to question it.

2. WHAT DO I DO WITH THE ASSESSMENT INFORMATION?

You use it to have a conversation *with* the learner about their progress. Feedback given in language that students will understand provides them with the answer to the questions *What did I do well?* and *What do I need to do next?*

Chapter 3 • Developing a Culture of SEL Assessment   **33**

3. WHAT'S NEXT?

The learner states what they have learned in alignment with the competency and, based on the learning progression, what their next step is. You, of course, facilitate this conversation using a variety of tools. You both agree on strategies to use to support the ongoing practice of implementing SEL competencies. It is vitally important that you carefully listen to the learner. Craft questions that will elicit responses to inform you. "Am I right when I say while you really did well on the portrait of the main character assignment, you struggled with the part where you compared Pony Boy to yourself? OK, let's talk about that."

You may be asking, so, this is it? Yes and no. You will need to create a systemic process for implementing effective SEL practices to create your ideal SEL learning environment. This includes a system for developing your feed forward, feedback, and feed up loop. Feed forward means that you set clear expectations via learning outcomes. Feedback is the information you provide about how the learner is progressing in acquiring the SEL competency presented in the outcome, and feed up is what the student needs to do next to continue growing. This looping system requires knowledge on how to embed SEL practices in your teaching and learning environment throughout the day. We believe that all teaching is SEL teaching. We already "do" SEL. It is not a separate "curriculum." It is a belief and value system that is integrated in the most effective practices of teaching and learning.

An important aspect in creating this culture includes allowing for community building and inclusion of student voices. Culturally responsive teaching is a framework for creating awareness for this kind of inclusivity. Culturally responsive teaching encompasses not only content and instruction but also assessing. Zaretta Hammond's (2013) model, *Ready for Rigor*, provides us with knowledge, skills, and dispositions for integrating culturally responsive teaching in SEL assessing.

The Ready for Rigor Framework includes four areas of instruction that promote a culturally responsive classroom: Awareness, Learning Partnerships, Information Processing, and Community of Learners and Learning Environments (see Figure 3.2). All indicate that the students are engaged in being part of this dynamic classroom experience, and they are ready for rigor and for independent learning. Hammond frames these actions and behaviors as giving learners feedback and affirmations, along with validation to develop rich and culturally inclusive conversations in a learning environment. Examine the Ready for Rigor Framework. Depending on the type of assessment practice applied, assessing through the lens of SEL can be used to help learners:

1. Gain a greater level of self-awareness
2. Process (and apply) information
3. Develop a variety of learning partnerships in the classroom
4. Create a community of learners and learning environment

FIGURE 3.2 • Ready for Rigor Framework

AWARENESS

- Understand the three levels of culture
- Recognize cultural archetypes of individualism and collectivism
- Understand how the brain learns
- Acknowledge the socio-political context around race and language
- Know and own your cultural lens
- Recognize your brain's triggers around race and culture
- Broaden your interpretation of culturally and linguistically diverse students' learning behaviors

LEARNING PARTNERSHIPS

- Reimagine the student and teacher relationship as a partnership
- Take responsibility to reduce students' social-emotional stress from stereotype threat and microaggressions
- Balance giving students both care and push
- Help students cultivate a positive mindset and sense of self-efficacy
- Support each student to take greater ownership for his learning
- Give students language to talk about their learning moves

INFORMATION PROCESSING

- Provide appropriate challenge in order to stimulate brain growth to increase intellective capacity
- Help students process new content using methods from oral traditions
- Connect new content to culturally relevant examples and metaphors from students' community and everyday lives
- Provide students authentic opportunities to process content
- Teach students cognitive routines using the brain's natural learning systems
- Use formative assessments and feedback to increase intellective capacity

COMMUNITY OF LEARNERS AND LEARNING ENVIRONMENT

- Create an environment that is intellectually and socially safe for learning
- Make space for student voice and agency
- Build classroom culture and learning around communal (sociocultural) talk and task structures
- Use classroom rituals and routines to support a culture of learning
- Use principles of restorative justice to manage conflicts and redirect negative behavior

Source: Reprinted from Hammond (2014).

CULTIVATING A CULTURE OF SE SEL ASSESSING

Cultivating a culture of SE SEL assessing is a mindset, as well as an art and science. It requires that you have an open and curious mind about how SEL can change the learning and teaching environment. It requires that you gain new knowledge, skills, and dispositions about both SEL and assessing. It requires that you question all of the assumptions you know about testing. It means you need to move from the culture of testing to seeing and knowing the value of ongoing formative assessment *for* learning. It means you allow yourself to experiment. It provides for nurturing the spirit of your learners. It allows for listening to and hearing what your students want and need in order to learn.

Students need autonomy, flexibility, and control, just as adults do. Your SEL culture of assessing has the potential for honoring student efficacy. Give student real choices rather than asking them to select from two forced options, such as show your learning by making a poster or giving a three-minute speech. We frequently think we are giving students choices, when in reality we are controlling their learning. Think about learning with them and explore what is possible. Ask them, "What do you think is the best way for you to show what you learned?" One innovative way to do this is via the Some Day strategy. What is a student's Some Day wish in relationship to assessing?

> Some Days are a practice developed by the team at the Rural Vitality Lab. They invite all students and teachers to share their wish for a special activity to promote student voices and empower schools to promote mental health, well-being, and emotional healing. We suggest you apply this concept to assessing. What are your students' wishes about how they are assessed? You may be pleasantly informed by their input.

Students are truly in the bullseye of the culture of SEL assessing. In this culture you value the feedback from your learners, and you honor their voices. On the other hand, students will feel they do not matter when data is used punitively. Students know that they do not matter when a concept is taught and they do not get it the first time, but the teacher just keeps on going. They know that they do not matter when a pacing guide dictates learning. They know that they do not matter when they are scared what will happen when they fail again.

In the culture of SEL assessing, the student is the center of all learning. All students feel valued and appreciated. They feel a sense of belonging. Students know their voices are respected because their input about their own learning is seen in the "what's next for me" conversations. Students know they are valued because their untapped potential is explored and allowed to blossom. Assessment needs to be owned by the students as a developmental aspect of the process of learning progressions.

Practitioner "Wondering" Reflection

Time for Your SEL Reflection Journal

In your SEL journal, reflect on what you have learned in this chapter. Consider these prompts:

- How might reframing your understanding of what excellence in assessing could be impact your teaching? And your students' learning?
- Why is student voice in the assessing process vital to positive SE SEL growth? How will you develop this concept in your own practice?
- What questions do you have about assessing SEL learning?

Takeaway to Practice

What is the one takeaway from this chapter you want to put into action? **Name it. Add it to your action plan.**

CHAPTER 4

Assessing and Assessments for Racial and Cultural Relevance

Co-Authored With L. Erika Saito

Even after implementing assessment reforms, we are still left with a system of teaching and learning (curriculum and assessment) that has produced racist outcomes for students of color, for hundreds of years. Whether we consider modern school segregation, inequitable funding for schools and communities of color, or (even in affluent schools) a racist, traumatic, curriculum, even the most equitable grading systems will still result in racist outcomes. This is because our schools, like most workplaces and organizations, uphold white supremacy cultures in many ways, from the expectations we hold of students to how we perceive our own power as educators. Thus, when educators employ a mindset of critical thinking and perpetual learning, we can mitigate these racist outcomes.

—Ken Shelton, Advocate (Keynote CUE Conference, March 2022)

> ## LEARNING OUTCOMES
>
> Colleagues on the assessing journey will be able to
>
> - Understand the necessary elements of an assessment (tests) or assessing practice (pedagogy) that addresses all learners
>
> - Examine assessment practices that are biased
>
> - Recognize when bias, hidden bias, or racism is included in assessment and how to move toward bias-free assessment practices
>
> - Identify culturally sustaining assessment practices that address diversity
>
> - Explore assessment practices that are culturally responsive

For educators, informal assessment occurs about as frequently as we make decisions, up to 1,500 times per day. As humans we are in a continuous state of assessing. We make decisions and choices and then assess. We assess how we dress, what we eat, how we speak, what we say, and dozens of other human behaviors. In K–12 education, assessment is normalized through more traditional means such as quizzes, tests, and inventories; assessments can and do occur on a daily basis. As we have discussed in earlier chapters, there are primarily two categories of assessing: formative and summative. Generally, all of the assessing practices we have described so far are formative assessments. The authors of this book concur that formative assessment is the most authentic form that tends to be more individualized, personalized, and differentiated by the educator for specific learners. Formative assessment is done through the lens of SEL.

ALL MEANS ALL

As we begin this very sensitive chapter, we would like to emphasize our beliefs about inclusion in assessment. We believe that involving all learners in the assessment process is essential. We believe that it is necessary to provide access to humanistic assessment practices, practices that address the individual learner, and practices that are grounded in social and emotional learning. In SEL, we assess the individual, not their place in society. Understanding what their "society" is will help us improve that assessing. Without inclusive assessment practices, exclusionary acts involving bias, prejudice, discrimination, racism, classism, sexism, heterosexism, ableism, and other "isms" will continue to perpetuate systemic and structural inequalities in assessment and in education.

In Chapter 3, we discussed the pivotal role of students in the assessment process and presented many types of formative assessment tools and conventions. This chapter will begin with a brief history of racism in assessment and present examples where racism is still evident in standardized tests and other assessment types. We address this issue of racism because it is a universal and persistent problem in many parts of the world, including the United States, Canada, the United Kingdom, and Australia, among others. We will then discuss an analysis of assessments that include racist language or other indicators of racism or exclusionary practices, and discuss solutions on how to address racism in teaching and learning. Through this lens, we will also address diversity, equity, and inclusion in assessment practices by all teachers and for all learners.

RACISM IN ASSESSMENT: A BRIEF HISTORY

Educational practices and schooling in the United States were adopted more than a century ago from European models that center on a climate of competition through test scores and grading (Schneider & Hutt, 2014). This has created a competitive mindset and practice influenced by ethnocentric European cultural norms that have led to testing development and grading practices that have largely ignored biases based on race and language nativity. As an example, standardized tests in the United States are historically rooted in racially divisive ways. The development of the Scholastic Aptitude Test (SAT) by Carl Brigham began as an intelligence test for the US military during World War I. From this self-made test, he determined the disparity in intelligence between white and Black test-takers, where Black individuals scored significantly lower. In short, he blamed the low test scores and future intelligence of Americans on the integration of Black people and did this without evidence, validity, and reliability of the test. This military test was later adapted to create the SAT as a commonplace entrance examination for college admissions. Having a historically racially biased test to then be the marker for college entrance exams across the United States is telling of the ways race can negatively impact opportunities for academic advancement and perpetuate the long-acknowledged achievement gap between Black and white students, rather than identifying the measurement tool as the issue (Rosales & Walker, 2021).

MEASUREMENT BY GROUP

By comparing test scores between ethnic groups, a standardized test can be culturally biased if a minority group consistently scores lower than the white group (Freedle, 2003).

The College Board admittedly states the SAT exam should not be the sole criteria for admission but should be used in conjunction with other variables, such as high school grade point average, class rank, or leadership ability, to determine eligibility. While the changes to the SAT are well-intentioned, standardized testing is not an effective tool in evaluating a student's ability to succeed in a university that focuses on a writing-based curriculum. In part due to the global COVID-19 pandemic but also recognizing the SAT as a roadblock for college entrance, particularly for underrepresented and historically marginalized groups, intentional shifts were made in 2022 by colleges across the United States to remove standardized testing as part of the college admissions process. This is a positive start toward equity in college access.

Many have researched this problem of inequity and the culturally insensitive nature of the SAT. Geiser (2015) wrote a paper on the growing correlation between race and SAT scores and shared that data connected to high-stakes standardized tests show that there are many factors related to the success of the test, including situational/environmental confounding factors, personal/emotional factors, and grade-spread requirement in standardized testing (see also QR code).

tinyurl.com/
geiser2015

EXAMINING RACE IN GRADING PRACTICES

Previous studies that have examined the role of bias in teacher grading practices indicate differences in grades based on student names. This association between students' names and perceived abilities and behaviors through grades are no longer grades that reflect student knowledge of a skill or standard, but instead reinforce the power dynamics between the authority figure (e.g., teacher) and the students. This can be damaging because it does not measure content knowledge or application, but instead sends negative messages to students about how they view themselves. In his experiment with 1,549 teachers, Quinn found that "teachers were 4.7 percentage points more likely to consider the white child's writing at or above 'grade level' compared to the identical writing from a Black child" (p. 75) (see Figures 4.1 and 4.2). Further, we find that there are grading practices that assess unrealistic situations for writing assessments that are not developed with purpose, except for the purpose of grading (Poe et al., 2018).

FIGURE 4.1 ● Quinn (2021) Side-by-Side Grading of Writing Sample, White Child Connor versus Black Child Dashawn

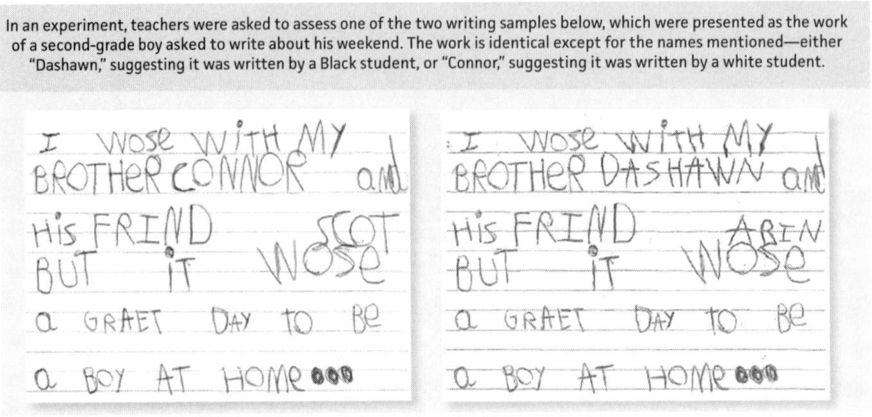

In an experiment, teachers were asked to assess one of the two writing samples below, which were presented as the work of a second-grade boy asked to write about his weekend. The work is identical except for the names mentioned—either "Dashawn," suggesting it was written by a Black student, or "Connor," suggesting it was written by a white student.

I wose with my brother Connor and his frind Scot but it wose a graet day to be a boy at home.

I wose with my brother Dashawn and his frind Arin but it wose a graet day to be a boy at home.

Source: Reprinted from Quinn (2021). Used with permission.

Quinn (2021) also revealed that when female teachers assessed a young boy's writing sample, they showed racial bias in their grading, but male teachers did not.

Quinn also investigated differences in grading based on the gender and race of the teacher. His prior research found that teachers show preference for students with identities similar to their own. In particular, white teachers tend to have lower expectations for Black students than for similar white students (Quinn, 2021). The most notable finding was that in all groups, when teachers use a specific grading rubric, estimates of bias are small and not significant.

EXAMINING LANGUAGE BIAS IN PROVIDING STUDENT FEEDBACK

Language bias in student feedback from teachers happens when the language used in evaluations exhibits microaggressions. Language bias and microaggressions in teacher feedback turn into teacher-centered statements that focus on telling the student what they did incorrectly, what is missing or needs to be fixed, and what the teacher thinks needs to be done. Rather, we recommend a more inclusive and bias-free approach, which is one that is student centered and allows students to think through their areas of growth with thoughtful questioning and guidance to seek the appropriate response (Reibel, 2021).

FIGURE 4.2 • Quinn (2021) Racial Bias in Grading (Using Rubrics) Comparing Black Student With White Student

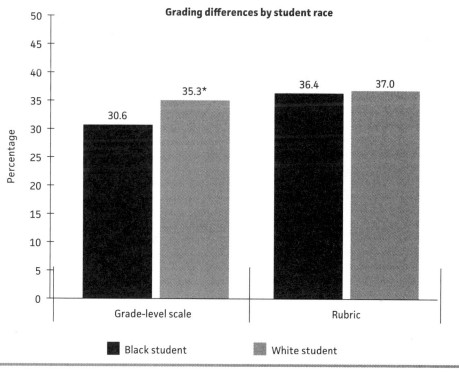

Source: Reprinted from Quinn (2021). Used with permission.

Note: Figure shows the percentage of teachers rating the assignment "at grade level" or above (grade-level scale) or "recounts an event with some detail" or above (rubric). Estimates are adjusted for teacher gender, grade level, race/ethnicity, experience, and school racial demographics.
* = difference in grades is statistically significant at the 95% confidence level

GENDER EQUITY IN ASSESSMENT

While this section does not have the breadth to wholly address gender inclusivity as it relates to assessment outcomes, or define gender-inclusive terminology and spaces, it will provide thought to the broader assessment practices as they relate to SEL. Research is still needed to understand the ways LGBTQ+ students are represented in K–12 classroom experiences and in assessment research. This section will highlight existing studies on gender bias and provide suggestions for ways to combat unconscious gender bias in assessment practices.

Unintentional gender bias favoring cisgender male students in K–12 continues to occur in classrooms across the United States despite efforts to create gender-equitable spaces for students (Sadker & Zittleman, 2009). This begins in elementary school as teacher time is spent with male students more often than female students. This increases cisgender male participation, resulting in more male students raising their hand and being called on to lead in-class discussion, asking questions, and responding to questions posed by the teacher. The teacher relies on male students for class participation (Alber, 2017). This also suggests a heteronormative divide between cisgender male and female students, with little information on nonbinary students' participation and support.

Creating gender-inclusive assessments can be attained through formative assessments, using check-in to determine student wellness, and seeking students' understanding through interactions with students, attention to the amount and quality of feedback provided to all students, and being cognizant of the amount of time spent supporting all students (Sadker & Zittleman, 2009).

SHIFTING TOWARD INCLUSIVE GRADING

With misperceptions of what it means to "shift" toward antiracist grading, some people believe if they adopt a specific aspect or practice, they are no longer racist in their grading practices. This is certainly not the case! To be antiracist in grading means a shift in mindset in the approach and adoption of the key practices. Antiracist grading is not a "pick and choose" set of items or selecting the easiest or most convenient practice. It is deeply reflective on one's own practices and addressing biases before evaluating student work.

CULTURALLY SUSTAINING SOCIAL AND EMOTIONAL ASSESSMENT PRACTICES

Culturally sustaining social and emotional learning builds on concepts of culturally relevant and culturally responsive teaching as well as funds of knowledge that leverages individual student backgrounds and experiences as an asset to learning (Mahfouz & Anthony-Stevens, 2020). Further, we see that when we recognize cultural assets of students in our classrooms, we can apply culture as an effective lens to learning and to mastering content. For teachers to become culturally responsive, they must implement evidence-based practices that incorporate culturally responsive instruction that works alongside their own teacher dispositions. While assessing collaboratively with the student, the teacher still holds high expectations for their students, has the ability to adapt instruction appropriately, and contributes to the overall wellness of students (Krasnoff, 2016). It is a two-way interaction where students' background knowledge is valued in the classroom and at the same time, teachers learn about their students and cultures. This co-construction of knowledge for teachers and students leads to considerations of assessment practices that relate directly to where students are in the process of learning. To meet this end, creating culturally sustaining, authentic assessments affords students to engage deeper in the learning process while simultaneously developing agency. Additionally, it addresses the equity gap by supporting the diverse cultural needs of students (Montenegro & Jankowski, 2017). Holding high expectations of both high- and low-performing students, as well as being conscious of the equitable pedagogical practices and attention provided to students, is a good place to start (Krasnoff, 2016).

STANDARDS-BASED GRADING

Standards-based grading is a method of evaluating student progress based on their mastery of specific learning objectives, or standards, rather than on overall averages or scores. This approach has been shown to promote more accurate and objective assessments of student learning and can help to address issues of equity in education.

One way in which standards-based grading can promote equity is by providing clearer and more transparent feedback to students and parents about what is expected of them. By clearly defining the learning standards and providing specific feedback on areas of strength and weakness, students are better able to understand how they are progressing and what they need to do to improve. Additionally, standards-based grading can help to mitigate the effects of systemic biases and other inequities in traditional grading systems. For example, traditional grading systems may penalize students who struggle with standardized tests or who come from disadvantaged backgrounds, whereas standards-based grading can provide a more nuanced and accurate assessment of their learning based on mastery of specific skills and concepts.

Overall, by focusing on mastery of specific standards rather than arbitrary grades or test scores, standards-based grading can help to create a more equitable and inclusive learning environment for all students.

Wilcox and Townsley (2022) identify the following key strengths addressed through standards-based grading:

- Grades are a reflection of student understanding.
- Grades and grading practices are transparent to the learner.
- Grades are not a mix of points and percentages, but rather a measure of attainment toward learning goals.
- The process addresses student understanding and levels of proficiency.

STANDARD	EXCEEDS 4	MEETS 3	APPROACHES 3	NOT MET 1

CONTRACT GRADING

Contract grading is rooted in critical pedagogy and allows students to negotiate the terms of their grades and results, thus creating a more equitable balance of power within the class structure. Students and teachers co-develop their determinations for maintaining a particular grade and are rid of pluses and minuses that can complicate the grading process. Providing a range for what constitutes a B allows students of varying abilities to attain a B even if they are closer to a C+ or an A-. Students and teachers can compromise on the descriptors for attaining a B or C in class. This can include a number of expectations that detail the completion of assignments and the submission process or a description for the level of classroom engagement for whole-class activities. Hybrid versions of this process have been challenged due to the lack of transparency in achieving higher grades such as an A that are recommended and determined by the teacher. This hybrid approach creates a level of autonomy (Danielewicz & Elbow, 2009; Poe et al., 2018). See the following example of holistic grading criteria for sixth-grade language arts.

SIXTH-GRADE LANGUAGE ARTS

To attain a grade of B you must:

- Submit all completed in-class work on time.
- Engage in all small-group discussions.
- Complete tests and quizzes to the best of one's ability.
- Complete test revisions.

CENTERING GROWTH AND MASTERY

Centering growth and mastery through grading practice means shifting the focus from grades as a way to rank or sort students to grades as a way to provide feedback and encourage learning. This approach values the process of learning and the progress students make toward mastery of specific learning objectives or standards, rather than the final grade or score they receive.

One way to center growth and mastery through grading practice is to adopt a standards-based grading system. This involves breaking down larger learning objectives into smaller, specific learning targets or standards, and evaluating student progress based on their mastery of these standards. By providing specific feedback on areas of strength and weakness, students are better able to identify what they need to work on to improve and can take ownership of their learning.

Another way to center growth and mastery through grading practice is to provide opportunities for students to revise and improve their work based on feedback. This approach emphasizes that learning is an ongoing process, and that mistakes and missteps are a natural part of the learning process. By allowing students to revise and resubmit work based on feedback, teachers can encourage students to take risks, make mistakes, and, ultimately, deepen their understanding of the material.

Overall, centering growth and mastery through grading practice requires a shift in mindset from grades as a way to measure student success to grades as a way to provide feedback and encourage learning. By focusing on the process of learning and providing specific feedback on areas of strength and weakness, teachers can create a more supportive and inclusive learning environment that encourages students to take ownership of their learning and strive toward mastery.

Another way to center growth and mastery through grading practice is to use rubrics to evaluate student work. Rubrics provide a clear and transparent set of criteria for evaluating student performance, which helps students understand what they need to do to improve and how their work will be evaluated. Additionally, teachers can use differentiated instruction to meet the diverse needs of their students. Differentiated instruction involves adjusting teaching methods and materials to match the learning needs and preferences of individual students, which can help students feel more engaged and motivated to learn.

Finally, teachers can prioritize student reflection as a way to encourage growth and mastery. Encouraging students to reflect on their learning process, including what they have learned, what they still need to work on, and how they can continue to improve, can help them develop metacognitive skills that will serve them well throughout their academic and professional careers.

Chapter 4 • Assessing and Assessments for Racial and Cultural Relevance   47

Centering growth and mastery through grading practice involves a shift in mindset from grades as the ultimate goal to grades as a tool for providing feedback and encouraging growth. By using formative assessments, rubrics, differentiated instruction, and student reflection, teachers can create a supportive and inclusive learning environment that prioritizes the development of student skills and knowledge.

FIVE KEY ASSESSMENT STRATEGIES THAT FOCUS ON GROWTH AND MASTERY

1. **Standards-based grading:** In a standards-based grading system, student progress is evaluated based on their mastery of specific learning objectives or standards, rather than on overall scores or averages. This approach provides a more accurate and objective assessment of student learning and can help to identify areas where students need additional support or instruction.

2. **Formative assessments:** Formative assessments, such as quizzes, class discussions, or group projects, are designed to provide ongoing feedback on student progress. By using formative assessments throughout the learning process, teachers can identify areas where students need additional support or instruction and adjust their teaching methods and materials accordingly.

3. **Rubrics:** Rubrics provide a clear and transparent set of criteria for evaluating student performance, which helps students understand what they need to do to improve and how their work will be evaluated. Rubrics can be used for a variety of assignments, such as essays, projects, or presentations.

4. **Revision and resubmission:** Allowing students to revise and resubmit their work based on feedback can encourage growth and mastery by emphasizing that learning is an ongoing process. By providing specific feedback and opportunities for revision, teachers can help students identify areas where they need to improve and develop a deeper understanding of the material.

5. **Differentiated instruction:** Differentiated instruction involves adjusting teaching methods and materials to match the learning needs and preferences of individual students. By tailoring instruction to the needs of each student, teachers can help to ensure that all students have the support they need to achieve mastery of the learning objectives.

We will further describe these practices in future chapters.

TEACHER EDUCATION AND INSTRUCTIONAL PRACTICE

In 1990, the American Federation of Teachers, National Council on Measurement in Education, and the National Education Association developed *Standards for Teacher Competence in Educational Assessment of Students*. Decades-long work has established evidence-based standards to guide schools and districts in how teachers should assess students. However, its application within schools and districts as well as training teachers in how to assess students is less known. Incorporating standards for teacher competency with educational assessments can serve as a preventative measure to the issues described in this chapter. Seven key standards are provided below with additional noncopyrighted material available on the Buros Center for Testing's "Standards for Teacher Competence in Educational Assessment of Students" web page, available via the QR code provided.

tinyurl.com/
burosstandards

Teachers need to be skilled in

1. **Choosing** assessment methods appropriate for instructional decisions.

2. **Developing** assessment methods appropriate for instructional decisions.

3. **Administering, scoring, and interpreting** the results of both externally produced and teacher-produced assessment methods.

4. **Using assessment results** when making decisions about individual students, planning teaching, developing curriculum, and school improvement.

5. **Developing** valid pupil grading procedures that use pupil assessments.

6. **Communicating** assessment results to students, parents, other lay audiences, and other educators.

7. **Recognizing** unethical, illegal, and otherwise inappropriate assessment methods and uses of assessment information.

Teacher Activity: Create a self-assessment to measure individual teacher competence in the skills that address educational assessment of students. Take the seven standards and turn them into "I" statements using a Likert Scale to rate your individual competency/perceived competency.

For example:

I can choose assessment methods appropriate to make instructional decisions.

Chapter 4 • Assessing and Assessments for Racial and Cultural Relevance   49

Ratings: (4) Always, (3) Almost always, (2) Frequently, (1) Only sometimes, or (0) Never

BEST PRACTICES: STRATEGIES FOR ASSESSING WITHOUT BIAS

Image source: Cleonard1973. https://creativecommons.org/licenses/by-sa/4.0/deed.en

CREATE A STANDARDS-BASED RUBRIC

Use a four-level scale with proficiency levels for grading.

1. Create and apply an objective approach to grading writing.
2. Provide students with grading rubrics and expectations for writing.
3. Have students write their name on the back or last page at the bottom and use numbers or other forms of identification to avoid student bias.
4. Provide student-thinking feedback: Use thinking questions to promote students to think about their progress and improve their skills to meet the standards.
5. Avoid teacher-centered comments that devalue and demotivate student learning.
6. Hold regular conferences with your students and also peer-to-peer conferences.

7. Conduct administrator and teacher training on teacher bias, with continuous discussion and follow-up on practices.

CRITICAL ISSUES FOR REFLECTION AND DISCUSSION

Another strategy to ensure that bias does not interfere with assessing is to hold frequent one-to-one conferences with your students. Why should we practice conferencing with our students/learners? The effectiveness of the student-led conference is dependent on several factors. Specifically, such conferences should:

1. Motivate the learner
2. Promote student responsibility
3. Help to focus students on quality work
4. Teach students the habit and power of reflection

THINK-ABOUTS AND WONDERINGS: QUESTIONS TO ASK YOURSELF

Use these questions to first ask yourself and then later to engage colleagues to rethink their grading practices and examine biases.

Q1: Do you grade students on the following?

- Homework
- Submitting work on time
- Attendance
- Quizzes/tests
- Projects
- In-class work
- Content knowledge

Q2: Are students penalized for:

- Incomplete work
- Late work
- Missing work
- Absence
- Tardiness
- Tests/quizzes
- Participation/engagement
- Behaviors

If you answered "yes" to any of the items in the list, we suggest that you reflect on the ways in which the list is damaging to students and consider changing your practice.

THINK ABOUT GRADING POLICIES AND CONSIDERATIONS

Q3: How do my grading policies support students who:

- Experience a family emergency
- Support family members through work, caretaking, etc.
- Have a household that is not conducive to studying

Q4: How do my current grading policies reinforce implicit biases?

NEW GRADING MINDSET

Assessing is grading, and the bottom line is that all learners must be given the opportunity to revise work, work to achieve their personal best, and feel small wins and accomplishments in order to keep learning. A recent digital headline in the *Wall Street Journal* reads, "Schools Are Ditching Homework, Deadlines Favor 'Equitable Grading'; Approach Aims to Measure Mastery and Accounts for Hardships at Home." The leading district in the grading for equity movement is Clark County, Nevada, which is the fifth largest district in the United States.

bit.ly/3DfGU1W

Dozens of school districts in California, Iowa, Virginia, and other states are moving toward "equitable grading" with varying degrees of buy-in. Grading for equity, mastery learning, and other nontraditional grading practices have caused educators to stretch their fixed grading mindset. Clark County's school district said the new approach was about "making grades a more accurate reflection of a student's progress and giving opportunities to all learners" (Randazzo, 2023). To read the full article from the *Wall Street Journal*, scan the QR code.

EQUITY IN DATA COLLECTION AND ANALYSIS: THE BIGGER PICTURE

In this chapter, we have examined assessing practices and analyzed these practices through the lens of diversity, equity, and inclusion. We have presented cases in our recent history that give examples of biased grading practices and racist grading practices, and we have suggested ways to make grading more equitable; equitable for all!

In previous chapters, we have described many types of assessments and assessing practices. We have shared practices that are student centered, practices and strategies that give students agency and ownership, and practices that offer students the opportunity to build their assessment identity.

BIAS IN DATA

In the 1990s, curriculum reform moved toward the application of data-driven decision-making and data-informed instruction. Before we briefly discuss this movement, let's first take a giant step back and think about the kinds of assessment data that are being collected. Let's think about whether or not the assessing processes and practices "influence equity goals": (1) are they "accountability-driven and data that are used for continuous improvement"; (2) do the data confirm assumptions and is the data used to challenge beliefs; (3) is the data continuously tracked and reassembled in flexible groups to promote student growth; and (4) are the data a compilation of authentic, formative assessment artifacts that are qualitative and combined with some quantitative data that reflect multiple means of representation of knowledge (Datnow & Park, 2018, p. 131)?

Datnow and Park (2018) frame data as a device that can either "open doors or close doors" depending on how it is collected and how it is applied in the educational setting. As they state, "data use can be an important lever for achieving equity" but we may not understand why and how data does this. In the name of educational reform, they say that "accountability policies have intensified the use of data to illuminate and address differences in achievement across racial, linguistic, and income groups" (pp. 131–132).

THE ISSUE WITH CURRENT RACIST ASSESSMENT PRACTICES

ASSESSMENT ANALYSIS ACTIVITY: IDENTIFYING THE ISSUE-IMPACT-SOLUTION

Now that we have unpacked racism in assessing and have provided solutions that promote humanistic assessment practices, we will now dive directly into scenarios, examples, and prevalent issues in classrooms. Let's take a look at issues with teacher-developed assessments and other assessing practices. Take a few minutes to jot down your reactions and the issues you have identified within the teacher-developed assessment and the impact it has on students, and come up with possible solutions. We would like you to add to your reflection journal, and document your thoughts, feelings, and impressions of the issues detailed in the scenarios. Think about your own bias, implicit bias, or awareness of inequitable assessing practices.

TEACHER-DEVELOPED ASSESSMENTS

Several issues within assessment arise that impact individual communities of color, each with nuanced and overlapping experiences of the ways race and racism are currently perpetuated in schools. What's worse is that some teacher-developed assessments lack inclusive language or are insensitive to the ways content knowledge is delivered without oversight. Instead, racist language is sometimes wrongfully incorporated, leading to racial stereotypes of communities of color and marginalizing them within their own classrooms. The result impacts the trust and relationship between students and teachers, school climate, and student self-efficacy. These unchecked practices lead to irreparable harm to students of color and suggest how "grades reflect the interplay between the work of the classroom and society at large" (Schneider & Hutt, 2014).

THE ISSUE: RACIST CLASS QUIZ CREATED BY EDUCATOR

Examine how the class quiz elicits reactions and demonstrates several concerns both in and outside of the classroom. After the scenario is presented, you will move through explicitly identified issues and ways the issue can be addressed.

Scenario: Despite being in the twenty-first century, several incidents of teacher-developed assessments have made the news for racist language. Take, for example, the Virginia chemistry teacher who created a class quiz and used an insensitive pun of how George Floyd died as a way to address a chemical element. In reporting this incident, the student, who identifies as half Black and half white, confronted the teacher and felt alone in addressing this incident. Her white classmates pushed back and even objected to her claim of racial insensitivity. It was only through her persistent push on social media that the issue finally gained coverage without any school support (Natanson & Meckler, 2020).

Brainstorm some solutions before you move on.

ISSUE: RECOGNIZING RACIST LANGUAGE

Racist language is never acceptable. In this real-life example, Black people are being objectified by a teacher within a school setting, which reinforces the language as being normalized. This also leads to concerns of what other types of racist comments or objectification of people are made at school that goes unnoticed.

54 Assessing Through the Lens of Social and Emotional Learning

Solution: Address and implement inclusive language practices in all school-related communication, assignments, and assessments (Capital Region BOCES, 2021).

ISSUE: THE NEED TO ADDRESS RACIAL BIAS BY TEACHERS

If racial bias is not addressed, these incidents will continue. A teacher made a racially charged comment and felt comfortable enough to include it in a class quiz without recognizing how it is racially biased.

Solution: Schoolwide training and ongoing professional development is needed in understanding and recognizing one's own biases. Explicit antiracist training is also necessary (Boudreau, 2020).

ISSUE: THE NEED TO ASSESS AND ADDRESS RACIAL SCHOOL CLIMATE

The students' pushback and siding with the teacher is evidence that there is underlying racial tension present within the student population as well as the rest of the school. Further, the reporting student had no school support when raising the issue.

Solution: A racial school climate survey should be administered to include all stakeholders; further, an outside evaluation of a schoolwide equity review should be made to determine strengths and areas of growth for actionable, accountable steps (Graham, 2022). For more information about the racial school climate gap, see Voight et al. (2015).

HOW DOES THIS RELATE TO SEL?

There are several connections to be made here that can be damaging to a student's social and emotional development. The incident(s) is traumatizing to the student because of the lack of acknowledgment by the teacher in listening to the student's concerns, lack of teacher support when other students begin to gaslight her, and lack of school support when seeking help. When the settings that are supposed to be safe and supportive, such as the classroom and school, turn out to be harmful, we start to question the way learning takes place and how continuous assessment is conducted. Beginning with the impact on student-teacher relationships, the racially charged language exhibited by the teacher can lead to a loss of trust and damage teacher-student relationships. As the student expressed that she felt marginalized within her own classroom, it is not only the teacher who is contributing to the negative class climate, but also the students and their complicity in avoiding racist behavior by the teacher and gaslighting students of color. She does not feel welcomed and this can impact her sense of self within the process. Within the larger school setting, social and emotional support is missing to meet her needs through this traumatizing event.

VALIDITY IN TEACHER-DEVELOPED ASSESSMENTS

One of the challenges in reviewing teacher-developed assessments is validity. An argument can be made that resolving racist assessment practices can occur if teachers meet within groups to peer review their colleagues' assessments. However, it takes more than having teachers present.

Scenario: In Texas, three teachers administered the same racist test in their middle school social studies class, asking students to select a list of stereotypes of Chinese people on a social studies exam and asking students to identify one of them as a "norm" (Escobado & Liou, 2021). This test was used by three different social studies teachers and their classes. The harm endured and the messages it sends impacts not only Chinese and Asian students taking the exam, but also reinforces messages to all students that stereotypes based on race are acceptable. This creates a greater divide between teachers and students, pits ethnic and racial groups against one another, and normalizes racist behaviors against Asians. What is worse is the district's statement that teachers were recently provided with diversity training. This problematizes the situation in several ways, including the aforementioned issues from the previous example.

CHALLENGES AND SOLUTIONS

The Need to Address More Than Just Diversity: Diversity training may be well-intentioned and can offer insight into understanding different cultures and ethnic and racial groups, but it does not always dive deep into concepts of bias and ways to address them. Further, diversity is a siloed concept and is not inherently anti-racist. The teachers may claim their test was diverse because it included Chinese culture; however, the teachers need to distinguish the difference between understanding culture and racial stereotypes about a particular culture. Several issues are raised in this particular case of district diversity training, and several possible ways to address this issue are noted here:

1. **Needs assessment:** District and school site training should begin with a needs assessment to capture the nuanced and particular needs of a school site in how diversity, equity, and inclusion are being implemented.

2. **Training beyond the concept of diversity:** Consider the purpose and intent of the training. Is it to understand the diversity of the student population at a surface level, or is the training intended to address teacher knowledge (Schwartz, 2019)?

3. **Reconsider assessment options:** Use a standardized or district- or department of education–approved curriculum and assessment or take a learner-centered approach. Avoid teacher-created assessments that lack equity checks because they may promote biased perspectives. If assessments are not provided by the curriculum or district, consider a review process for approving teacher-created assessments using a rubric to ensure testing language is inclusive and bias-free.

4. **The need to assess content standards:** Each item on a test should demonstrate mastery toward a specific content and grade-level standard. The teacher-created assessment in the Texas example did not address a specific content standard.

5. **Teacher knowledge of content standards and how to assess them:** Consider the question or statement being made and how student responses demonstrate knowledge or meeting the content standard. Higher order thinking can occur within multiple-choice and even in true/false testing options.

6. **Address the difference between stereotype and fact:** The teachers should be trained in understanding the difference between a stereotype and a fact. Instead, the teacher created three stereotypes to appear to be true through language use such as "it is normal in China to . . ." which sounds like it must be true. The issue is to confuse students into seeing stereotypes as equaling truth. Separately, the assessment was delivered online using a multiple-choice format, with three stereotypes as the only possible options, none of which were true.

7. **The need for oversight in implementation of practices:** There is an apparent disconnect between how teachers were trained to understand the content versus the intention of the training. Separate is the lack of monitoring implementation into practice.

8. **Changes are needed in assessment development or practices:** Structures should be in place for administration to monitor and evaluate teacher-created assessments, particularly if they are being used across an entire grade level. Consider alternative methods to assessment, such as a learner-centered approach to demonstrate mastery through project-based learning or self-assessment.

HOW DOES THIS CONNECT TO SEL?

In adult SEL, let's think about what collective message the teachers who administered this test are sending to all of their students about people from China. Altogether it is bad decision-making, but beyond this is the reinforcement of stereotypes that is damaging to students who are guided to think racism is normalized by seeing it developed by teachers in printed classroom materials. Further, this disrupts any efforts of building social awareness on the part of the adults—they are not able to distinguish what is socially acceptable and appropriate. At the same time, it also demonstrates the teachers' limitations and lack of development in one's self-awareness due to the lack of self-examination of biased behavior. Adults require the necessary social and emotional skills to effectively communicate with students and model the positive behaviors and interactions they want their students to continuously progress toward as they face challenging experiences, such as this.

For student SEL, we should address the immediate impact a racist assessment had on student experience with schooling and how students are internalizing these messages as truths. Specifically, Asian American students who took the test were the students who identified the wrongs of the adults and called it out.

LOOKING AHEAD

Not every case of racism in teacher-created assessments or inequitable-based assessment practices reaches the media because test-takers are not able to copy the evidence due to restrictions on phone use during an exam. There continues to be limited awareness of students not realizing the language is racist, districts and schools avoiding unwanted attention, and private settlements between districts and impacted families. These explicit examples demonstrate the ways racist assessments persist under the radar within schools until students recognize the wrongs of their trusted teachers. We need to reconsider best practices for the development and approval process for assessments in schools and districts that center on content standards.

Traditional grading is embedded with ambiguity, including what qualifies as an A, and we know that the more ambiguous the situation, the more likely that implicit bias will operate and let a teacher's (Feldman, 2018, p. 189) "background experience and automatic associations shape his or her impressions of the scene" (Ogletree et al., 2012).

Traditional grading is embedded with ambiguity, including what qualifies as an A, and we know that the more ambiguous the situation, the more likely that implicit bias will operate and let a teacher's (Feldman, 2018, p. 189) "background experience and automatic associations shape his or her impressions of the scene" (Ogletree et al., 2012).

Let's continue to move forward with equitable grading, tests, and testing in our classrooms and in our work environments on this assessing journey.

Practitioner "Wondering" Reflection

Time for Your SEL Reflection Journal

In your SEL journal, reflect on what you have learned in this chapter. Consider these prompts:

- What is one way you can ensure that you are grading with equity?
- Are assessment and data practices conducted with diversity in mind?
- When you create groups and subgroups, how can you ensure this is done through the lens of equity?

Takeaway to Practice

What is the one takeaway from this chapter you want to put into action? **Name it. Create your action plan.**

CHAPTER 5

Assessment Pedagogy and Design

Assessment should not be a mere snapshot in time; it should be a video of a student's growth over time.

—Carol Ann Tomlinson

LEARNING OUTCOMES

Colleagues on the assessing journey will be able to

- Explore the pedagogy of assessment
- Apply Universal Design for Learning (UDL) to social and emotional learning skills, competencies, and dispositions
- Discover research on differentiation, learner variability, and accommodations
- Dive into the "why" of formative assessment
- Explore how assessment practices and strategies can be culturally relevant for certain populations

---

This chapter will prepare you for the chapters that follow, which focus on many tools and strategies that are aligned to social and emotional learning pedagogy, skills, and competencies. Later, in Chapter 9, you will apply some of the strategies to build an SEL assessment plan that works for you and your learners.

Our goal is to front load you with sound assessment practices that ensure *every* learner's goals are met, continuously measured, assessed, and re-assessed. To make this a reality, we must first discuss designing learning for instruction through the lens of SEL.

UNIVERSAL DESIGN FOR LEARNING AND SOCIAL AND EMOTIONAL LEARNING

WHAT IS UNIVERSAL DESIGN FOR LEARNING?

SEL assessing is achieved by applying Universal Design for Learning principles. According to CAST (formerly the Center for Applied Special Technology), "Universal Design for Learning (UDL) is a framework to improve and optimize teaching and learning for all people based on scientific insights into how humans learn." (See also QR code.) The framework applies learning theory to guide the design of instructional goals, assessments, methods, and materials so that all learning can be customized and adjusted to meet individual needs. When UDL is applied to assessments and assessing, it allows for individualization that is inherently connected to meet the social and emotional needs of all learners. In order for assessing and assessments to be designed and deployed in an SEL manner, they must also be UDL compliant.

The three main principles of UDL are:

1. Providing multiple means of representation—presenting information in multiple ways to support diverse learning needs and preferences. (Various assessment types address SEL competencies.)

2. Providing multiple means of action and expression—offering students multiple ways to demonstrate their knowledge and skills. (An assessment is a means for demonstrating knowledge; formative, summative, performance-based, self-assessment, peer assessment, and project-based assessments give learners varied options to demonstrate their knowledge and skills.)

3. Providing multiple means of engagement—fostering a variety of ways for students to be motivated, interested, and engaged in learning. (Culturally relevant assessments, gamified formative assessments, and age-appropriate assessments all allow for optimal engagement of learning and demonstrating mastery of content.)

Chapter 5 • Assessment Pedagogy and Design • 61

HOW DOES ASSESSMENT MEET UDL STANDARDS AND PRACTICES?

bit.ly/3PWTb2Z

CAST quotes Salvia and colleagues' 2009 text, *Assessment in Special and Inclusive Education*, which says that assessment is the process of gathering information about a learner's performance to make educational decisions. UDL encourages "assessment by design" (see Figure 5.1).

FIGURE 5.1 • UDL Tips for Designing Assessments for All Learners

UDL ASSESSMENT TIP (CAST)	CONNECTIONS TO SEL
Accessibility of all materials need to be free from bias	Accessibility built into items from the beginning, along with necessary bias review procedures ensure that quality is retained in all items.* Thompson et al. (2002)
Alignment of assessments to learning goals	Goal setting is grounded in SEL. Goal setting supports self-management and self-awareness.
Offer authentic opportunities for assessment	Authenticity connects to the learners' interests and to their lived experiences making assessment more meaningful. Meaningful assessment is accompanied by meaningful learning.
Assess engagement as well as content knowledge	Engagement practices need to meet social norms, address the diversity of the learners, and help to motivate learning in a culturally responsive way.
Include frequent formative assessment	Formative assessing is authentic assessment.
Reduce unnecessary barriers to access	Access to assessments supports inclusion and allows fair and equitable practices for all.
Use and share rubrics to clarify expectations	Assessing by rubric supports all SEL skills and competencies. Each learner can move toward individual mastery by understanding expectations and outcomes. Rubrics can also be accompanied by exemplars or mentor texts.
Involve learners in the learning process	Just as instruction is adapted to meet the individual's needs, SEL assessing should always be learner centered.
Reflect on summative assessments	Reflection is a necessary component to support continuous improvement for all learners. Question to ask: Do summative assessments really measure what they need to measure?
Build communities of practice that support	Community-building practices establish stronger relationships among educators, within grade level teams, and throughout the schoolwide community when reflective design is practiced.

Source: Adapted from © CAST (2023).

DIFFERENTIATION OF SEL TOOLS: DIVERSITY AND LEARNER VARIABILITY

Differentiation also used synonymously with learner variability, exists in every classroom. In special education, accommodations are made to adapt to the individual needs of the students. Although diversity is often thought of in relation to students' backgrounds and abilities (e.g., students receiving special education services, English language learners, culturally and linguistically diverse students), *variability* is not limited to any particular category of students. Learner variability comes in many forms and applies to all students and includes individual and personal attributes of students that impact how they experience schooling (Rao & Meo, 2016, p. 1).

DIFFERENTIATED ASSESSMENTS FOR INCLUSION: NATIONAL CENTER ON EDUCATIONAL OUTCOMES

The National Center on Educational Outcomes (NCEO) focuses on the inclusion of students with disabilities, English learners, and English learners with disabilities, in instruction and assessments. The scope of NCEO's work includes issues related to accessibility of assessments across the comprehensive assessment system, including formative assessment practices, classroom-based assessments, diagnostic assessments, interim assessments, and summative assessments.

NCEO (also see QR code) states how assessments need to adhere to standards of clarity, text type, font size, etc. so that access is ensured. For example, the clarity of instructions and procedures needs to be simple, clear, and presented in understandable language. Readability and plain language increases the likelihood that learners can read and comprehend the materials. A variety of readability and plain language guidelines need to be followed (e.g., sentence length and number of difficult words are kept to a minimum). With state and national laws playing a regulatory role in accessibility for all assessment materials and practices, we still do not see clear and explicit connections that meet the social and emotional needs for learning.

nceo.info

SELECTING, ADAPTING, AND DESIGNING ASSESSMENTS THAT ARE INCLUSIVE

Selecting assessment tools and strategies that adhere to UDL principles, accommodate, differentiate, and are adjusted to individual learners can be a very complex task, but it doesn't have to be. You will be amazed by how many of the assessing practices we currently use every day in the classroom meet the social and emotional learning needs for our learners.

THE CASE FOR FORMATIVE ASSESSMENT

As we have emphasized in previous chapters and will continue to stress in the subsequent chapters of this book, formative assessment practices are prepared, delivered, and received by learners with social and emotional literacy in mind.

> Since 2001, Federal Laws such as the Elementary and Secondary Education Act (ESEA) and the Individuals with Disabilities Education Act (IDEA) 2004 have made raising student achievement standards the center of our national conversation. Consequently, educators have increasingly turned their attention to exploring the potential of formative assessments as one approach to increasing student outcomes (Black & William, 1998) in order to meet federal and state accountability requirements. Meanwhile, the upcoming reauthorization of ESEA and the work of the Partnership for Assessment of Readiness for College and Careers (PARCC) consortium and SMARTER Balanced Assessment Consortium (SBAC), funded through Race to the Top (RTT), have heightened and expanded the need for formative assessment practices in American classrooms (Davidson & Frohbieter, 2011; Dorn, 2010). SBAC has designed a comprehensive system that strategically balances formative, interim, and summative assessments (K–12 Center at ETS, 2011). (Madison-Harris & Muoneke, 2012)

FACTS ABOUT FORMATIVE ASSESSMENT

Formative assessment is an ongoing process of assessing that aims to evaluate and improve student learning throughout a course or unit, as opposed to a summative assessment that measures achievement at the end of it.

1. Formative assessment can take many different forms, including quizzes, class discussions, homework assignments, peer evaluations, and teacher observations.
2. The goal of formative assessment is to provide feedback to both students and teachers, allowing them to adjust their teaching and learning strategies to better meet the needs of the students.
3. Formative assessment helps students to develop their metacognitive skills, which are the skills necessary for self-directed learning and problem-solving.
4. Effective formative assessment requires clear learning objectives, aligned assessments, and meaningful feedback.
5. Formative assessment can be used to identify students who may need additional support or intervention, allowing teachers to provide targeted assistance.
6. Formative assessment is different from summative assessment, which measures student achievement at the end of a course or unit.
7. Formative assessment is an ongoing process and should be used throughout a course or unit to ensure that students are making progress and mastering the content.

FORMATIVE ASSESSMENT TECHNIQUES FOR THE CLASSROOM

Many educators use culturally responsive assessment techniques, such as interactive games and online quizzing. (See chapter on Digital Tools and Technologies).

Many of these techniques fall into the category of "Checking for Understanding" or what one author refers to as "Quick Check" strategies (Berger et al., 2014). In their book, *Leaders of Their Own Learning*, Berger and colleagues show dozens of examples of how students can be engaged through assessment (see QR code).

tinyurl.com/cfudailycheckins

RESOURCES FOR CHECKING FOR UNDERSTANDING (CFU)

NAME OF CFU TECHNIQUE	DESCRIPTION
Traffic Light	When teachers want to make sure that concepts are being understood, they ask students to hold up green, yellow, or red signs (cards, sticks, paper strips). Green means "I know, I can do it myself," yellow means "I'm not sure or I have a question," and red means "I don't understand, I need help."

(Continued)

(Continued)

NAME OF CFU TECHNIQUE	DESCRIPTION
Glass, Bugs, Mud	Similar to traffic lights, glass = crystal clear understanding, bugs = a little fuzzy, mud = I can barely see.
No Hands Up	Pause with wait time, then select individuals.
Thumb-o-meter **Fist to Fives**	Show degrees of agreement with thumbs and fingers.
Go Around	When a one- or two-word answer can show understanding for a task, teachers can ask students to say their word or words and go around the room in secession.
Popcorn	Shout responses out randomly like popcorn popping.
Do Now	A do now is any activity that you have at the very beginning of class that helps you set the tone for that day. Quickly, quietly, get started right away. Go ahead and get started right now on your do now.
Think, Pair, Share	Turn and Talk/Think, Pair, Share interactions give students an opportunity to deepen their understanding while practicing their verbal skills.
Double Think, Pair, Share	Two teams are involved in this activity. After the allotted time of sharing with their partner, each pair then finds another pair to share answers with. As the first team reads their answers aloud, the second team adds new ideas to their list or puts a check mark next to items they also thought of. The second team then shares answers that were missing from the first team's list.
Explain It Back (similar to Turn and Talk)	Ask students to repeat or summarize instructions or content to a group or a partner in their own words to check for misinterpretations.
Sticky Note Storm	Also referred to as a "snowstorm" if white pieces of paper are used.
Sage and Scribe	One student plays the role of teacher, and the other plays the attentive student. Explaining concepts clearly is a difficult skill that requires a lot of practice, and recording information helps students build note-taking skills.
Inside Out Circle **Parallel Lines** **(also called Tea Party, Face-to-Face, Serpentine, Ladder)**	1. The teacher poses a question, sets a time limit, and gives students a moment to think before writing. For example, "In two minutes, how many words about photosynthesis can you write down?" or "In 45 seconds, write down as many adjectives as you can." 2. Each student writes down as many answers as they can think of—one idea per sticky note—and sticks it to the center of the table. 3. Some teachers allow students to throw the papers up in the air to represent a "snowstorm."

66 Assessing Through the Lens of Social and Emotional Learning

NAME OF CFU TECHNIQUE	DESCRIPTION
Detective **(steps adapted from We Are Teachers;** **also known as a Scavenger Hunt)**	1. Give each student a prepared worksheet featuring several questions. Students then circulate and find a partner, just as in Mingle, Pair, Share. Just like a detective, they are off in search of answers! Partner 1 asks partner 2 one question from their worksheet. 2. Partner 2 provides an answer, and partner 1 writes it on their own worksheet. Partners then switch roles. After both students have asked and answered one question, they split up and each look for a new partner. 3. Students continue circulating until all answers on their worksheet have been filled in. Then they return to their seats until everyone is finished. 4. Once they are back in their desk groups, teams compare answers. If there are discrepancies among the answers and they cannot come to a consensus, they may raise their hands as a team and ask the teacher for clarification.
Quiz, Quiz, Trade	1. Prepare review cards with questions and answers. (This sounds time consuming, but it can be as simple as cutting up one review sheet into individual cards or having students be involved in preparing the cards.) 2. Pass out one review card per student. 3. Students stand and circulate with one hand in the air, searching for a partner. 4. Once they pair up, partner 1 asks partner 2 the question on their card. Partner 2 answers. If they get the answer correct, partner 1 offers praise. If not, partner 1 coaches partner 2 until the correct answer is revealed. 5. Partners switch roles and repeat the question-answer process. 6. After both partners have asked and answered, they trade cards and set off to find a new partner. The process continues for whatever amount of time the teacher determines is appropriate.

(Continued)

(Continued)

NAME OF CFU TECHNIQUE	DESCRIPTION
Flash **(good for review!)**	1. Prepare question and answer cards. Each student will also need a dry-erase board and a marker or scrap paper and a pencil. Explain the concept of "think time" to your students before you begin so that slower processors don't feel anxious. 2. Assign one student in each desk group to be the leader. 3. Have question-answer cards stacked face down on the table. 4. The leader draws the top card and asks the other three team members the question on the card. 5. The leader calls "think time" and counts to ten. Students may not pick up their pen or pencil until think time is over. 6. Then, each individual writes down their answer, shielding their answer from their desk mates. 7. The leader says "flash." Each student turns their board (or paper) face out and "flashes" their answer for the others to see. 8. The group discusses the answers shown. If they are all the same, they ask the captain to verify that the answer is correct. If there are different answers, the students discuss the discrepancy and try to come to agreement on one answer. The leader (who has the answer) can coach but cannot just tell the answer. 9. For the next round, the role of leader rotates to the right, and the process repeats. Continue until all cards have been asked and answered.
Write Around	1. A fun activity for creative writing or story summarizing or collaborative writing. 2. The teacher provides a sentence starter for the class, both verbally and in writing (on a doc cam or white board). For example: *If you give a mouse a cookie* . . . or *in the beginning of* Because of Winn Dixie . . . 3. Ask each student to copy the sentence starter and finish the sentence on their own piece of paper. 4. After they have written their answer, each student passes their paper to the team member on their right. 5. Next, the student reads the paper they have received from their neighbor and adds a new sentence to that page. 6. Again, they pass the paper to their right. 7. After a few go-rounds, four great stories or summaries emerge. 8. Give students time to read their final versions, add a conclusion, and/or edit their favorite one to share with the class.

And for an example for checking for understanding in action, see the QR code.

68 • Assessing Through the Lens of Social and Emotional Learning

ASSESSMENT TOOLS THAT SUPPORT SEL SKILLS AND COMPETENCIES

In the next chapter, we will present a tool chest full of assessment tools and assessing strategies that support SEL skills, competencies, and dispositions by the category of user, tools for student use, and tools for teacher use. In Chapter 7, we will discuss the role technology and digital tools play in the assessment. We will also present considerations of why we use the tools, when to use these tools, and how to integrate technology through the lens of a humanistic or social and emotional experience.

https://vimeo.com/43990520

Practitioner "Wondering" Reflection

Time for Your SEL Reflection Journal

In your SEL journal, reflect on what you have learned in this chapter. Consider these prompts:

- What are some pedagogical features of assessment?
- Do my everyday assessing practices apply Universal Design for Learning (UDL)?
- Do my assessing tools and practices support differentiation, learner variability, and accommodations?
- Why is formative assessment so critical to practice?

Takeaway to Practice

What is the one takeaway from this chapter you want to put into action? **Name it. Create it. Add it to your action plan** (which you will be writing in Chapter 9).

CHAPTER 6

Assessment Tools and Strategies

Assessment should not be a tool for ranking, grading, or judging students, but rather a tool for promoting learning and growth.

—Linda Suskie

> **LEARNING OUTCOMES**
>
> Colleagues on the assessing journey will be able to
>
> - Explore various assessing processes and understand how we apply them through the lens of SEL
> - Explain and understand the SEL connection to student-centered assessing
> - Demonstrate how conventional tools and strategies can be used for assessing
> - Have the knowledge, skills, and motivation to change the assessing culture beginning in your own learning environment

BEGIN WITH LEARNER IDENTITY

When we examine assessment through a social and emotional lens and from a learner-centered perspective, we can apply the SEL skills of self-awareness and self-management. When learners are more self-aware and apply management skills during learning, then they will achieve greater success. Let's begin this journey by first addressing learner identity. Learner identity consists of a learner's own perceptions, emotions, and feelings, and what they believe is their capacity for learning. It's unfortunate that in our schools today, there is a spotlight shining on mental health, severe anxiety, stress, test anxiety, and a perceived sense of failure. Our students understand early on that their perception of self and perception of learning directly impacts their success. Self-perception is often clouded by general distress, by mental or emotional problems, or sometimes by feeling anxious about a task or performance. Anxiety of all types can and do impede learning.

Anxiety disorders are some of the most widespread mental health issues worldwide. In educational settings, individuals may suffer from specific forms of test and performance anxiety that are connected to a knowledge domain. Unquestionably, the most prominent of these is math anxiety (Luttenberger et al., 2018, p. 311).

MATH ANXIETY

According to the Programme for International Student Assessment's (PISA; OECD, 2013) examination of middle school students across thirty-four participating Organisation for Economic Co-operation and Development (OECD) countries, 59 percent of the fifteen- to sixteen-year-old students reported that they often worry math classes will be difficult for them; "33% reported that they get very tense when they have to complete math homework, and another 31% stated they get very nervous doing math problems" (p. 312). These statistics continue to show evidence of the widespread issue of math anxiety and academic performance anxiety among school-age children and in all learners.

Learner identity applies an asset mindset of learning rather than a deficit mindset. A recent SEL graduate (2020) who teaches sixth-grade math had been faced with the problem of her students (both male and female) reporting math anxiety. Rather than focusing on deficit language, we turned her research around and looked at it through the lens of a growth mindset. We changed the title of her work from a focus on math anxiety to "Developing a Positive Math Identity in Middle School Mathematics" (Holden, 2021). With this new direction, we were able to address the issue of math anxiety, as well as the fear and obstacles of learning mathematics. We proved that learners could develop a positive sense of self and strengthen their personal math identity by adopting a growth mindset and an "I can do" attitude to help build strength, persistence, and resilience. Students in her class approached their learning through a success model, applying master learning, self-checks, and a learning progression. They were able to track their emotions, and their mindsets, and take personal responsibility for their learning. Many of the software tools in mathematics, such as iReady®, are designed to track progress in mathematics, so the individual learner can see their personalized growth in learning on a dashboard.

Chapter 6 • Assessment Tools and Strategies   71

FLEXIBLE AND GROWTH MINDSET APPLIED TOWARD LEARNING

When faced with learning, making progressions through content, and gaining growth in knowledge and application of the content, learners need to not only have a positive sense of self but also be challenged by work that is "just right." In their pivotal work, Vygotsky and Cole (1978) define the Zone of Proximal Development (ZPD) as

> The distance between the actual developmental level as determined by independent problem-solving and the level of potential development as determined through problem-solving under adult guidance or in collaboration with more capable peers. (Vygotsky & Cole, 1978, p. 86)

In other words, learning is the result of being in "just the right zone"—one that is challenging, but not too challenging; one that, with instructional guidance, allows the learner to meet, exceed, and set new goals.

When learners are assessed on concepts, topics, or even terms they do not know or have never been exposed to, this can cause extreme cognitive dissonance. No amount of grit or determination to achieve learning mastery can be substituted by extrinsic motivation or even praise. While they need to be challenged, learners are faced with a belief system about testing and assessment that is not in alignment with ZPD or other theories associated with brain science. Failure is associated with perceptions of learning that are not favorable and often lead to negative learner identity, guilt, shame, and a loss of worth. We often hear from our graduate students that they are devastated when they earn a B grade on their assignments. The desire to reach for that A and to achieve excellence is sometimes not grounded in reality. After all, is it the grade or the learning that matters? Somewhere along the way, the instruction did not include enough scaffolding, knowledge checks through formative assessment, authenticity, connection to the real world, or being grounded by "what's in it for me." Often, the answer to the question, "Teacher, why do we have to learn this?" is "Because it's on the test." We must teach our learners to reframe their perceptions of intelligence and their responses to failure. The adage "failure is not an option" should not be embedded into the fabric of learning; rather, we need to see failure as an opportunity for growth.

72　Assessing Through the Lens of Social and Emotional Learning

TRIAL AND ERROR

Trial and error are the foundation of science and innovation. Take, for example, Audri (Littlepythagoras, 2012), a then seven-year-old who became a YouTube sensation by sharing his Rube Goldberg machines (a machine that creates a chain reaction). "Rube Goldberg machines do not always work on the first try," noted Audri. Predicting the number of times he would experience failure with his machine, he further created a hypothesis: "I think it will have ten to twenty failures and two successes." Watch the video available at the QR code and see the joy he experiences when he is successful after just three trials!

As the old saying goes, "if at first you do not succeed, try and try again" (first credited to Robert the Bruce, king of Scotland, in 1314 although it has been used in history by many others, including W. C. Fields and Benjamin Franklin).

Another SEL competency applied in trial and error applications is responsible decision-making, which often leads to solving problems. Trial and error science is endemic to problem-solving; we learn by making attempts and then by changing our direction to find workable solutions. Trial and error require formulating a hypothesis, testing, predicting, extending, imagining, visualizing, and many other processes to solve problems. Adopting and embracing the process of problem-solving through trial and error can lead to mastery learning. Mastery learning is an SEL-focused, fair, and equitable assessment practice where learning depends on mistakes. Feldman (2018), in his text *Grading for Equity*, mentions the practice of "retakes" (which is taking summative assessments over again until the content is mastered). This process allows students to "fix their errors and give it another try until they succeed" (p. 165). To put this process in context, Feldman describes who the learner is and the circumstances that would justify a retake. First of all, as previously mentioned, test taking, especially summative test taking, is a daunting process for many humans. When a person performs poorly on an assessment, there are likely to be conditions that caused this. Moving into test taking with a mindset of failure causes guilt and shame, and discourages the learner from succeeding.

youtu.be/
0uDDEEHDf1Y

Feldman (2018) lists three conditions for allowing retakes in education:

1. Student had some kind of interfering event that prevented them from performing their best.
2. The format or design of the test itself impeded the student from communicating their knowledge (trick questions, confusing syntax, complicated word choices, and complex sentence structure).

3. Student was inadequately prepared or had a weak understanding. (p. 166)

Applying the practice of retakes will help open the door for students' success; the more you try different approaches, the better you will be at learning, and the more you will be successful in academics, through summative and formative assessment practices.

This philosophy of learning takes into consideration brain science and how we tap into our neural networks. Research shows the optimum number of repetitions needed by humans for knowledge to be transferred into the long-term memory of the brain is seventeen. Seventeen repetitions for learning are widely researched and proven to be the number of times required to learn vocabulary words and other concepts (sometimes even a math formula). The number of repetitions must involve a variety of methods over planned periods of time. Take, for example, what my children's Suzuki violin teacher always said: "You need to practice every time you eat." If you eat three times a day, with snacks included, in a week's period of time, you will have practiced at least twenty-one times, which is definitely an optimum number (Sistek-Chandler, personal conversation).

The US Department of Education, Institute of Education Sciences, and National Center for Education Evaluation and Regional Assistance (Kamil et al., 2008) released a learning guide that directs educators to provide explicit instruction of vocabulary. Repetition is the key to memory, especially long-term memory. We will discuss the importance of repetitions and the importance of meaningful instruction and how they support learning and learning progressions across the curriculum later in the chapter.

FIXED MINDSET AND GROWTH MINDSET

How do the concepts of fixed and growth mindset address assessment, and how are they connected with learner identity? A fixed mindset is associated with the philosophy and belief that intelligence is fixed and cannot be changed. On the contrary, intelligence is malleable and can be changed by adopting a different mindset, called a "growth mindset," as coined by psychologist Carol Dweck of Stanford University. Dweck argues that a fixed mindset prohibits humans (students) from developing to their full potential. As previously described, we should not protect students from failure, mistakes, and challenging tasks. Many noted practitioners and researchers have stated that a comfort zone does not provide a challenge or incentive for growth.

> Many educators think that lowering their standards
> will give students success experiences, boost their

self-esteem, and raise their achievement. . . . Well, it doesn't work. Lowering standards just leads to poorly educated students who feel entitled to easy work and lavish praise. (Dweck, 2006, p. 193)

When learners adopt a growth mindset, their abilities, intelligence, and talents can be developed through effort, persistence, grit, determination, and, most importantly, by purposeful instruction from an assessment-literate educator. Instruction that includes formative assessment and provides individualized feedback on assignments paves the way for higher achievement.

In Chapter 4, we discussed the achievement gap in the United States and explored some reasons why this gap is so prevalent in our multiracial schools today. As Muhammad (2020) theorizes in her book *Cultivating Genius*, this gap exists due to a superior or victim mindset; she offers hope by suggesting that we embrace a liberation mindset. Assessment literacy is indeed impacted by mindset and is inextricably connected to social and emotional tenets.

Of course, we cannot talk about a growth mindset without making a connection to intrinsic and extrinsic motivation. Students need both kinds of motivation to learn, achieve, and succeed. With a positive assessment mindset, learners will intrinsically be motivated by tracking their individual learning progressions and applying strategies for self-assessment those that are based on social and emotional learning practices. When was the last time you heard a learner boast about their accomplishments, beam with joy, and be proud of themselves? Extrinsic motivation must be balanced not by praising students for success on easy tasks, but rather by rewarding success through challenge, encouragement, guidance, and by creating a safe environment for risk-taking. In a learning environment that is extrinsically motivating, the educator creates a trusting relationship with the learner, one that provides many opportunities for personalized authentic experiences and assessments.

In this next section we will:

- Share assessment practices that are grounded in SEL, as well as those that are student-centered.
- Frame learning through goal setting and address the assets of the learner (not the deficit).
- Present various types of check-ins for assessing.
- Show models of learning using sentence frames and templates.

Chapter 6 • Assessment Tools and Strategies 75

- Share culturally responsive practices from Zaretta Hammond's (2018) Anchor Framework.

- Explain how self-assessments and self-reflection support learning, and present a relatively new method of assessing exit tickets (written and digital).

- Show how various strategies, practices, and tools address the five SEL competencies. (see Figure 6.1).

FIGURE 6.1 ● Assessment Strategies for Teaching and Student Learning

PRACTICE/ STRATEGY	SEL COMPETENCIES	REFERENCE
Individual Goal Setting SMART Goals	Self-Awareness Self-Management	Goal-Setting Theory (Locke & Latham, 2013)
Check-ins for Formative Assessment	Self-Awareness Self-Management	Classroom Techniques (Cross & Angelo, 1993)
Emotional Check-Ins	Self-Awareness Self-Management	Zones of Regulation Mood Meter RULER (Brackett et al., 2019) Impact on Behavior
Entry Tickets Exit Tickets	Self-Awareness Self-Management	Fowler et al. (2019) K-W-L (Ogle, 1986)
Sentence Frames	Self-Awareness Self-Management Responsible Decision-Making	Block (2019) Roe (2014) Westby (2013)
"I" Statements Narrative Writing with Affirmations	Self-Awareness	Dillon (2010) Dillon et al. (2009, 2011)
Writing Frames	Self-Awareness Recognizing Relationships	Writing Frames (Lewis & Wray, 1996)

PRACTICE/ STRATEGY	SEL COMPETENCIES	REFERENCE
Self-Assessment	Self-Awareness Self-Management	Devaney et al. (2006) Yoder (2014) Self-Assessing Social and Emotional Instruction and Competencies: A Tool for Teachers, Center on Great Teachers and Leaders
Self-Reflection Metacognition	Self-Awareness	McMillan & Hearn (2008)
Student Self-Assessment Reflection and Journaling	Self-Awareness Self-Management	Numerous references, including Allport (1942, journal as self-reflective autobiography), Bromley & Powell (1999), and Bromley (2007)

GOAL SETTING AS A PLANNING AND ASSESSING STRATEGY

Goal setting addresses two main areas of SEL, self-awareness (SA) and self-management (SM). How goal setting works and how it strengthens SA and SM skills and competencies can be explained by brain science. *Executive function* is a term used to explain cognitive processes, including planning, working memory, attention, inhibition, self-monitoring, self-regulation, and initiation carried out by prefrontal areas of the frontal lobes. Planning is a critical piece to goal setting. Goal setting involves brain-based practices that promote learning, many of which focus on the sequential, linear processing of information. In order to activate executive function to initiate pre-planning and predict steps and processes, applying a goal-setting strategy helps to build a foundation, incremental steps for progressing, meaningful memory, and success with learning. Experts say that it is important to set short-term, medium-term, and long-term goals. Making a visible timeline of goals can assist students with a sequential aid for anticipating and attending to what is next. Goals are your steppingstones that guide students along the path to personal success.

Chapter 6 • Assessment Tools and Strategies 77

SMART GOALS

Goal-setting steps are often summarized by the acronym SMART, developed by Dr. Edwin Locke in the 1960s while examining the relationship between motivation and goal setting in a factory environment. Locke found that when employees were motivated, given clear goals, and provided with feedback about their performance that this process would in turn increase their overall performance (original work by Locke, 1968, in Locke & Latham, 2013). The application of SMART goals is a tangible model for developing "actionable" learning goals. SMART goals are Specific, Measurable, Attainable, Realistic, and Time bound. For a SMART goal to be effective, we must pay close attention to the word "actionable." It is through a series of actions, steps, and the completion of objectives that we will reach a desirable outcome and an overall goal.

1. **Specific**—define your goal in detail, and describe exactly and precisely what is being pursued

2. **Measurable**—decide how success will be tracked through completion (are there deliverables, artifacts, or projects?)

3. **Attainable**—set realistic goals and challenging goals that can be achieved

4. **Realistic and Relevant**—determine whether this goal can realistically be accomplished

5. **Timely or Time Bound**—establish a timeframe for completion

FIGURE 6.2 ● SMART Goals PowerPoint Template

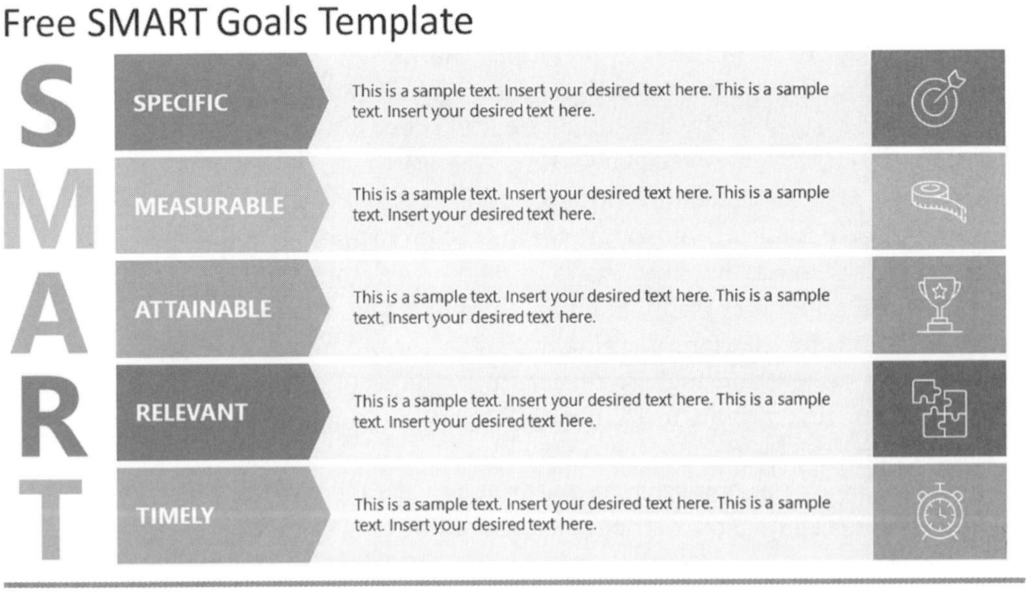

Free SMART Goals Template

Source: slidemodel.com.

78 ● Assessing Through the Lens of Social and Emotional Learning

Students use the SMART goals method for tracking personal success, meeting deadlines, and reaching attainable outcomes (see Figure 6.2). Another successful application is for peer review between teams.

tinyurl.com/
pptsmartgoals

CHECK-INS AS AN ASSESSMENT STRATEGY

Using check-ins as an assessment strategy supports formative assessment as a means to reveal gaps in understanding and remove assumptions about what students know and are able to do. Check-ins may take various formats, such as written, verbal, gesture-based (thumbs up, down, or sideways), or via an interactive device through polling or even a response to a question related to content. In instructional pedagogy, check-ins are an important part of any lesson to "check for understanding" (Hunter, 2004). Typically, check-ins occur throughout the lesson as quick spurts of checking for comprehension. Finally, check-ins are premier formative classroom assessment strategies that have "very low stakes, can be ungraded or reflect a minor grade" (Caldera, 2020, p. 178).

EMOTIONAL CHECK-INS AND EMOTIONAL LABELING

Emotional check-ins have been proven to be an authentic measure for identifying emotions and heightening a learner's self-awareness. Emotional check-ins also help students learn to recognize emotions in themselves and in others, "offering students the opportunity to practice navigating emotions and building strong relationships... maybe most importantly, a check-in sets the ideal context for learning" (Johnson, 2022, para. 5).

Why are emotional check-ins such a critical process for learning? Without emotional check-ins and emotional awareness, learning cannot occur. This is a strong statement that is connected to numerous research studies about cognition, emotions, and the brain. Neuroscience shows us through highlighted brain scans that when words, ideas, thoughts, and concepts light up in the brain, the emotional state of the human plays a part in brain activity. Dr. Marc Brackett and colleagues from the Yale Center for Emotional Intelligence have studied this emotional phenomenon for more than a decade. In Brackett's book *Permission to Feel*, he examines the premise that learning cannot be achieved without a connection to acute self-awareness and self-management. Emotions are the foundation of learning. There are many conditions that aid in the complex process of learning and make up the

tinyurl.com/
circumplexgame

learning ecosystem, such as interpreting visual representation, graphics, and models; connecting through oral-aural communication; and developing community and trust building in the learning environment. Pointing back to educating the whole child in specific settings, "the success of any attempt to educate the whole child is dependent upon the extent to which learning occurs in caring, supportive, safe, and empowering settings" (Brackett & Rivers, 2014, p. 368).

The RULER approach is anchored in the "achievement model of emotional literacy" (Rivers & Brackett, 2011, p. 78), which states that "acquiring and valuing the knowledge and skills of recognizing, understanding, labeling, expressing, and regulating emotion (i.e., the RULER skills) is critical to youth development, academic engagement and achievement, and life success" (Brackett & Rivers, 2014, p. 374). Another reason why labeling emotions is a powerful tool for learning is to provide a model to examine an emotional outcome. Russell's 2D Distribution of Emotion (Russell, 1980; Russell & Barrett, 1999) helps differentiate between core affect and prototypical emotion episodes (PEE). According to Russell, "any emotion can be described using an unpleasantness/pleasantness dimension (valence) and a high arousal/low arousal dimension (activation)" (Guthrie Yarwood, 2022).

You may want to play an emotional labeling game using the QR code.

EMOTIONAL LABELING DIAGRAMS

There are many visuals that support the labeling of emotions: Mood Meter, Zones of Regulation, Plutchik's Wheel of Emotion, Gloria Wilcox's Feeling Wheel, and Vygotsky's Zone of Proximal Development.

Another visual aid used effectively to reinforce memory is Edgar Dale's Cone of Experience. This is also referred to as the Learning Experience Model (see Figure 6.3).

IDENTIFYING OUR EMOTIONS

How many emotions do humans have and why is it important to measure emotional regulation? Psychiatric science points to four core emotions—happiness, sadness, fear, and anger—which are differentially associated with three core effects: reward (happiness), punishment (sadness), and stress (fear and anger). Depending on whose research you study, there are many categorical lists. Scientific reports state that we as humans can potentially experience and name a total of 34,000 emotions. For a deeper analysis of emotions, refer to Keltner and Haidt (1999) and their

FIGURE 6.3 • Example Learning Experience Model

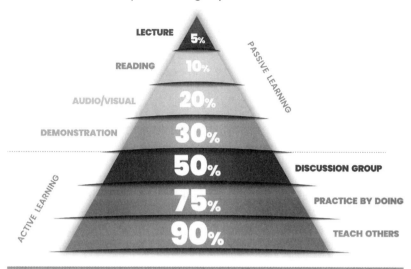

Image source: iStock.com/Chavapong Prateep Na Thalang

taxonomy of analysis of the social functions of emotion by classification of individual emotion, dyadic emotion, group emotion, and emotions that are related to culture.

SPOTLIGHT ON THE SCIENCE OF EMOTION

Hoffman and colleagues (2020) from Yale have studied how the science of emotion identification and emotion regulation applies in a classroom setting. Hoffman et al. propose that it is essential to explicitly teach emotion regulation skills and that it is critical for students to develop emotional vocabulary. Their work notes that it is essential to explicitly teach emotional regulation skills not as an isolated practice but through integration of "emotion skills into academic content, school routines, and regular practices that make emotion regulation skill building as part of everyday learning" (Hoffman et al., 2020, p. 105).

> *It is essential to explicitly teach emotion regulation skills not as an isolated practice but through integration of "emotion skills into academic content, school routines, and regular practices that make emotion regulation skill building as part of everyday learning" (Hoffman et al., 2020, p. 105).*

EMOTIONAL PRESENCE

Experiences that impact your emotional presence help develop self-compassion. By recognizing and labeling an emotion, you can take appropriate compassionate action. Your kind inner voice can tell you that you are human and that it is okay to experience emotions that are unfavorable. You can try to learn from the experience to see how you can do it differently next time; thus, assessing one's emotions allows you to move through the emotion making space and time in the brain for learning and transformation.

ENTRY TICKETS AND EXIT TICKETS

An entry ticket can be as simple and quick as a well-known strategy called K-W-L, which requires recalling what they *know*, determining what they *want* to learn, and identifying what they *learned* (Ogle, 1986). Entry assessment tickets promote assessing for prior knowledge, obtaining feedback from your learners about what they want to learn by tapping into their passions and insights, and gaining an understanding of how the content might be personalized to relate to the student's culture and background.

An exit ticket is a powerful way to assess the effectiveness of a lesson. Fowler and colleagues (2019) conducted a "mini experiment" where they analyzed exit tickets as a formative assessment. Their participants included middle and high school science teachers from varying science disciplines. A variety of exit ticket types were predesigned that included specific prompts. (See Fowler's 2019 article for a more in-depth description and examples of the exit tickets). Teachers collected these tickets and did not review them until they were together. To simulate an actual exit-ticket review experience, teachers were only given seven minutes to look through their exit tickets, make sense of the results with a partner, and consider the next steps. Adding the seven-minute time limit for the review emulated the need for the exit ticket to be "quickly interpreted after school or during a single planning period" (Fowler et al., 2019, p. 20). The exit-ticket process created a start-to-finish loop that included how this formative assessment tool not only provided assessment of learning data, but also offered numerous reflective data points that would impact students' opportunities to learn and participate in future lessons. For the learner, this quick assessment of knowledge gives them the opportunity to summarize their learning and provide examples of where they may have gotten stuck in the learning process.

Hammond (2014) and others share the exit-ticket approach as "culturally relevant," allowing voice from each student. For the teacher, this activity identifies gaps in learning, participation, and engagement, and shifts the instruction to the learner to allow them to give feedback. Exit tickets provide closure. CASEL refers to the culmination of a lesson, a session, or a block of instruction as "an optimistic closure." This process is one of the three signature practices in delivering an SEL lesson (2019). This is a great strategy not only for ending the lesson on a positive note, but also for promoting self-awareness since it encourages young learners to check in with themselves. The three CASEL SEL signature practices are (1) a welcoming activity, (2) engaging strategies, and (3) an optimistic closure. Exit-ticket strategies can be a great opportunity for establishing an "optimistic" lesson closure.

In an action research study conducted by a student in a Master of Arts in Social and Emotional Learning (MA SEL) program, the evidence clearly showed that the implementation of a closing routine, similar to exit tickets, increased communication between the students and teacher and also provided strong insights into areas of student need. The SEL competencies of self-awareness and self-management were targeted in the study.

Hammond's research (2021) indicates that engagement, belonging, and academic achievement often correlate positively. Her research specifically examined the role of closing routine protocols and class discussions as tools by which to access student voice, process content collectively, and create a social learning environment, thereby facilitating increased engagement and a sense of belonging within the class.

Moore's (2022) study found that students experienced a greater sense of belonging after engaging in closing routines and class discussions, in which they were prepared and certain behavior protocols were established and practiced. Student feedback indicated various benefits from the activities, both academically and in the realm of social emotional learning. Further, students reported a greater appreciation for group work and collaboration as a result of the learning routines. A greater sense of belonging and improved self-esteem was also shown in the data analysis, suggesting a correlation between being challenged academically, taking social emotional risks, and a positive learning environment.

EXIT TICKET FEEDBACK LOOP

1. Create exit ticket

2. Administer ticket

3. Analyze feedback

4. Shift instruction and give feedback

As one-to-one computing becomes more ubiquitous and more affordable, there is a movement to make entry and exit tickets digital. In our practices in higher education, we have used Google Docs formatted to prompt desired responses to learning, for posing questions, and for obtaining immediate feedback on student understanding. We have also used Google Forms and Sheets. Microsoft Excel can also capture digital data. The good news is when exit tickets are submitted digitally, educators can quickly look for patterns in the data, sift and sort through categories of understanding, and capture both quantitative and qualitative data. We will share more digital tools for assessing in Chapter 7.

"I" STATEMENTS AND SELF-EFFICACY

When learners take a stand on who they are using "I" statements, this increases positive learner identity and allows for an increase in emotional literacy. We often need to examine the world around us from the inside out, to apply strategies such as self-examination and identifying self-beliefs. Bandura (1989) recognized that "self-efficacy and self-beliefs can enhance or impair performance through their effects on cognitive, affective, or motivational intervening processes" (p. 729).

English Language Arts (ELA) curricula contain many instances of first-person writing and composition. Opinion writing, autobiographical writing, and reflective writing allow a first-person perspective (or lens) and the use of affirmative "I" statements. Using the first-person voice in writing or in poetry assesses feelings, thoughts, and ideas. We will later discuss how reflective writing and journaling can act as assessments.

SENTENCE FRAMES USING "I"

I feel _____.

I imagine _____.

I need/want _____.

I agree/disagree _____.

I noticed _____.

I observed _____.

I am _____.

bit.ly/44KYAOH

Author and illustrator Peter H. Reynolds, along with his coauthor Susan Verde, has a series of "I Am" books that develop a learner's sense of self. Through these "I Am" statements, self-identity can grow and develop (see more at the QR code).

SENTENCE FRAMES

Sentence frames, "close/cloze" sentence format, sentence stems, or sentence starters give learners a choice in vocabulary to complete sentences. While these terms are used interchangeably, they are not all the same.

Sentence frames give students an opportunity to use vocabulary that they would not be able to use without the supporting sentence "framework" that surrounds the word. Unlike sentence starters, which, as the name implies, simply start the sentence off, sentence frames provide more clues to the learner. Sentence formats offer a visual organization for developing a sentence. All spur the same cognitive activity and are strong conventions for writing and reading (Block, 2019; Roe, 2014; Westby, 2013). Westby (2013) notes that using these conventions helps students learn vocabulary and strengthens academic language.

How does this apply to SEL? Why do frames work? Learners decide what word or words to use either by selecting from a word bank, a list of frequently used words, a dictionary, or a thesaurus. Using SEL-related vocabulary and concepts is aligned to the SEL skill of decision-making. Oftentimes the act of identifying "just one word" makes a concept more accessible for all types of learners. Writing a long passage without a prompt or guide can be very daunting for any emerging reader and especially English learners.

Sentence frames based on SEL competencies can increase awareness of the range and complexity of emotions, therefore helping learners to identify more clearly their own emotions and the emotions of others. Happy, sad, and angry have their limitations. For example, giving students a word bank with alternatives to the words *happy* and *sad* with a sentence frame provides both new vocabulary and a better understanding of feelings.

SENTENCE STEMS

A sentence stem or starter is often the beginning of a sentence that prompts thinking and writing. According to CultivatingLiteracy.org, sentence stems promote complete thought and "contain a subject (person, place, or thing) and a predicate (tells what is happening). The subject and predicate must compliment [sic] each other" (Cultivating Literacy, 2020). Complex sentence stems are a phrase or portions of a sentence with a missing part. Sentence stems give learners the basic foundation to grow their ideas; they motivate the learner to get their thoughts going and assist in developing semantic skills like inference. Sentence starters are often used as a prompt for writing across the curriculum in science for lab reports, in social studies for recalling content, in word problems in mathematics, in phrases for essay writing, and

Chapter 6 • Assessment Tools and Strategies **85**

more! Using sentence starters in SEL reflection journals helps students to move to deeper levels of thinking and understanding.

20 REFLECTIVE SENTENCE STARTERS

1. Today I am inspired by _____.
2. There is no easy way to say this, but _____.
3. How do I know _____?
4. I thought it would be fun to share_____.
5. I often ask myself, _____?
6. I am curious about _____.
7. I wonder why _____.
8. There is one thing that annoys me: _____.
9. When I need inspiration, I _____.
10. For me, change is _____.
11. When I was younger _____.
12. When I am older _____.
13. How often have I heard _____?
14. It's silly to think _____.
15. One of the earliest lessons I have learned is ____.
16. Why have I never considered _____?
17. An interesting thing that happened to me was ____.
18. I laugh when I hear _____.
19. A thing that always makes me cry is _____.
20. What I can do differently next time is _____.

WRITING FRAMES

Lewis and Wray (2002) developed a framing process called Writing Frames. Based on writing genres, frames are segmented by (1) Recount Genre Frames, (2) Report Genre Frames, (3) Explanation Genre Frames, (4) Procedural Genre Frames, (5) Persuasion Genre Frames, and (6) Discussion Genre Frames (p. 4). Lewis and Wray include templates to help learners scaffold their experiences and their writing. This is a particularly useful writing practice and assessment strategy since the learner uses a format that helps focus on key elements.

1. **Recount Genre Frames.** This frame allows the learner to remember, recount, and capture through writing. Examples include (a) Orientation: a "scene setting," e.g., I went on a field trip to the zoo; (b) Events: I sat next to Juan in first period; and

(c) Reorientation: When we returned from our field trip we wrote about our experiences.

2. **Report Genre Frames.** The Report Genre Frame prompts a learner to summarize, classify, and describe. An example might use structure, function, and visual representation as a model or to describe a phenomenon. This type of report uses "being and having" clauses.

3. **Explanation Genre Frames.** Writing frames with sentence starters help explain how, what, what's next, and results.

4. **Procedural Genre Frames.** These writing frames include descriptive procedures and instructions with sequenced steps.

5. **Persuasion Genre Frames.** Persuasive writing usually consists of a thesis or point of view, an argument, elaborations, statistics, and a supporting summary that restates the narrative.

6. **Discussion Genre Frames.** One template prompts the learner to identify a topic for discussion, identify an argument for and against a topic, and then draw a conclusion. See other examples in Lewis and Wray (2002, pp. 37–39).

CLOSE/CLOZE

Close/Cloze is a reading technique that leaves out words for the learner to insert. This technique can be very game-like and is sometimes used as an assessment. Instructors use fill-in-the-missing word _____ (blank) on quizzes. Remember Mad Libs, the game where you could insert types of words and create a funny sentence or story? In case you have never filled out a Mad Lib, it consists of a phrasal template for writing and is read out loud after it is completed (Price & Stern, 1953/2008). The rules include one player prompting other players for a list of words to substitute for blanks in a story. The words are categorized by type: noun, verb, adverb, place, celebrity, exclamation, or part of the body. This game is now owned by Penguin Random House and is still being produced. Students can create their own missing word paragraphs or stories as a means for assessing understanding.

Finally, Wikipedia defines a cloze test as a close deletion test or occlusion test. Certain items, words, or signs are removed (cloze text), and the learner is asked to replace the missing language or word. This type of assessment allows for critical thinking and understanding words and vocabulary in context. This exercise is commonly administered for the assessment of native and English language learning and instruction.

Chapter 6 • Assessment Tools and Strategies   **87**

STUDENT SELF-ASSESSMENT

In this next section, we share how academic and personal success for learners is greatly impacted when they assess their own learning. Students are an intrinsic part of the information-sharing process. Students need to be clear about what they have learned and through this process apply self-reflection, emotional self-assessment, and self-assessment in the content areas by using rubrics or checklists, self-reflection, and journal writing. They can reflect on their learning and be involved in a number of ways.

McMillan and Hearn (2008) make a direct connection between self-assessment and motivation to perform. "When students set goals that aid their improved understanding, and then identify criteria, self-evaluate their progress toward learning, reflect on their learning, and generate strategies for more learning, they will show improved performance with meaningful motivation" (p. 44).

Brown and Harris (2014) strongly recommend that student self-assessment (SSA) is so important it should no longer be treated as an assessment, but instead as an "essential competence for self-regulation" (p. 22).

Brown and Harris (2014) strongly recommend that student self-assessment (SSA) is so important it should no longer be treated as an assessment, but instead as an "essential competence for self-regulation" (p. 22).

In their earlier research, Brown and Harris (2013) have classified SSA according to how the self-assessment has been carried out through three methods: (1) self-ratings or self-marking, (2) self-estimates of performance, and (3) criteria- or rubric-based assessments. Self-rating and self-marking types tend to be the most meaningful. Self-assessment is highly personalized, giving the learner control of the assessment.

SELF-RATING/MARKING TYPES

- Rating system
- Checklists
- Task completion
- Ordinal ranking/agreement

- Smileys to judge quality
- Grade own quiz/test
- Objective-based scoring guides
- Rubrics for meeting levels of competency

Tan (2007) designed a continuum of types of self-assessing associated with the level of teacher involvement (see Figure 6.4).

FACTS ABOUT SSA STUDENT GAINS

- Greater learner autonomy is developed
- Self-efficacy increases
- Learners take responsibility for learning
- More buy-in obtained from learner
- Learners value their work
- Learners monitor growth and progress
- Learners realize strengths and areas to improve
- Gains in self-regulation are realized

FIGURE 6.4 • Continuum of Types of Self-Assessing Associated With the Level of Teacher Involvement

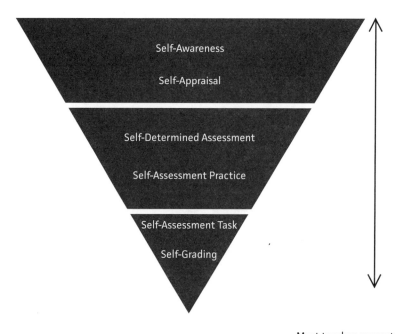

STUDENT SELF-REFLECTION

Self-reflection is a form of assessment. When students evaluate their learning and realize their strengths and direction for improvement, the learning becomes less rote and less superficial. We know that deep learning occurs when the learner is emotionally connected to the content. We also know that learners need to be motivated both intrinsically and extrinsically in a learning and thinking environment. Self-reflection is highly personal and meaningful. Student self-assessment supports SEL skills, specifically the competency of self-awareness.

What is reflection? Dewey (1910/1966) in his seminal work defines reflection as, "active, persistent and careful consideration belief or supposed form of knowledge" (p. 9). Reflection also includes self-analysis, self-evaluation, self-dialogue, and self-observation. Cambridge professor Donald Schon, who created the Reflective Practice Toolkit, defines reflective practice as "the ability to reflect on one's actions so as to engage in a process of continuous learning." As practitioners and educators, we strive to be in a continuous process of learning and improving. As humans, we learn by doing and often learn from our failures. Ask yourself, "How might I improve that lesson? What can I do next time? We need to take time to think about our experiences, learn from them, and develop an action plan for what we will do next. Another important part of the reflective process is that learners need to think about their thinking and engage in a metacognitive process. Vanderbilt University's Center for Metacognition has developed this definition: "Metacognition is, put simply, thinking about one's thinking. More precisely, it refers to the processes used to plan, monitor, and assess one's understanding and performance. Metacognition includes a critical awareness of (a) one's thinking and learning and (b) oneself as a thinker and learner" (Chick, 2013, Libguide).

Reflection is a highly personalized experience, one that we often don't take the time to fit into our daily lives. Reflection can take the form of mindful activities, such as meditation, chanting, sitting, lying down in silence, yoga, or practicing breathing strategies. Mindful reflection allows us to reflect without judgment and with curiosity and openness to our experiences, thoughts, feelings, and actions. Mindfulness is directly connected to self-awareness. Through mindful self-reflection, we not only enhance our relationship with ourselves but also with others.

JOURNALING

While grounded in therapeutic practices, journaling can be a powerful form of self-assessment for adults and learners of all ages. Journals can be kept as evidence of learning for all subjects.

90 Assessing Through the Lens of Social and Emotional Learning

Some journals are personal, some are used for formative assessment to check for understanding, and others are used for personal notetaking. Digital journaling is commonly known as blogging or a web log (Jorn Barger, 2023). Blogs are filled with personal expression, written for an audience and for a specific purpose, on thousands of topics by millions of people worldwide. As a matter of fact, in 2022 there were 31 million blogs in the United States alone (statista.com).

IMPACT OF JOURNALING

One essential question is, what impact does journaling have on learners' social and emotional literacy skills? While the primary medium for journaling is writing, we also include other visual media practices for demonstrating the meaning and application of knowledge. Journaling also includes graphics and other visuals such as sketches, drawings, and various media (glued in or taped in leaves, photos, and clippings that can be inserted into a journal). For an example of a multimedia print-based journal, see Joni Chaucer and Zena Rester-Zodrow's (1997) book *Moon Journals*, which demonstrates a way to make nature and writing mesh. Nature journals are quite common with social scientists and with scientists who work in outdoor settings. In her outdoor science camp with adolescents, a graduate of the Master of Arts in Social and Emotional Learning used journaling and sketching to measure the impact on their connection with nature. Andersen (2023) discovered that a week-long outdoor experience using journals increased the camper's level of connection with nature at the outdoor science camp.

WRITING JOURNALS

A writing journal can be an indicator of writing skills and skills improvement, and thus a very tangible assessment of learning. A journal can also serve as a tool to improve the fluency of writing skills. The writing journal can be a regular tool for daily Writer's Workshop, free writing sessions at the start of a lesson, summary for closure (exit ticket writing), short responses, directed writing, and as a journal for collecting thoughts, feelings, and ideas. Some journals track experiments, keep a calorie count (or food log), and serve as tools for brainstorming and other personal expressions of writing.

Lew and Schmidt (2011) conducted a study to evaluate whether reflective journal writing was effective in promoting self-reflection and learning and whether students became better at self-reflection if they engaged in continuous reflective journal writing (p. 532). The findings on reflective journal writing suggest that "self-reflection on both how and what students have learned does lead to improvements in academic performance" (p. 529).

CONTEMPORARY JOURNALING

Sketchnoting is a relatively new form of journaling, used to help develop visual communication skills, improve critical thinking, and promote creative confidence in many subjects including engineering and design. Perry, Wimer, & Bell (2017) in their book *Sketchnoting in School* describe the power of visual note taking and concur that sketchnoting can be an exhibition of understanding. We know that a picture tells a thousand words and can represent concepts and connections between them. More recently, bullet and dot journaling, cartooning, coloring, and creating graphic novels are all examples of journals or chronicles of learning. In summary, all journals, sketches, and mind and concept maps are excellent forms of formative assessment.

tinyurl.com/baughcum

Sketchnoter Sylvia Duckworth, a Canadian educator, has an extensive library of sketchnotes on Flickr.

See a beautiful sketchnote by Carrie Baughcum via the provided QR code, which features a November 2019 KQED article by Katrina Schwartz titled "Why Teachers Are So Excited About the Power of Sketchnoting."

To get started with sketchnoting, here are some tips:

1. Choose a focus: Decide on the main idea or topic you want to capture.
2. Use simple shapes and icons: Draw simple shapes and icons to represent key concepts, ideas, or actions.
3. Use color: Use color to highlight important information and make your notes more visually appealing.
4. Add text: Write short phrases or key words to summarize and clarify your ideas.
5. Experiment with layout: Use different layouts to organize your ideas and make connections between them.
6. Practice: Like any skill, sketchnoting takes practice, so don't worry about making mistakes and keep experimenting with different techniques.

EMOTIONAL SELF-ASSESSMENT = COMPASSION

In order to develop self-compassion, it is important to pay attention to the experiences that impact your emotional presence. By recognizing and labeling an emotion, you can take appropriate compassionate action. Your kind inner voice can tell you that you are human and that it is okay to experience emotions that are unfavorable. You can try to learn from the experience to see how you can do it differently next time; thus, assessing one's emotions allows you to move through the emotion creating space and time in the brain for learning and transformation.

PUTTING STUDENT ASSESSING INTO PRACTICE

Assessing strategies in this chapter can be put into action by applying them through explicit teaching practices in the classroom. In order for student assessing to be authentically applied and measured through formative practice, we recommend an approach called Teaching Moves, which is a set of strategies created by teachers to move learning forward (Pressley et al., 1992). These twelve strategies also allow students to move their assessing practices forward (see McEwan, 2004, for the complete list). As practitioners, we and others understand that what the teacher does to advance student assessment greatly impacts student learning.

PRACTITIONER MOVES + LEARNER MOVES = ONGOING AND CONTINUOUS ASSESSMENT: WHAT DOES THIS LOOK LIKE?

SEL FOCUS AREA OR STRATEGY	PRACTITIONER MOVES	LEARNER MOVES
Learner Identity	Share personal attributes with learners, personal strengths, and areas of improvement. Demonstrate and model asset-based teaching through vulnerability. Personalize and individualize assignments to meet the learner's needs and create a learning environment that is welcoming, safe, and just.	Demonstrates learning both individually and cooperatively in groups. Work represents levels of self-awareness, self-identity, and cultural awareness.
Flexible, Fixed, and Growth Mindset	Praise and encourage	"I can," not "I can't." Strength to move forward without judgment. Making mistakes is learning. Goal setting, small chunks at a time. They have written positive affirmations.

(Continued)

Chapter 6 • Assessment Tools and Strategies • 93

(Continued)

SEL FOCUS AREA OR STRATEGY	PRACTITIONER MOVES	LEARNER MOVES
Writing as Assessment	Present multiple means of writing and expressive opportunities	Check-ins Emotional check-ins Journal writing
Student Self-Assessment	Individual goal setting Entry and exit tickets Mastery learning	Individual goal setting
Student Self-Reflection	Offer writing prompts for thinking before and after assignments	Engagement in ongoing self-reflective activities. Develop comfort with the reflective process for learning and growing

FINAL THOUGHTS

SEL assessing is not something that is done to the learner. SEL assessing is done with the learner to provide ongoing formative feed forward (where am I going?), feedback (how did I do?), and then feed forward again (what is next?). Keeping students at the center of all SEL assessments is critical to their SEL competency growth. Pairing the strategies and tools discussed in this chapter with student learning progressions may result in a rich SEL environment where the student is the focus and they flourish.

Practitioner "Wondering" Reflection

Time for Your SEL Reflection Journal

In your SEL journal, reflect on what you have learned in this chapter. Consider these prompts:

- Which SEL tool or strategy are you currently using in your classroom?
- Which SEL strategy would you like to try out in your workplace?
- How might you integrate SMART goals with your students?
- Which SEL-based writing strategy are you most eager to use?

Takeaway to Practice

What is the one takeaway from this chapter you want to put into action? **Name it. Create it. Add it to your action plan** (which you will be writing in Chapter 9).

CHAPTER 7

Assessment, Assessing Strategies, and Digital Tools

When we think about tests in schools, we often picture students shuffling papers at their desks. They fill in short answers to questions, respond to multiple-choice-style options, or write brief essays. The majority of their cognitive effort is focused on searching their memory to find appropriate responses to the test items or applying formulae to familiar problems. This style of educational assessment targets the types of skills that were seen as important throughout the twentieth century—the skills of storing relevant information and retrieving it upon demand, often as these processes related to literacy and numeracy.

—Esther Care, Global Economy and Development, Center for Universal Education, and Alvin Vista, former Brookings Institution Fellow

---

LEARNING OUTCOMES

Colleagues on the assessing journey will be able to

- Discover the history and background of online assessments, standards-based assessments, and summative assessment tools

- Explore digital tools for assessing

- Understand the function and structure of quizzes, polls, and other assessment tools

- Learn how formative digital assessment tools work

- Reexamine the connection between assessing and culturally responsive practices

- Learn about the role of artificial intelligence, intelligent tutors, and other aides for practicing concepts and for assessing

We need to develop an educational culture that uses technology for the "greater good" and *not* just for computerized, standardized tests. In the twenty-first century, computer-based tests (CBT) have become the norm, even for children as young as four years old. There are fewer and fewer #2 pencils and Scantrons® in schools; instead, students sit in front of a laptop, a Chromebook, or a computer terminal and complete multiple-choice, and forced-choice responses, and true/false questions all the while checking boxes. Our students have become box checkers, not critical thinkers. Some in education refer to these types of tests as "multiple guess" because the answer is mostly "C." Tens of thousands of students in schools nationwide have also interacted with large amounts of content in the classroom by using clickers, cell phones, and other interactive handheld devices. As we pointed out in Chapter 1, we have become a nation of computer-based test-takers.

Generation Z has been replaced by the new Alpha Generation, children who were born after 2010 and who have known advanced technology since birth. The Alpha Generation is different from previous generations in many ways. We now have a generation that has increased its digital literacy skills and has been taught both formally and informally through the gamification of learning via technology. Our neuroplastic brains continue to change and adapt to new forms of technology, artificial intelligence, augmented reality, virtual reality, mixed reality, and the metaverse (a combination of these components along with the internet).

MACHINE LEARNING VS. HUMAN LEARNING

As early as 1978, computer-aided instruction (CAI) was being studied as a promise for teaching and for learning. That same year, Suppes and Macken (1978) published a paper on the historical path from research and development to the operational use of CAI. What is interesting about this is that CAI and computer-based teaching (CBT) were precursors to computer-based assessments and computer-based tests. Dr. Patrick Suppes, a computer programmer, later used artificial intelligence and adaptive learning to change the learning experience. He moved on to found Computer Curriculum

Corporation and spearheaded network-based instruction and assessment through an integrated learning system. Picture for the first-time students sitting in front of the terminal where content could be delivered just-in-time, personalized, and through an individual pathway to achievement, while adjusting levels of difficulty either upward or downward. Fast forward to the twenty-first century and computer scientists have created a system called the Adaptive and Intelligent Education System. Reinforcement learning is often used in conjunction with the development of teaching strategies, and this reinforcement learning–based system is known as RLATES. While we are not going to discuss the history of computer-based digital assessments, we will categorize these tools by the type of assessing they perform.

Bunderson and colleagues (1998) reported there are four generations of computer-based assessment:

1. **Computerized testing**—administering conventional tests by computer (CBT).

2. **Computerized adaptive testing**—tailoring the difficulty or contents of the next piece presented or an aspect of the timing of the next item on the basis of examinees' responses.

3. **Continuous measurement**—using calibrated measures embedded in a curriculum to estimate dynamic changes continuously and unobtrusively in the student's achievement trajectory and profile as a learner.

4. **Intelligent measurement**—producing intelligent scoring, interpretation of individual profiles, and advice to learners and teachers by means of knowledge bases and inferencing procedures.

ASSESSMENT AND ACCOUNTABILITY SYSTEMS

By 2001, the federal No Child Left Behind Act required states to set standards for all content areas, measure student performance against the standards, and hold schools accountable for the results. Then, in 2009, the Common Core State Standards were introduced and adopted in forty-five states, making standardized tests "standard" across the United States. This testing climate is again in transition. According to a report from FutureEd (Olsen, 2019), "an increasing number of states are designing new tests for grades 3 through 8 that reflect their individual state content standards and meet accountability requirements under the federal Every Student Succeeds Act (ESSA)" (p. 1). Overall, there continues to be a shift to online testing through a variety of means, adaptive testing, automated scoring, and other performance tasks that are now embedded in the software or systems.

SUMMATIVE TESTS

Over the past two decades, the state and national standardized testing markets have raked in billions of dollars. As of 2023, the market is dominated by five major companies: American Institute of Research (AIR), now owned by Cambian; Data Recognition Company; Pearson (joined by Prentice Hall, Addison Wesley, Longman, Scott Foresman, Waterford, and many more); Questar, acquired by NWEA along with Educational Testing Services; and Smarter Balanced. A newer player is the Partnership for Assessment of Readiness for College and Careers.

Fast forward to March 2020 at the start of the worldwide pandemic when the US Department of Education announced that it would temporarily suspend federally mandated testing requirements for the school year. As of the writing of this book, this was still the case. Along with this announcement, many colleges and universities, including the California State University system, changed admission requirements to not require the American College Test (ACT) or the Stanford Achievement Test (SAT). So where is summative assessment going? We posit that reforms are on the way to move toward more frequent assessing, and to more comprehensive methods that include formative and authentic assessment.

TYPES OF ASSESSMENTS IN THE DIGITAL AGE

We have categorized assessments by (1) premade assessments/tests, (2) digital exams with auto-grading capabilities, and (3) user-created assessments. Premade assessments/tests are readily available in a digital format and delivered via computer or through the internet. These tests have historically been created by companies that are "for profit" textbook publishers. There are many benefits to taking digital exams with auto-grading features, such as giving learners immediate feedback on their work. Artificial intelligence and its built-in algorithms drive the auto-grading processes. The third category, user-created assessments, can maximize open-source tools to create and customize summative assessments.

In Chapter 2, we noted that formative assessment is a planned, ongoing process used by students and teachers during learning and teaching to elicit and use evidence of student learning with the intention of improving student understanding. Formative assessment guides students to become self-directed learners. Evidence indicates that the use of technology-based formative assessment in the classroom impacts students' learning outcomes. Why use *digital tools* for assessing? Digital tools are purposefully constructed to support many theories of learning. Digital tools in the assessment category are supported by the application of the following theories:

- **Engagement Theory**—real-time, immediate, with participation from all users, anonymously.
- **Immediacy**—through real-time responses and connections.
- **Interactive Learning Theory (ILT)**—dynamic interactive discourse between the teacher and students, between students and resources, and among students (Steinaker & Bell, 1979).
- **Collaborative Learning Theory**—rooted in Vygotsky's representation of the Zone of Proximal Development, a situational opportunity, promotes peer-to-peer learning and develops critical thinking skills when working in groups.
- **Asynchronous Processes**—think time, wait time, more anonymous.
- **Cognitive Load**—helps to process information by chunking.
- **Constructivist Theory**—building knowledge and constructing evidence for learning.
- **Gamification**—teamwork or competitive (e.g., e-sports).

How does formative assessment use digital tools to support learners? Learner-empowered practices that are rooted in formative assessment help to:

1. Activate respect, collaboration, engagement, and agency as well as social-emotional and academic needs.
2. Clarify the learning goals, elicit thinking, and engage in self, peer, and teacher feedback.
3. Promote practice using actionable feedback and evidence (Nordengren et al., 2021, p. 22).

Categories of Digital Tools for Teaching, Learning, and Assessing

- Quizzes and short assessments
- Surveys
- Polls
- Gamified platform
- Classroom response systems
- Rubrics and rubric creators (self-assessing, student centered, content focused with criterion)
- Simulations and intelligent tutoring systems

DIGITAL TOOLS FOR ASSESSING FORMATIVE WORK

Many digital tools for assessing can be categorized as formative assessment tools. Here is a list of contemporary, formative tools for assessing, along with some vendor-provided details about accessibility and availability, which was current at the time of publication. Tools are categorized in a matrix later in this chapter.

1. **Nearpod,** www.nearpod.com

   Nearpod is an online system to create original multimedia assessments or select from a 15,000+ item library of pre-made interactive content. Creators may choose from polls, multiple-choice or open-ended questions, draw-its, and gamified quizzes.

2. **Pear Deck,** https://www.peardeck.com/

   Pear Deck is a Google Slides add-on that lets educators incorporate interactive or formative assessments into slideshow presentations. Sample questions, templates, and Microsoft and Google integration are included with a free account; paid premium access unlocks additional features.

3. **ClassFlow,** www.classflow.com

   ClassFlow is a collaborative tool for building interactive lessons and activities. Choose from free and paid digital resources or upload your own. Among the assessment types offered are multiple-choice, short answer, true/false, and essay. Student polls and questions provide real-time formative feedback.

4. **GoClass,** www.goclass.com

   GoClass allows educators to create lessons with embedded assessments. Students can interact with the teacher-generated learning materials on mobile or other internet-connected devices, and teachers can track student participation on the platform.

5. **Formative,** www.formative.com

   With Formative, teachers can automatically create assessments from their existing content, or use something from the platform's library. As students respond to these assessments with text or drawing, the teacher's screen is updated in real-time to help assess student progress. Both free and paid accounts are available; the free version comes with grading tools and Google Classroom integration.

6. **Kahoot!,** www.kahoot.com

   Kahoot! is an engaging learning platform that allows educators to create live and asynchronous game-like quizzes for their students. Teachers can select from the 50 million games in the existing library or create custom games based on classroom content. The free basic plan provides access to the quiz library, question bank, customization tools, and more.

7. **Padlet,** www.padlet.com

Padlet is like a bulletin board for the digital age. Whether for collaboration, communication, or assessment, students and educators can add almost any type of file to the platform's digital blank "wall." A free basic plan allows users to create three padlets at a time, while paid versions have unlimited padlets and higher file size uploads.

8. **Jamboard,** https://jamboard.google.com/

Jamboard is part of the Google Suite of tools. Similar to Padlet, the tool promotes visual collaboration through a common whiteboard accessible in real time. Combine graphics, text, and sticky notes of all shapes, sizes, and colors.

9. **Socrative,** www.socrative.com

The Socrative platform allows teachers to create polls and gamified quizzes to assess student progress, with real-time results visible on screen. Socrative's free plan permits one public room with up to fifty students, on-the-fly questions, and something called "Space Race" assessment.

10. **Google Forms,** https://docs.google.com/forms/u/0/

This open-source tool has a lot of assessment capabilities. You can create video quizzes and multiple-choice or short-answer questions. The tool also lets educators design surveys and then analyze responses in Google Sheets.

11. **Survey Monkey,** www.surveymonkey.com

Survey Monkey allows users to create surveys, quizzes, and polls, then gather feedback via email, chat, social media, and more. The tool also has web-based analysis features and exporting capabilities.

12. **Quizlet,** www.quizlet.com

Quizlet is a digital database with millions of study sets. Educators can use its flashcards, multiple-choice or true/false quizzes, matching games, and more to assess student progress. Quizlet is free for basic features; premium accounts allow for customization and tracking student progress.

13. **Quizizz,** https://quizizz.com/

This site has thousands of quizzes and resources for educators ranging from professional development to teacher certification to dozens of content areas and all grade levels. Quizizz has formative, standards-aligned quizzing resources.

14. **Flip,** https://info.flip.com/ (Formerly Flipgrid)

Flip is a video discussion application, offered completely free through Microsoft. Teachers, educators, and students can create and post video responses that can be further customized with emoji, stickers, and text. Flip is an effective tool for audio/video peer review.

15. **Edpuzzle,** https://edpuzzle.com/

Edpuzzle is not really a puzzle-building program, but is actually a video-based learning and assessment platform that helps educators turn one-way videos into interactive formative assessments. Upload or link to YouTube, TED, Vimeo, or other videos, then add interactivity by inserting questions, links, or images to create meaningful evaluations. Free storage space for twenty videos is available.

16. **Quia,** www.quia.com

Quia gives educators the tools to create, customize, and share learning activities, from flashcards and matching games to concentration and word search activities. It comes with a huge repository of premade learning objects you can customize. After a thirty-day free trial, the premium account license is $49 per year.

17. **i-Ready,** www.iready.com

i-Ready provides personalized instruction across the curriculum. The system relies on research-based, stored data from more than 1 million students. This is a fee-based program. The major benefit is the personalization and individualized learning paths.

18. **BrainPOP,** https://www.brainpop.com/

BrainPOP has a database with both free and fee-based access to more than 1,000 animated videos plus quizzes and related materials that teach and assess many content areas. BrainPOP is for students in grades K–12, and it covers science, social studies, English, math, engineering and technology, health, arts, and music. BrainPOP is standards-based aligned.

19. **Poll Everywhere,** https://www.polleverywhere.com/

Polls can be delivered via smartphone or other interactive device, and educators can create surveys, questions and answers, quizzes, word clouds, and more.

RUBRICS AND RUBRIC CREATION: LEARNER-CENTERED ASSESSING THROUGH RUBRICS AND RUBRIC CREATION

All of the resources that follow direct you to sites for creating rubrics and adapting premade rubrics. You may even want to

Chapter 7 • Assessment, Assessing Strategies, and Digital Tools 103 allow students to create their own. Begin your rubric search by navigating to Kathy Schrock's Guide to Everything, and then continue exploring on the list.

- Kathy Schrock's Guide to Everything (Assessment and Rubrics): https://www.schrockguide.net/assessment-and-rubrics.html
- iRubric: http://rcampus.com/
- Roobrix: https://roobrix.com
- Rubistar: http://rubistar.4teachers.org/index.php
- Rubric Machine by The Landmark Project: http://landmark-project.com/rubric_builder/index.php
- TeacherVision lesson planning rubrics: https://www.teachervision.com/lesson-planning/rubric

A LOOK AT SIMULATIONS

Simulations are real-life (or almost real-life) computer-based scenarios created and delivered via software, gaming systems, and, most recently, through virtual worlds using mixed reality or virtual reality with 3D systems (with VR goggles). Mixed reality is augmented reality, artificial intelligence, virtual reality, and 3D immersive environments. The US military has used simulations for decades to train soldiers, pilots, navigators, and Navy SEALs. Scientists have used simulations for modeling, 3D rendering, and problem solving. Medicine has used simulations to develop interactions with anatomical models, role play with patients and other mannequins, and simulate experiences for nurses, doctors, and other medical personnel. Patient care, operations, and other medical procedures can all be simulated. Have you seen the hologram of a walk-through of a virtual body? In his book *Simulation and Learning: A Model-Centered Approach*, Landriscina (2013) comments that simulation is "not only transforming scientific practice, but it is also leading scientists and philosophers of science to reexamine relations between models, theories, and experiments" (p. 1). All of this is done in a simulated environment to prevent harm from humans but to also enhance learning through repetition and practice.

In early 2023, Almaki and colleagues reviewed the use of simulation games in K–12 education and determined that there is still a lack of understanding of using simulations games:

> Despite simulation games (SGs) being a novel pedagogical tool that can soundly represent real environments to enhance students' learning outcomes, knowledge, and skills, there is still a lack of an overview of the current theoretical understanding of using simulation

104 Assessing Through the Lens of Social and Emotional Learning

games as a pedagogical method to develop K-12 learning outcomes. (Almaki et al., 2023, p. 1)

A systematic review of twenty-five studies determined that SGs could indeed "develop student learning outcomes, increase learner engagement, be motivating, provide a safe interactive environment, and increase academic performance and achievements" (Almaki et al., 2023 p. 1).

SCIENCE AND MATHEMATICS WITH SIMULATIONS

How is simulation being used in education for assessing? In K–12 education, there are many computer-based simulations that are used in science, mathematics, and the social sciences. One in use in junior highs and high schools is PhET Interactive. PhET Interactive was founded in 2002 by Nobel Laureate Carl Wieman and developed by the PhET Interactive Simulations project at the University of Colorado Boulder. These interactive math and science simulations are available at no cost and are research-based. Due to the nature of the simulation, they are highly engaging, intuitive, and can provide a game-like experience where students learn through exploration and discovery. A simulation may be used for visual assessment of processes or for learners to explain their interpretation of a phenomenon. At the University of Colorado, ongoing research is being conducted on both the design and use of interactive simulations to better understand: (1) Which characteristics make these simulation tools effective for learning and why (2) How students engage and interact with these tools to learn; and what influences this process; and (3) When, how, and why these tools are effective in a variety of learning environments (PhET Interactive Simulations, n.d.). To further this research on engagement, interaction, and effective learning, the field will continue to examine the simulated environment to include efficacy of immersive simulations through virtual reality (VR).

SOCIAL SCIENCE SIMULATIONS IN TEACHER EDUCATION

In teacher education programs across the United States, preservice educators are using simSchool® to simulate a "real" in-person classroom environment. Students can interact with cartoon-like characters (who imitate behaviors of K–12 students) through a web-based simulation. SimSchool is controlled by an artificial intelligence–based system that is programmed to react to decisions made by the future educator. According to the website, the simSchool program has more than 10 trillion learner profiles (simSchool, n.d.). This tool has been especially useful during the pandemic, giving future teachers work experiences in diverse environments with diverse "virtual" students.

HIGHER EDUCATION FOR PROFESSIONAL DEVELOPMENT

In higher education, many virtual assessments are being conducted in various simulated environments. In an experiment by Koster and Soffler (2021), traditional assessments such as checklists, global rating scale, and objective-based evaluations were used in a faculty development workshop that compared the user experience. The researchers concluded that more high-stakes assessment in the virtual environments will take place in the future. Educators are now searching for solutions to deliver and assess instruction in the metaverse.

SIMULATIONS IN NURSING AND HEALTH CARE

Simulations have been proven to be a valuable tool for nursing and health education and provide students with the opportunity to practice and develop clinical skills in a safe and controlled environment. There are a range of simulations from online, scenario-based simulations to physical models (patient simulators). These simulators combine robotics and technology to mirror a variety of medical conditions. They allow students to practice clinical skills such as vital sign assessment, medication administration, and wound care, as well as communication and critical thinking skills.

Some online simulations are carried out in virtual worlds with VR to simulate emergencies, medical procedures, and interactive training. Students can also prepare for disasters and receive advanced training for triage care and can practice critical and ethical decision-making. The literature also emphasizes the value of interprofessional education from different health care disciplines to practice collaboration and teamwork skills. Simulations can mimic complex cases that require collaboration between nurses, physicians, and other health care professionals. All simulations provide training, practice, and just-in-time assessing without harming patients.

DIGITAL TOOLS	FORMATIVE ASSESSMENTS & QUIZZES	POLLS	GAMIFIED PLATFORMS	WEB 2.0 COLLABORATIVE LEARNING	RUBRICS & RUBRIC CREATORS	SIMULATIONS	VIRTUAL REALITY & METAVERSE
Nearpod	✓	✓	✓				
Pear Deck	✓	✓	✓				
ClassFlow	✓	✓	✓				
GoClass	✓	✓	✓				
Formative	✓	✓	✓				
Kahoot!	✓	✓	✓	✓			
Padlet	✓			✓			
Jamboard	✓			✓			
Socrative	✓		✓				
Google Forms	✓			✓	✓		
Survey Monkey	✓	✓					
Quizlet	✓	✓	✓				
Quizizz	✓	✓	✓				
Flip	✓			✓			
Edpuzzle	✓		✓				
Quia	✓		✓				
i-Ready	✓		✓				
BrainPOP	✓		✓			✓	
Rubric Creators							
iRubric					✓		
Roobrix	✓	✓	✓		✓		
Rubistar					✓		
Rubric Machine					✓		
TeacherVision					✓		
Simulations and VR						✓	
Open SciEd Library						✓	
PhET						✓	
simSchool						✓	
School Sims						✓	
Mursion						✓	✓

INTELLIGENT TUTORING SYSTEMS

Intelligent tutors and intelligent tutoring systems are computer-based programs that provide instruction that is adapted to the needs of individual students. Intelligent tutors can be automated to respond to specific scenarios with a voice or typed message or even with an avatar who speaks to the learner. Some learning management systems have an intelligent agent setting that enables instructors to set up just-in-time messaging and notifications. For example, if an assignment is late, the intelligent agent sends a reminder message to the student. In online buying scenarios, oftentimes "bots" show up to help the end user to troubleshoot or answer questions. All of these systems are based on artificial intelligence and are evolving as intelligent tutors and artificial intelligence-based assessors.

EMERGING/EMERGENT ASSESSING PRACTICES

From a computer science perspective, digital assessment systems (programs) collect real-time data and information, such as keystrokes, mouse movements, clickstreams, video, and voice/audio imprints (von Davier et al., 2021). Some systems also use haptics to track and monitor eye movements and simulated environments and measure interactivity and engagement. Mixed reality systems, which include virtual reality, augmented reality, artificial intelligence, and 3D immersive environments, delivered over the internet are being developed for use in the metaverse. What is the metaverse and how can we utilize it for teaching, learning, and assessing learning? The metaverse is a virtual world completely delivered over the internet. It has also been referred to as a medium for communication that bridges physical and virtual experiences, a digital environment complete with augmented reality and virtual reality technologies. The prediction is that the metaverse will change how we connect, communicate, and access information; this includes how we are assessed in the future. Assessment practices in the metaverse will provide a multimodal, interactive environment, one that can be personalized, individualized, and be responsive to all learners' needs.

NEW ON THE HORIZON OF APPLICATIONS: CHATGPT

ChatGPT is a variant of an Open Artificial Intelligence (OpenAI) that enables language to be generated through software. ChatGPT stands for Chat Generative Pre-Trained Transformer. Classified as a chatbot, it is designed to carry conversations with people. Some of its features include answering follow-up questions, challenging incorrect premises, rejecting inappropriate queries, and even admitting its mistakes. ChatGPT as AI was trained on an enormous amount of text data. As cited in Brown et al. (2022), Bern Elliot reported that the AI learned to recognize patterns and then produce its own content that resembled different writing styles. OpenAI won't share exactly what information was used to train ChatGPT, but according to a report by the company, it in part uses archived books and Wikipedia (p. 1). As humans continue to develop multimodal systems of interaction, ways of assessing will evolve and so will the tools that deliver and grade assessments.

CULTURALLY RESPONSIVE ASSESSING

In Chapter 4, we shared evidence and gave justification on why we need to make assessing more fair, equitable, and culturally relevant. Part of the picture includes personal identity. In Chapter 3 we discussed learner identity and a learner's perception of self when taking assessments. Taking into consideration a person's identity, including their race, ethnicity, birthplace, gender, social class, socioeconomic status, family role, and varying abilities, assessing needs to be personalized to meet each individual. Part of the consideration of identity includes the individual's values, emotions, interests, talents, goals, physical features, beliefs, and principles (Learning for Justice, n.d.).

Building a sense of community is critical to support social and emotional learning. When students identify their social and personal identities in online or virtual settings, this can open up the online learning environment (OLE) to be a powerful medium. The OLE can be a place that supports active learning and openness toward building community attitudes and beliefs about assessing. Also, when learners are engaged in online assessment practices that are culturally responsive, age appropriate, address their individual strengths, and support scaffolding for strengthening areas of weakness, this helps position students at the center of their learning. As we have pointed out in previous chapters, when learners focus on leveraging their personal affective and the cognitive processes of learning, this in turn builds confidence and self-esteem for learning and for self-assessing. Whether in an online or in-person learning environment, the sense of community helps support students.

Learners today embrace formative assessment for these same reasons. Assessing our youth with digital tools increases engagement and learning, and is associated with achieving learning outcomes and expectancies. Along with these generational differences due to technology affordances, the culture of assessing and assessment will continue to grow and adapt to new methods of teaching and learning.

Chapter 7 • Assessment, Assessing Strategies, and Digital Tools 109

It is important to recognize and discuss the ethics and social worth of these emerging technologies. How will they be used for assessing? Ask yourself, does the culture you are living in and working with "value" online assessments, artificial intelligence systems, simulations, and virtual worlds as valid learning environments and ethical humanistic tools for assessing?

Practitioner "Wondering" Reflection

Time for Your SEL Reflection Journal

In your SEL journal, reflect on what you have learned in this chapter. Consider these prompts:

- When assessing your leaners, are you using a model or strategy that is geared to their interests, emotional connection, and beliefs about the subject matter being assessed?
- How do you feel about machine learning and assessing?
- What do you wonder about in using digital tools? Which concepts or ideas about computer-based learning strongly resonated with you?
- What do you think about assessing in a virtual world with multimodal and immersive capabilities?
- Are there digital assessment practices you would venture to change in your practice?
- Is using OpenAI systems a form of cheating?
- What do you want to know more about?

Takeaway to Practice

What is the one takeaway from this chapter you want to put into action? Select one digital tool to try out for formative assessment. Conduct a mini-research study to assess the effectiveness of the tool. How did your learners grasp concepts, what was the effectiveness, and was it *fun*?

CHAPTER 8

Practitioner Reflection

Reflection is not just about looking back; it is about looking forward, learning from the past, and applying that knowledge to the future.

—Simon Sinek

LEARNING OUTCOMES

Colleagues on the assessing journey will be able to

- Learn the importance of self-reflection as a self-assessment tool and strategy
- Practice self-assessment of SEL skills and competencies
- Create a reflection plan that is aligned with analyzing personal teaching practice

---

We have explored the historical overview and context of social emotional learning and have presented SEL assessing practices to guide our implementation of the SE SEL standards and competencies. In this chapter, we think about how we can provide data that clearly show the impact of SE SEL competencies on teaching and learning, with a specific focus on the teaching process. We begin with one of the most powerful tools to support lifelong learning—reflection. Reflection is an ongoing process that enables us to grow and develop both personally and professionally.

TEACHER INQUIRY

Teacher inquiry is also known as teacher research, classroom research, practitioner research, and action research. Later in this chapter, we will highlight practitioner research and action research as formalized methods of teacher assessment.

> Teacher inquiry is a vehicle that can be used by teachers to untangle some of the complexities that occur in the profession, raise teachers' voices in discussions of educational reform, and ultimately transform assumptions about the teaching profession itself. Transforming the profession is really the capstone of the teacher inquiry process. (Dana & Yendol-Hoppey, 2008, p. 6)

As in all professions and in life, we go through daily assessing practices. Many daily living practices are autonomous and "dependent upon cognitive (e.g., reasoning, planning), motor (e.g., balance, dexterity), and perceptual (including sensory) abilities" (Mlinac & Feng, 2016, p. 505). Other daily assessment

FIGURE 8.1 • Practitioner Assessment Cycle

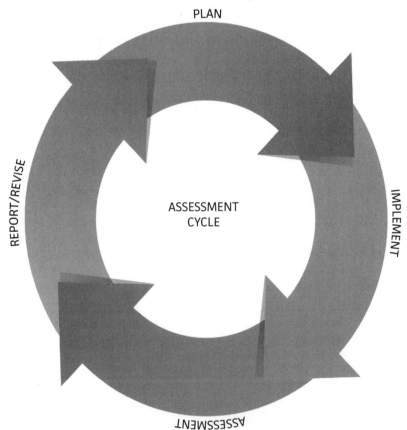

actions are more overt and conscious. In order to become a humanized "thinking and assessing" being, we must be proactive and purposeful with all of our actions. Instead of being a cog in the wheel of life, our role is one of being independent thinkers and assessors of our own actions. Lifelong learning requires that individuals be able not only to work independently but also to assess their own performance and progress.

Self-assessment may be regarded as a skill and, as such, needs to be developed in all educators. One would say that as practitioners, we are in a continuous state of assessment through actions, decisions, and analysis of the results of our actions. We refer to this as the Practitioner Assessment Cycle (see Figure 8.1).

TEACHER SELF-ASSESSMENT

"In order to guarantee adequate self-assessment and the formulation of criteria and standards, practitioners need to realize feelings of ownership, as well as contribute to the process of formulating the assessment criteria" (Van Diggelen et al., 2013, p. 117).

METACOGNITION

Along with the continuous cycle of self-assessment, we need to consistently engage in the process of metacognition. Teachers need to reflect using metacognitive strategies for themselves and for their learners. "Teachers can facilitate metacognition by modeling their own thinking aloud and by creating questions that prompt reflective thinking in students. Explicit instruction in the way one thinks through a task is essential to building these skills in students" (Malone, 2020). High-performing educators who engage in metacognitive activities and who monitor and adjust their teaching become more actualized and self-aware. You learn from your discoveries, taking note of what strategies you use, and evaluate which ones seem to bring you the most success and which ones don't seem to work. Learning how you come to understand something is more important than what knowledge you accumulate.

METACOGNITION, ASSESSING, AND SELF-ASSESSING

Here is a quick guide to practicing metacognition and making the connection to teaching and assessing yourself and the learning environment:

1. Work to understand how your brain learns and how you teach—be in a continuous cycle of self-reflection.

2. Develop awareness of how you prefer to approach (and avoid) teaching and learning tasks. Maximize your own strengths; improve weaknesses.

3. Honestly monitor and assess teaching and assessing strategies you use and their effectiveness.

4. Adjust assessing strategies when appropriate to increase and improve learning.

5. Self-consciously apply, analyze, and manage new understandings about your teaching with the goal of improving long-term performance and retention.

6. Strive to move from the state of teaching dependency (waiting for an expert to give you the right answer) to teaching autonomy (figuring things out for yourself and teaching your learners to do the same).

DEVELOPING A PRACTITIONER REFLECTIVE PRACTICE

PRACTITIONER REFLECTION

Practitioner reflection is more than picking up a journal and writing about what happened during a class. Practitioner reflection requires a personal reflection system that guides the thoughtful critical analysis of your teaching. Asking hard questions will reveal areas of strength, areas of need, and a direction to go to improve your practice. You may ask, what did I do well during that learning activity? What did my students do well as a result of my instruction and their exploration? What did not go well? How am I going to improve? How will I know I improved and that my students learned? Creating a personal reflection template provides you with a way to wonder about "How am I doing as a teacher?" and be engaged in continuous lines of inquiry for teacher action research.

Why reflective practice? Research supports both the teaching of how to be an active reflector and the impact of developing effective reflective practice. Moradkhani and colleagues (2017) state that teachers who thoughtfully examine their teaching practices on a regular basis aid in enhancing them through the critical examinations of their beliefs about teaching and learning. Farrell (2016) reports that teachers who are supported in a reflective practice gain new insights into how they are impacting student learning.

Our work with educators shows a strong correlation between meaningful reflection and intentional planning for increasing knowledge and skills. Educators who consistently reflect on their practice quickly identify patterns of behaviors, areas of success, and areas for improvement. There is no guessing. The data support their growth and direction.

UNPACKING THE REFLECTIVE PROCESS

According to Dewey (1933), reflection may be defined as the "active, persistent, and careful consideration of any belief or supposed form of knowledge in light of the grounds that support it" (p. 9). As educators, we make more than 1,500 decisions each day, and over the course of each day we are in a continuous reflective stage of our practice.

Note: Before any adult learner begins a reflection, the practitioner must agree to approach the issue with openness and willingness to actively engage in the process. This "buy-in" is necessary so that the practitioner thoroughly understands "why" they are engaging in the reflective process.

The purpose of this reflective process results in these seven multiple cognitive and SEL discoveries, which enhances teaching and learning practices.

1. Make meaning and begin to understand the experience or problem.

2. Develop an acute personal awareness of the issue or situation. This is done through listening to words, observing actions, and examining any written text.

3. Engage in metacognitive activity, thinking about one's own thinking.

4. During the reflective process, continue to gain an awareness of personal bias, assumptions, judgment, denial, and other feelings that may impede the process of true and honest self-reflection.

5. Through the process of self-reflection, this new awareness may be a trigger that initiates discomfort, dissonance, and an overall lack of understanding (Thorpe, 2004). Engage in a clarification process and regroup by acknowledging these feelings in your reflections.

6. After your written or oral reflection experience, describe what you learned about yourself or your role at that moment. What have you discovered and what is still causing you cognitive dissonance?

7. Plan what you will do next and reflect on lessons learned to pay close attention to changing your approach.

Another approach uses the Five Rs of Reflection: Reporting, Responding, Relating, Reasoning, and Reconstructing to help make sense of a learning experience (see Figure 8.2).

FIGURE 8.2 • Five Rs of Reflection

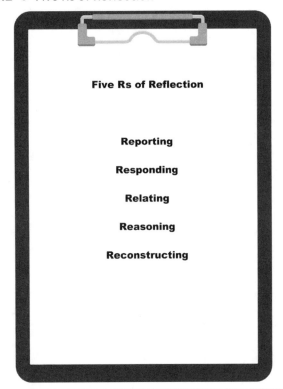

Source: iStock.com/IRYNA NASKOVA

TEACHER ACTION RESEARCH—CONNECTING REFLECTION TO ACTION

Let's briefly explore how practitioner reflection and teacher action research intersect to provide ongoing "data" that elevate your teaching practice. In the two action research case studies that follow, we will uncover how reflection and self-awareness strengthen self-assessment in the daily practices of educators. Later, in Chapter 9, we will explore teacher action research in greater detail along with assessment of SEL skills and competencies in context in two preschools, two elementary schools, and two middle schools.

EDUCATOR REFLECTION: ACTION RESEARCH ON THE EFFECTS OF SYSTEMATIC REFLECTION ON TEACHER SEL SKILLS (JANUSZKA, 2022)

Master's graduate student Dana Januszka is applying the results from this action research on systematic reflection to her work as a consultant with school leaders. Januszka's research delved into how the level of adult SEL competencies as reflected in their essential knowledge, performances, and dispositions impact their teaching and modeling of SEL in their classrooms.

An excerpt from Januszka's action research report:

> Reflective teaching requires that teachers examine their values and beliefs about teaching and learning so that they can take more responsibility for their actions in the classroom (Korthagen, 1993). This practice frees teachers from impulsive and routine activity and enables them to act in a more deliberate and intentional manner (Dewey, 1933). Experience alone is actually not the greatest teacher, for we do not learn as much from the experience as we learn from reflecting on that experience (Farrell, 2003). There is no question that when teachers combine experience with reflection, professional growth and effective teaching occur (Dewey, 1933, 1958).
>
> Teachers may wonder why they should invest time and effort into reflective practice, time that many feel they do not have to spare. They may even view the reflective practice as another thing to add to their plate. But if teachers do not take the time to reflect on their work, they have no evidence to show what are effective strategies for teaching and learning in their classrooms. They are implementing learning through "guessing." In addition, they may become prone to burnout.

Januszka's research findings support the regular use of reflection as a tool for increasing SEL skills in adults.

> When looking specifically at the strategies for reflection, it appears that (8/9 or 88.8%) of those who report collaboration, verbal processing with colleagues or outside professionals, and identifying strengths and weaknesses also report that the practice of self-reflection allows them to be more aware of their emotions, feelings, and mindset. They report that this helps them to have stronger relationships and make decisions that lead to next steps and planning (p. 17).

ACTIVITIES FOR REFLECTION (JANUSZKA, 2022, P. 13)

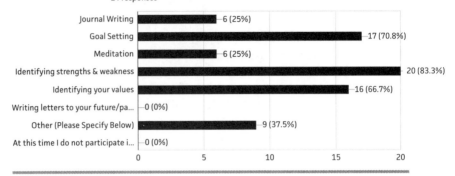

Source: Januszka (2022). Used with permission.

OTHER REFLECTIVE PRACTICES REPORTED (P. 13)

IF YOU SELECTED OTHER ABOVE, WHAT OTHER TYPES OF REFLECTION DO YOU PARTICIPATE IN?
Discuss thoughts and reflections with my spouse or close friends
Setting aside time to do things in nature such as walks, camping, or kayaking
I verbally process with others too
Deep breathing so I guess that's kind of meditation
Teacher collaboration
Constructive conversations with colleagues or people in the field of what I am interested
Group conversations with the people that participated in an activity or event that I am in
Prayer and Bible reading
Collecting evidence for evaluation system
Talk therapy
Speak with therapist

Source: Januszka (2022). Used with permission.

In analyzing the findings to see how teachers' beliefs about reflection affect their personal SEL skills, specifically self-awareness, self-management, and responsible decision-making, Januszka's data show that "teachers who use reflection as a regular part of their routine use their personal SEL skills with more frequency" (p. 13).

Januszka is applying the information from her study to create a series of professional development opportunities for use with her clients who are school leaders to assist in establishing schoolwide SEL implementations. Along with consistent reflective practices, goal setting and personal self-care addressing these areas of need will ensure a successful SEL implementation.

SHERRY ROBERTSON, TEACHERS' PERSPECTIVES IMPACT ON THE IMPLEMENTATION OF AN SEL PROGRAM

In another study on teacher reflection and the implementation of an SEL program, Sherry Robertson (2022) was concerned with how school climate and teacher perspectives impact the implementation of a social and emotional learning program. Her school was in the early stages of developing a plan for the selection and implementation of a schoolwide SEL program. Robertson's study focused on administrators, teachers, and staff at a suburban middle school. The results from the study would be used to guide the creation of a needs-based plan for the most effective implementation of social and emotional learning at her school.

Robertson gathered evidence of the need for her study. She reports,

> Recent research has shown that in order to create a sustainable SEL implementation, it is essential to allow the staff members to have a voice in the process. These approaches should be organized around a "developmental model of SEL," focus on flexible and evidence-based strategies, and be responsive and adaptable to student needs (Bailey et al., 2019). (Robertson, 2022, p. 14)

Educators need to begin with self-awareness, and reflection is the first step to examine what we are already doing. In order for schoolwide implementation of SEL, schools must begin with a lens of self-reflection and develop the social and emotional competencies of the staff.

THE POWER OF PEER REVIEW FOR ASSESSING PRACTICE

Another powerful process for assessing educator practice is peer review. Peer review, while a form of assessment, is not intended to be a strict application of teacher evaluation; instead, we see it as a critical embedded professional development opportunity for continuous improvement.

What are some of the benefits of peer review? Dufour and Eaker (1998), in their observation and research conducted during a professional learning community (PLC), share that when peer review is done well, the observation, feedback, and reflection have a high impact on improving professional practice. In fact, PLCs in and among themselves have the power to allow practitioners to "work together in collaborative teams rather than in isolation and take collective responsibility for student learning; and to establish a guaranteed and viable curriculum that specifies the knowledge, skills, and dispositions students are expected to acquire, unit by unit" (Dufour & Reeves, 2016, p. 69).

PEER REVIEW: USING PEER OBSERVATION, FIVE KEY PHASES

The cycle of peer observation provides a basis for the implementation of peer observation, feedback, and reflection, and includes five key phases for successful peer observation (see Figure 8.3):

1. **Teacher self-reflection:** Self-reflection informs future peer observation activities.

2. **Preobservation conversation:** Underpinned by supportive and collaborative whole-school protocols and developmental approach.

3. **Peer observation:** Teachers learn from one another, building a shared understanding of effective practice.

4. **Teacher and observer reflection:** Provides an opportunity for structured feedback and reflection, based on agreed criteria with a focus on progressing student learning.

5. **Postobservation conversation:** Implementation of new strategies and improved teaching and learning. (State Government of Victoria, Australia, ©2019)

FIGURE 8.3 • Cycle of Teacher Self-Reflection

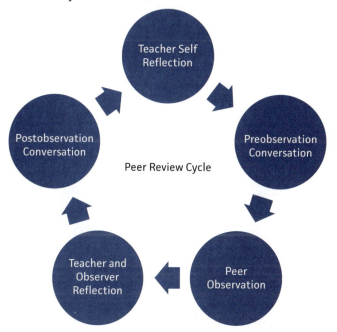

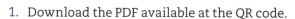

THE SEL SELF-ASSESSMENT

The American Institute of Research, under the guidance of Dr. Nicolas Yoder, created an SEL self-assessment tool for teachers. The tool is based on the CASEL 5 competencies.

1. Download the PDF available at the QR code.
2. Take the assessment.
3. Reflect on your results.

bit.ly/42Wintw

Note: Take the assessment before you implement new tools or strategies. Take the assessment again after six months to a year.

Description: This tool is divided into the following three sections, with Section 1 and Section 2 each divided into two parts:

Section 1. Social Interaction Assessment

Part A. Self-assess implementation of teaching practices.

Part B. Self-assess teachers' own SEL competencies.

Section 2. Instructional Interaction Assessment

Part A. Self-assess implementation of teaching practices.

Part B. Self-assess teachers' own SEL competencies.

Section 3. Culminating Activities and Action Planning

Sections 1 and 2, Part A—Educators have the opportunity to self-assess on the teaching practices; Section 1 focuses on social interactions and Section 2 focuses on instructional interactions.

RATINGS

Ratings are based on how often and how well educators implement each practice on a scale of 1 to 5, from "I do not implement this practice" to "I implement this practice extremely well."

1—I do not implement this practice: I am not implementing these practices.

2—I struggle to implement this practice: I sometimes attempt to implement these practices, and when I do, I have a difficult time implementing them.

3—I implement this practice reasonably well: I attempt to implement these practices and do a reasonable job. I think with more practice and/or some support, I could implement these practices well.

4—I generally implement this practice well: I implement these practices well on a regular basis. These practices are not implemented perfectly, but my students benefit when I implement them.

5—I implement this practice extremely well: I consider these practices to be among my regular practices. I use these practices all of the time, and they are highly successful with my students.

Sections 1 and 2, Part B—Educators consider their own social emotional competencies (SECs) and how their SECs influence their ability to implement (1) social teaching practices and (2) instructional teaching practices.

Teachers will rate their SECs on a four-point scale, from 1 = strongly disagree to 4 = strongly agree.

Section 3—Total scores are computed, and educators can reflect on their self-ratings with guidance from questions and points provided for further consideration.

 Available for download at https://resources.corwin.com/AssessingThroughtheLensofSEL

EXTENDING YOUR PRACTICE TO INCLUDE PEER OBSERVATIONS AS TEACHER ASSESSMENT

Add to your personal assessment plan peer observation as part of your circle of teacher self-reflections. Select one of the instruments in this list and use the corresponding QR codes.

PREOBSERVATION CONVERSATIONS

https://tinyurl.com/peerobservationtemplate

TEACHER SELF-REFLECTION TEMPLATE

https://tinyurl.com/teacherselfreflectiontemplate

PEER OBSERVATION TEMPLATE

https://tinyurl.com/observationpeer2

POSTOBSERVATION TEMPLATE

https://tinyurl.com/postobservationtempl

PEER OBSERVATION FEEDBACK AND REFLECTION, A PRACTICAL GUIDE FOR TEACHERS

https://tinyurl.com/peerfeedbacktempl

Practitioner "Wondering" Reflection

Time for Your SEL Reflection Journal

In your SEL journal, reflect on what you have learned in this chapter. Consider these prompts:

- In what ways do you use reflective practice to inform your teaching?
- In what ways can you create an inquiry process that informs your practice?
- How might you integrate a peer assessment/observation in your plan?

Takeaway to Practice

What is the one takeaway from this chapter you want to put into action? **Name it. Create it. Add it to your action plan** (which you will be writing in Chapter 9).

CHAPTER 9

Developing a Practical SEL Assessment Plan That Supports Teaching and Learning

By failing to prepare, you are preparing to fail.

—Benjamin Franklin

LEARNING OUTCOMES

Colleagues on the assessing journey will be able to

- Develop a plan that includes assessment for learning
- Apply an SEL assessment strategy for each lesson
- Develop an SEL assessment plan that supports the daily integration of SEL dispositions, knowledge, and performance for student growth
- Select effective tools that align with student SEL needs
- Align everyday SEL assessment practices with the CASEL framework

125

et's return to the "why" of this book. As we mentioned in the Introduction, assessment needs to be owned by the students as a developmental aspect of the process of learning. Assessment to inform both teaching and learning needs to be embraced by the practitioner. While data collected for accountability may be needed at the school, district, or state level, practitioners tell us that what they need are the "whys" and "hows" in using SEL formative assessment to impact student social and emotional knowledge and skill acquisition that will increase both their SEL competencies and support their academic journeys. We have described the "why" in previous chapters, and this chapter addresses the "how."

DEVELOPING AN SEL ASSESSMENT PLAN

In Chapter 2 we explained the roles of the teacher and the student in SEL assessing. Since we know and believe that social emotional learning is about the learner, then it makes sense that an SEL assessment plan will have the learner at the center of all decisions. SEL assessing is the process of gathering information in an ongoing manner to provide feedback by offering information (how did I do?) and feed forward by planning (what do I need to do next?) for the purpose of supporting teaching and learning. We refer to this in the world of assessment as continuous assessment for ongoing improvement.

All SEL assessing results are intended *for supporting students' SEL growth.* We have stated this before, and it deserves repeating: SEL assessing is not about collecting data for reporting, grading, or compliance. Now with your newly found knowledge, you may realize that your role as the practitioner is to create an optimal learning environment for every student so that they can gain new knowledge and skills for SEL competence; your SEL assessment plan is focused on learner success.

FIRST, ENVISION YOUR IDEAL SEL LEARNING ENVIRONMENT

In the ideal SEL learning environment, the practitioner who guides learners in the acquisition of SEL competencies knows SEL standards and their competencies and learning progressions; has self-assessed; has an action plan for increasing personal SEL competencies; and knows how to integrate SEL learning throughout the period, day, week, and year across all subject disciplines and extracurricular activities—always with the student at the center. The teacher is assessment (not testing!) literate and knows that SEL assessing is a process. SEL assessing is an ongoing process that provides formative assessment via feed up (What am I expected to learn?), feedback (How am I progressing?), and feed forward (What do I need to do next to keep increasing my SEL competencies?).

What are the students doing in this ideal SEL classroom? They are engaged in learning. They are empowered because they feel competent, connected, and heard. They are effectively working on the day's academic and SEL learning outcomes, which are clearly explained in the morning/beginning of class routine. Both the academic and SEL learning expectations guide the student's work of learning.

Because students know the SEL competencies and the expectations of self-awareness, social awareness, self-management, relationship skills, and responsible decision-making, they work toward increasing those competencies. Whether they are pursuing the learning outcomes individually, in teams, or as a whole class, they collaborate to ensure that the SEL and academic learning environment is safe and engaging for all learners. When expectations are not met, there is a clear process and pathway for dealing with issues.

Student self-assessment and reflection is a part of the positive assessing culture for the class. Students' journals/agendas help them to think about what they accomplished, what they need to do next, and what challenged them. They freely let the teacher know what kind of help they need to move forward—whether SEL or academically. They own their progress.

Parents, guardians, families, and the community are partners in understanding, knowing, and supporting the SEL learning environment. They know they play essential roles in the continuing SEL growth of all family and community members. They help plan, lead, attend, and participate in the development of community-based SEL events—seminars, workshops, and learning events. The family integrates many of the SEL routines and rituals at home. The family knows they have allies to support their children. The families participate in ongoing feedback and feed forward, via surveys and informal and formal meetings, for a continuous improvement cycle.

In the ideal SEL learning environment, all roles—student, teacher, family, community—are interconnected. The educators do not "give" voice to anyone; they honor the many voices in their community. When all members of the community feel their voices are heard and honored, it has a significant impact on the development of the SEL culture. For example, first responders are known and visit the school, participating in several activities and events. Social services support is readily available inside the school and in the community. And all aspects of SEL growth are known, respected, and supported—whether it is at the grocery store, the gas station, the doctor's office, or the community library. Learning, then, does not just take place within the walls of the school; the entire community embraces helping youth to learn and grow.

Chapter 9 • Developing a Practical SEL Assessment Plan That Supports Teaching and Learning   127

"DOING" STUDENT-FOCUSED SEL ASSESSING

To do student-focused SEL assessing right and well, you will begin with a series of questions:

1. Why am I assessing SEL competencies?

This sounds straightforward. You are assessing SEL competencies to determine where each learner is on the progression of acquiring specific SEL knowledge, skills, and performances. If you are assessing for any other reason, you need to ask why. Who is requiring this assessment (or testing)? How will the data be used? If it is for any reason other than to get feedback on where students are in their progression of SEL learning, then you really need to question it.

2. What do I do with the assessment information?

You use it to have a conversation *with* the learner about their progress. Feedback given in language that students will understand provides them with the answer to the following questions: What did I do well? What do I need to do next?

3. What's next?

The learner states what they have learned in alignment with the competency and, based on the learning progression, what their next step is. You, of course, facilitate this conversation using a variety of tools. You both agree on strategies to use to support the ongoing practice of implementing SEL competencies. It is vitally important that you carefully listen to the learner. Craft questions that will elicit responses to inform you. "Am I right when I say you really did well at lunch today with self-control? You did not push or shove. You cleaned up your eating area. Is there anything you struggled with? OK, let's talk about that."

You may be asking, "So, this is it?" Yes and no. You will need to develop a plan for implementing effective SEL practices to create your ideal SEL learning environment. This includes a system for developing your feed forward, feedback, and feed up loop. Feed forward means that you set clear expectations via learning outcomes. Feedback is the information you provide about how the learner is progressing in acquiring the SEL competency presented in the outcome, and feed up is what the student needs to do next to continue growing. This looping system requires knowledge on how to embed SEL practices in your teaching and learning environment throughout the day. We believe that all teaching is SEL teaching. We already "do" SEL. It is not a separate "curriculum." It is a belief and value system that is integrated in the most effective practices of teaching and learning.

YOUR SOCIAL EMOTIONAL LEARNING ASSESSMENT PLAN

Components of the SEL Assessment Plan: Steps to Consider

(See specific guidelines included in each step.)

Step 1: Identify the Focus of the Plan—Who are you assessing? Answer these questions: What or who is the focus of the plan? A class? A subset of learners in the class? An entire grade level? Describe who you are assessing.

Step 2: Decide How You Will Use the Data—Who will be using the data you gather and for what purpose? Who will be using the results of your assessment plan? Are you gathering information from your students for the purpose of increasing their SEL skills, knowledge, and dispositions? If not, you are *not* doing formative ongoing assessing for student learning.

The results of the SEL assessment plan are appropriate for your use in planning learning activities and for sharing with students to help them gain SEL competencies. At the appropriate time, these results may be used with parents to support ongoing SEL skills. Explain how the results will be used and by whom.

Step 3: Identify the Social Emotional Learning Competencies—What SEL competencies are you assessing? Do you first need an overall assessment of the five core SEL competencies? Do you then need to drill down to specific competencies based on behavior or skills you have observed that this group of learners need to gain competency in? Are you following a commercially created SEL curriculum? Does it contain effective assessment tools? If the program does not contain the kinds of assessments you need, are you creating more useful assessment tools?

Step 4: Select the SEL Assessment Tools and Strategies—Choose developmentally and culturally appropriate tools and strategies presented in this book aligned to your assessment purposes. Align those tools and strategies to the SEL competencies using the CASEL framework. Or, develop the SEL tools you need in order to assess the SEL skills of your learners. Self-reports, self-assessments, checklists, exit slips, and other strategies presented in this book are all examples of SEL tools.

(Continued)

Chapter 9 • Developing a Practical SEL Assessment Plan That Supports Teaching and Learning • **129**

(Continued)

> **Step 5: Create a Tracking Process**—How will you collect data, analyze it, use it, and track student progress? Create a process that works for you and your learners. Do not skip this. Without a plan for keeping track of student growth, you have no evidence of SEL effectiveness. Without the evidence of progress, students have no idea how they are doing.
>
> **Step 6: Reflect, Learn, and Repeat**—Take the time for reflection. Review your SEL assessment plan to determine what is working well, what didn't work, and what needs to be changed. This is an ongoing iterative process. Be sure your students are part of the reflection and learning process too.

A NOTE ON THE PROGRESSION OF SEL

An important point to note for those who implement social emotional learning is to understand that students' social, emotional, and cognitive growth is uneven and nonlinear. Piaget's theory of cognitive development assumes that all children go through the same sequence of development, but they do so at different rates. Practitioners well-versed in SEL knowledge make a special effort to provide learning assessments and activities based on individual progress, rather than on the normal standards of peers of the same age. Individuals construct their own knowledge during the interaction with the environment. If the COVID-19 pandemic has done nothing else, it has made us aware of the impact of isolation on acquisition of SEL skills. Educators around the globe are dealing with students who lack social and emotional competencies.

There are a variety of factors that impact the acquisition of SEL competencies, just as there are many factors affecting cognitive growth. Family cultural norms, trauma, disasters, and environmental events such as Hurricane Irma, floods, and earthquakes disrupt the acquisition of SEL competencies. Knowing this allows the teacher to create learning opportunities that are aligned to the needs of students in a specific learning environment.

ONE WAY TO CONSIDER ASSESSING SEL COMPETENCIES: A LEARNING PROGRESSIONS MODEL

Since students do not uniformly acquire SEL skills, a framework or model that provides the progression of learning may be useful as you assess the competencies. The following chart unpacks the self-awareness competency into subcompetencies followed by a continuum from emerging to developing to use as students' skills grow.

FLOW OF THE PROGRESSION'S CHART

The first part includes the SEL competency and moves to the subcompetency, delving into the essential knowledge, performances, and critical dispositions.

> **Teacher Action 1:** The teacher chooses and/or creates learning activities to support the acquisition of new knowledge and skills with the needs of the learner at the forefront. This step also includes creating rubrics for meaningful assessment.

> **Teacher Action 2:** The SEL practitioner thoughtfully gathers information and data about the SEL needs of their learners, provides continuous and meaningful feedback, and allows time for reflection. All artifacts are put together. In the effective SEL classroom, students' voices are honored and respected.

The practitioner and the students reflect on their growth and determine next steps as a team.

STUDENT SEL LEARNING PROGRESSIONS

Let's take a moment to apply some of our knowledge of self-awareness.

Self-Awareness—The Conscious Knowledge of One's Own Feelings, Desires, and Motives. Competency 1—Develop Self-Awareness Knowledge, Performances, and Dispositions to Achieve Academic and Life Success.
Sub-Competencies
S.A.* C-1.** Identifying emotions and each student's specifically
S.A. C-2. Knowing how to express emotions constructively
S.A. C-3. Identifying personal abilities and strengths
S.A. C-4. Creating goals for self-awareness improvement
S.A. C-5. Knowing when to ask for help
S.A. C-6. Monitoring progress in increasing self-awareness knowledge, skills, and performance
Student Learning Progressions

(Continued)

(Continued)

Sub-Competency 1
Competency 1–S.A. C-1. Identifying emotions and each student's specifically
Essential Knowledge
S.A. C-1. Identifying emotions and each student's specifically
Emerging: The student can clearly identify and describe emotions such as happy, surprised, proud, excited, bored, distracted, sad, afraid, confused, etc. **Developing:** The student can identify, describe, and explain their own emotions in the context of the situation.
Performances
S.A. C-1. Identifying emotions and each student's specifically
Emerging: The student names a range of emotions from positive to negative and identifies the emotions that they feel and express. **Developing:** The student identifies, describes, and explains a continuum of emotions in the context of their own situations and when these emotions can be categorized as negative or positive.
Critical Dispositions
S.A. C-1. Identifying emotions and each student's specifically
Emerging: The student is committed to learning about emotions and wants to understand their own and why they have them. **Developing:** The student seeks to understand their emotions and how and why they vary in different situations.

*S.A.—self-awareness, **C-1—competency and the number relates to the first student-focused competency

Using this model, create your own learning progression (LP) for an SEL competency.

CASEL Competency
Subcompetencies
S.A. C-1.
S.A. C-2.
S.A. C-3.
Student Learning Progressions (SLP*)
Sub-Competency 1
Competency 1–S.A. C-1.

132 Assessing Through the Lens of Social and Emotional Learning

Essential Knowledge (EK**)
S.A. C-1. Identifying . . .
Initial—Emerging—Developing—Highly Developed (Select One) The student can _____.
Performances
S.A. C-1. Identifying . . .
Initial—Emerging—Developing—Highly Developed (Select One) The student _____.
Critical Dispositions
S.A. C-1. Identifying . . .
Initial—Emerging—Developing—Highly Developed (Select One) The student _____.

*SLP—student learning progressions, **EK—essential knowledge

UNPACKING THE LEARNING PROGRESSIONS MODEL

DEFINING KNOWLEDGE, SKILLS, AND DISPOSITIONS

In education, knowledge, skills, and dispositions are often referred to as the three key components of learning (see Figure 9.1).

1. **Knowledge:** Knowledge is the information, concepts, and ideas that learners acquire through study, research, observation, and experience. It includes both factual and theoretical knowledge, and can be acquired through various sources, including books, lectures, experiments, and personal experiences.

2. **Skills:** Skills refer to the ability to perform a task or activity competently. They can be developed through practice, instruction, and feedback. Skills can be cognitive (such as problem-solving or critical thinking) or physical (such as playing an instrument or performing a sport).

3. **Dispositions:** Dispositions are the attitudes, values, and beliefs that underlie a learner's behavior and actions. They are often referred to as habits of mind, and include traits such as curiosity, persistence, flexibility, and open-mindedness. Dispositions can be developed and strengthened through intentional learning experiences and reflection.

Chapter 9 • Developing a Practical SEL Assessment Plan That Supports Teaching and Learning 133

FIGURE 9.1 • Learning Progressions Model

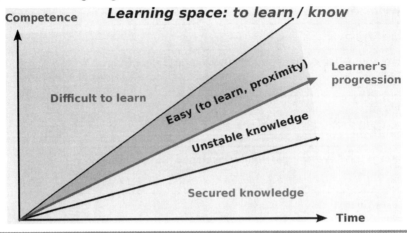

Here, we reflect more on each of the three components of learning.

KNOWLEDGE

Knowledge as we have previously noted is pivotal as the end goal of assessment and evaluations. An individual's knowledge is generally evaluated through written or oral assessments. We provide four practices that would be used for assessing. Each of the four represents an SEL appropriate measure.

1. **Performance evaluations:** This involves assessing an individual's knowledge by observing their performance in a practical situation.

2. **Interviews:** This involves assessing an individual's knowledge by asking them questions about their understanding of a particular subject.

3. **Portfolio assessments:** This involves evaluating an individual's knowledge by reviewing their collection of work samples.

4. **Self-assessments:** This involves individuals reflecting on their own knowledge and assessing their level of understanding in a particular field.

SKILLS

When we further examine the dynamics of essential skills development for learners, we find there is a deep connection to assessment. Assessing students requires a combination of various skills that can help teachers evaluate the learning progress of their students. Some essential skills needed for assessing students may include:

1. **Communication:** The ability to communicate effectively with students and understand their strengths and weaknesses is crucial in assessing their progress.

2. **Observation:** The ability to observe students' behaviors and activities can provide insight into their level of engagement and understanding.

3. **Analytical skills:** Teachers need to have strong analytical skills to evaluate student performance data, identify patterns, and draw conclusions.

4. **Problem-solving skills:** Teachers should be able to identify problems with students' learning and develop strategies to address them.

5. **Planning and organization:** Teachers should be able to plan and organize assessments in a structured and effective manner.

6. **Attention to detail:** Teachers need to pay close attention to detail when evaluating student work to ensure accuracy and fairness.

7. **Patience and empathy:** Teachers should possess patience and empathy to understand the unique needs and learning styles of their students.

8. **Technology skills:** In today's digital age, teachers must be proficient in using technology tools and software to create and administer assessments.

9. **Assessment literacy:** Teachers should have a good understanding of various types of assessments, their purposes, and their appropriate use.

10. **Collaboration:** Teachers should be able to collaborate with other educators, parents, and students to gather additional insights and perspectives on student learning.

Question: Are we missing any skills? If so, what are they?

DISPOSITIONS

DISPOSITIONS OF EFFECTIVE TEACHERS

Grant and Gillette (2006) identified the following eight dispositions of effective teachers:

1. Understanding and accepting themselves

2. Being able to accept criticism

3. Willing to change

4. Having open minds and being free from prejudice

5. Desiring to learn new things

6. Having a well-constructed philosophy of education and using it as the basis of teaching

7. Having a multicultural view of learning and human development

8. Knowing and connecting with the community in which they are teaching (Grant & Gillette, 2006, pp. 76–79)

STUDENT DISPOSITIONS AND ASSESSING

There are many possible dispositions that students may demonstrate when taking tests or when engaging in any assessment activity. This, of course, is dependent on a variety of factors such as their personal traits, academic preparation, testing experience, and the test format. Here are some common dispositions that students may exhibit:

1. **Confidence:** Some students feel confident in their ability to perform well on tests, and this may lead them to approach testing with a positive attitude and a sense of readiness.

2. **Anxiety:** On the other hand, some students experience test anxiety, which can manifest as feelings of stress, nervousness, or fear. This may result in decreased performance or difficulty concentrating.

3. **Preparedness:** Students who have studied and prepared for a test may feel more confident and less anxious, because they have a sense of control over the outcome.

4. **Lack of preparedness:** Conversely, students who have not adequately prepared for a test may feel overwhelmed, anxious, or unsure of what to expect.

5. **Motivation:** Students who are motivated to perform well on a test may approach it with a positive mindset and a desire to succeed.

6. **Lack of motivation:** Conversely, students who lack motivation may feel indifferent or apathetic toward the test, leading to lower levels of engagement and effort.

7. **Mindset:** Students with a growth mindset, who believe that their abilities can be developed through hard work and dedication, may approach tests with a sense of optimism and a willingness to learn from their mistakes.

8. **Fixed mindset:** Conversely, students with a fixed mindset, who believe that their abilities are innate and unchangeable, may be more likely to give up or feel discouraged if they struggle during the test.

Why are dispositions important? For teachers and students, developing positive dispositions is an important life skill that transcends from the formal learning environment to the informal learning environment.

STUDENT EFFICACY IN ASSESSING

As we have mentioned in previous chapters, in the culture of SEL assessing, the student is the center of all learning. All students feel valued and wanted. Students know their voices are respected because their input about their own learning is seen in the "what's next for me" conversations. Students know they are valued because their untapped potential is explored and allowed to blossom. Assessment needs to be owned by the students as a developmental aspect of the process of learning progressions.

Developing an SEL assessment plan is both an art and a science. It requires that you have an open and curious mind about how SEL can change the learning and teaching environment. It requires that you gain new knowledge, skills, and dispositions about both SEL and assessing. It requires that you question all the assumptions you know about testing. It means you need to move from the culture of testing to seeing and knowing the value of ongoing formative assessment *for* learning. It means you allow yourself to experiment. It provides for nurturing the spirit of your learners. It allows for listening to and hearing what your students want and need in order to learn. Your SEL assessment plan places students at the center of all assessing strategies. The student is your "why" you assess; your plan ensures that learning will take place.

CREATE YOUR OWN ASSESSMENT PLAN

Explore the resources that follow and any others you find to create a presentation of the steps to develop an SEL assessment plan within a specific context:

- Classrooms
- Schools
- Districts
- Organizations

SOCIAL AND EMOTIONAL PROFESSIONALLY DEVELOPED ASSESSMENT RESOURCES TO REVIEW

1. **Are You Ready to Assess Social and Emotional Learning and Development? (Second Edition, 2019, American Institutes of Research): A Decision Tree and Toolkit (PDF Document)**

   The free *Stop, Think, Act: Ready to Assess* toolkit is intended to assess learning and development conditions, as well as student SEL competencies (see QR code).

   tinyurl.com/readytoassess

2. **XSEL Labs**

   Dr. Clark McKown, world renowned SEL assessment expert and co-creator of XSEL Labs, provides educational stakeholders with a handout to guide steps for developing an SEL assessment plan and also provides specific SEL assessments tools aligned with many SEL programs in use by schools and districts currently (see QR code). It's an excellent website for exploring resources, downloading free worksheets, and for reviewing recommendations for steps to develop SEL assessment plans.

   xsel-labs.com/

3. **RAND Education Assessment Finder**

   An excellent site to use for exploring and locating existing SEL assessments aligned with specific SEL competence attributes that are developmentally appropriate (see QR code).

   bit.ly/3JXOmmb

4. **SEL Assessment Guide from CASEL: A Sample of Tools That Assess SEL in Educational Settings**

   The SEL Assessment Guide at the CASEL website is a digital guide from the Assessment Work Group, which consists of seven organizations including CASEL (see QR code). While CASEL is not an approval agency for assessing SEL, the website provides several resources for leaders and implementation teams in grades pre-K–12 settings who are making decisions about selecting and using measures of student SEL. This includes guidance on how to select an assessment and use student SEL competency data. CASEL requires that a form be filled out in order to enter the portal to the Assessment Guide.

   bit.ly/3JXOmmb

5. **Explore SEL (EASEL Lab) at Harvard**

   To drill deeper into SEL skills at the developmental level, the Ecological Approaches to Social Emotional Learning (EASEL) Laboratory, led by Dr. Stephanie Jones of the Harvard Graduate School of Education, explores the "effects of high-quality social-emotional interventions on the development and achievement of children, youth, teachers, parents, and communities" (EASEL, 2021; see QR code).

According to the EASEL website, the "lab's approach stems from Bronfenbrenner's bio-ecological model of human development, which situates individuals in the everyday contexts in which they live, learn, work and play. This means studying children and youth in their everyday settings: exploring interactions with peers, the quality of relationships with adults, the impact of broader influences such as culture, climate, and the policy landscape on children's experiences and development, and the impact of individual characteristics (e.g., temperament) and environmental factors (e.g., risk factors such as exposure to poverty, trauma or violence; and protective factors such as high-quality relationships with a caregiver) on developmental trajectories" (EASEL, n.d.).

easel.gse.harvard.edu/

MORE ABOUT THE LEARNING PROGRESSIONS MODEL FOR TEACHING STANDARDS

The Interstate New Teacher Assessment and Support Consortium (InTASC) and the Council of Chief State School Officers (2013) created a master document of Learning Progressions for Teachers. Our LPs for SEL were modeled after the LP developed by this agency. The InTASC LP model includes knowledge, skills, and dispositions for Teaching Standards (see QR code).

These agencies are nonpartisan, nonprofit organizations of public officials who head departments of elementary and secondary education in the US states, the District of Columbia, the Department of Defense Education Activity, the Bureau of Indian Education, and five US territories.

tinyurl.com/intascteacherprogressions

Practitioner "Wondering" Reflection

Time for Your SEL Reflection Journal

In your SEL journal, reflect on what you have learned in this chapter. Consider these prompts:

- My biggest "aha" in this chapter was . . .
- One strategy, idea, or activity I will immediately implement is . . .
- One thing I am not quite clear on is . . .
- What I am curious about is . . .
- In what ways can I integrate assessing in a meaningful way in every lesson?
- How will I move forward with developing a practical assessment plan for SEL knowledge, skills, and dispositions?
- How can I best apply the Stop, Think, Act toolkit for assessing social and emotional learning and development?

Takeaway to Practice

What is the one takeaway from this chapter you want to put into action? **Name it. Create your action plan.**

CHAPTER 10

Evidence-Based SEL Assessment

Practitioner Action Research

Over the years and across the country, we have repeatedly observed individual teachers and teams of reflective practitioners relentlessly examining the manner in which each of their diverse students experiences their instruction. Those same teachers then use that information to purposefully modify their teaching to ensure that each day, each and every student experiences feelings of competence, belonging, usefulness, potency, and optimism through their schoolwork.

—Sagor and Williams (2017, p. xi)

LEARNING OUTCOMES

Colleagues on the assessing journey will be able to

- Examine action research studies from master's degree graduates that implement and measure SEL in the pre-K through middle grade classrooms

- Explore case studies according to age group and grade bands

- Know the importance and impact of teacher action research on self and others

- Connect the results of thoughtful practitioner reflection to the improvement of their own teaching and to the development of ongoing teacher action research

141

ASSESSMENT TOOLS, SEL, AND DEVELOPMENT

There are a plethora of assessment tools that apply to all developmental and academic levels: birth, early learning, pre-K, transitional K (TK), grade level specific, exit examinations, pre-college testing, tests in college, graduate education, professional certifications, and examinations. Some assess readiness, while others are employed as a preassessment (pretest) and postassessment (posttest) method of assessing knowledge and learning.

The main purpose of this chapter is to examine six studies that were conducted in a graduate-level program that applied the action research methodology. These studies exemplify the assessment of social emotional learning skills and competencies.

CASE STUDIES IN ACTION RESEARCH IN TK THROUGH GRADE 12 CLASSROOMS

For more than three decades, the authors have worked in teacher education programs advising students on developing action research projects and proposals, and on completing AR studies. Since 2020, the researchers have worked with more than 200 graduates from a Master of Arts (MA) program in SEL. All students in the program complete an AR project for program fulfillment. While developing the MA SEL program, we selected action research as an inclusive, participatory research model that can take place over a short period of time to test an SEL strategy or practice to measure improvement. We feel that when action research is applied directly to the researcher's environment (education or workplace), the process of researching is more authentic than using a quantitative approach to studying impact. According to Bradbury-Huang (2010), the purpose of action research is to study action through intervention or change in practice:

> Action research is an orientation to knowledge creation that arises in a context of practice and requires researchers to work with practitioners. Unlike conventional social science, its purpose is not primarily or solely to understand social arrangements, but also to effect desired change as a path to generating knowledge and empowering stakeholders. We may therefore say that action research represents a transformative orientation to knowledge creation in that action researchers seek to take knowledge production beyond the gate-keeping of professional knowledge makers. (p. 93)

Carr and Kemmis (1986) used the term *action research* as a unique approach to research, different from most quantitative and qualitative experimental research. Carr and Kemmis believe that action research has many benefits:

1. Theories and knowledge are generated from research grounded in the **realities** of educational practice.

2. Teachers **become collaborators** in educational research by investigating **their own problems**.

3. Teachers play a part in the research process, which makes them more likely to **facilitate a change** based on the knowledge they acquire. (originally cited in Carr & Kemmis, 1986, adapted by Dana & Yendol-Hoppey, 2008, p. 6)

Teacher action research is "a continual set of spirals consisting of reflection and action" (Elliot & Dweck, 1988).

Teacher action research is "a continual set of spirals consisting of reflection and action" (Elliot & Dweck, 1988).

Teacher action research, in our opinion, is an area that is highly underutilized and too often dismissed. Teacher action research is a strand of ongoing competency that is foundational in any program but particularly when studying social and emotional learning. We believe that action research is the most authentic research a practitioner can engage in. It is personal, it helps examine problems in the learning environment, and it is a catalyst for facilitating real change, not just hypothesizing about it. In SEL, action research is conducted through the process of examining which learning activities impact SEL growth and how the implementation of the activity and assessing process supports student learning so that we know we are using effective teaching and learning activities. The challenge is in creating, developing, and sustaining an ongoing inquiry approach to teaching practice. How can we ensure practitioner action research becomes an ingrained part of our professional practice?

In our MA SEL program, graduate students are immersed in action research. The process unfolds over a period of ten months. We enjoy watching our graduate students as they make the connection between their research questions, the implementation of the study, and the data analyses and findings.

Our term for this paradigm shift is moving from *being a teacher* to *being a change agent*. Once you really "get" how practitioner reflection paired with teacher action research has the potential to move the perception of the teacher from a manager of students (or

Chapter 10 • Evidence-Based SEL Assessment **143**

worse—a babysitter) to a highly skilled and knowledgeable professional, you will discover the benefits of embedding teacher action research into practice.

Many of us have experienced this "knowing." For example, when, during an administrative observation, a principal questioned a particular vocabulary activity seventh-grade students were completing, the teacher confidently shared the research behind the activity and their data that showed this particular learning activity increased vocabulary acquisition in 90 percent of their students. They were able to defend their practice with both external peer-reviewed research and their own action research. This new "knowing" that reflection plus action research equals increasing knowledge and skills in teaching practice is transformative. You become a change agent for the teaching profession.

> Knowing + Action Research = Transformative Practice

Students in our MA SEL program conduct action research that is purposeful. The findings from their research are used to create a plan, called an implementation brief, that guides the next steps in their SEL journey. It is through reflection followed by an action research cycle that transformative change can occur. Our students are leaders in implementing action research to effect change, and they continue to make transformative changes in SEL practice at the classroom, school, district, and statewide levels.

ASSESSING SEL THROUGH ACTION RESEARCH IN EARLY CHILDHOOD EDUCATION

In the following sections we will use case studies to illustrate SEL assessing at various levels of education. In the first and second cases, two graduate students, both practitioners in early childhood education, conducted human-subjects–approved action research with children in two preschool classrooms.

Case Study 1—*The Impact of Morning Meetings in an Early Childhood Classroom* (Sima, 2022)

Case Study 2—*Mindfulness as a Tool: Strengthening Inhibitory Control in Preschoolers through Self-Awareness* (Movsisyan, 2022)

CASE STUDY 1

The Impact of Morning Meetings in an Early Childhood Classroom (Sima, 2022)

Overview: This action research study was conducted in Kristen's early childhood classroom in Colorado, with students ranging between three and five years of age. The study examined the impact of a daily morning meeting with preschool students. In addition, the research explored how the explicit teaching and modeling of social and emotional learning skills in the morning meeting and throughout the day might increase student-teacher relationships and student-to-student relationships, as well as decrease unwanted and negative behaviors.

Social and emotional skills were assessed looking for growth and overall understanding of SEL skills and concepts. Data were collected and triangulated through a student questionnaire, the Teaching Strategies GOLD assessment, and through direct observation.

Findings: The end results were that when a daily morning meeting was implemented, students did show growth in SEL skills not only during the morning meeting but also throughout their school day. They were demonstrating a great deal of independence and showed growth in self-regulation skills. Kristen discovered that when SEL was integrated into the classroom, students had a better grasp of self-management, relationship skills, social awareness skills, responsible decision-making skills, and self-awareness skills. Overall, this study had a tremendous impact on Kristen's teaching; her role has changed to be more of a facilitator and her preschool students became greater stewards of their learning.

Assessing Practices:

1. Teaching Strategies GOLD, an early childhood assessment product (https://teachingstrategies.com/product/gold/)
2. Direct observation (Measuring social and emotional skills)
3. Student questionnaire

CASE STUDY 2

Mindfulness as a Tool: Strengthening Inhibitory Control in Preschoolers Through Self-Awareness (Movsisyan, 2022)

Overview: This study investigated the impact of mindfulness practices on inhibition in the development of four- to five-year-old preschoolers. The study strived to have preschool participants develop an increase in overall self-awareness. This research applied daily mindfulness practices to decrease impulsive behaviors. The overall intention was to promote a calmer, safer, and happier classroom environment. What the researcher discovered was that explicit use of mindfulness practices increased the preschoolers' focus, impulse control, self-awareness, and emotional recognition, thus promoting and strengthening their inhibitory control.

Instruments and Data Collection: Several data points were collected from the classroom teacher and instructional aide that were then triangulated in this study. These included (1) an entry and exit questionnaire about impulsive behaviors, (2) an interview with the teacher and aide as well as a reflective, pre/postintervention survey on the topic of mindfulness, and (3) two observational

FIGURE 10.1 ● Student Emotional Vocabulary and Recognition Data

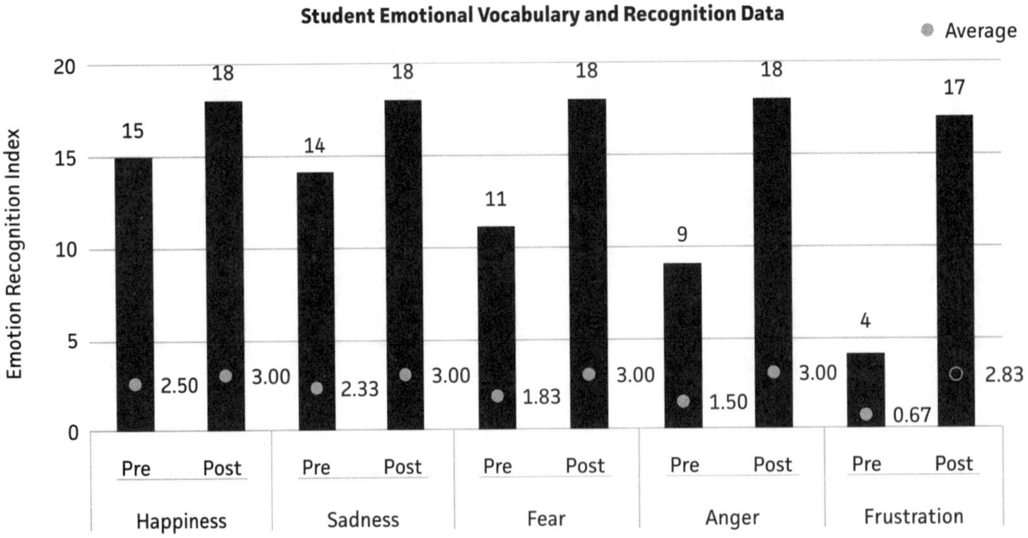

Source: Movsisyan (2022). Used with permission.

checklists that focused on emotional vocabulary knowledge and emotion recognition/observational assessment. (See Figure 10.1.)

Developmental Assessment: In addition to the measures above, one of the researcher's direct assessments was the Head-Toes-Knees-Shoulders (HTKS) task that is used with children between the ages of four and five years. The HTKS task has been conceptualized by Ponitz and colleagues (2009) as a measure of behavior regulation also known as inhibitory control. The HTKS is a reliable and valid screener of kindergarten readiness and early achievement for English- and Spanish-speaking children between four and five years of age. The test consists of two parts. During the first part, the child is instructed to touch their head, then their toes. After the instruction and practice, the child is told to do the reverse of what the child is instructed to do. If the child is told to touch the head, the child should touch their toes. If the child is instructed to touch their toes, the child should touch their head. If the child performs 50 percent of the tasks correctly (the reverse), the instructor proceeds to the second part of the test. If the child performs fewer than 50 percent of the tasks correctly, the testing stops. The second part of HTKS is of increased difficulty, as the child is instructed to touch their knees and shoulders. And when the instruction and practice are completed, the child is instructed to remember and do the reverse. This time the child is told to touch the head, toes, knees, and shoulders, and the child needs to remember, focus, and control impulses, so the child would be able to perform the reverse of the instructions. The instructor should administer the task while seated, with the child standing in front of the instructor at about a three-foot distance. If the child produces the correct response immediately, the item is scored as "2." If they self-correct right away, without prompting, the item is scored as "1." If they do not touch the correct part of their body at all, the item is scored as "0."

Conclusion: This action research started with the question of how daily mindful practices impact inhibitory control in preschoolers, with two subquestions regarding the choice of age-appropriate mindful practices for four- and five-year-old preschoolers and productive ways to incorporate mindfulness in daily academic instruction. Through tests, observations, field notes, and surveys, it was discovered over the six weeks that mindfulness could efficiently be adopted by four- and five-year-olds and used as a tool to control impulses and manage emotions and reactions. The overall goal was to discover how mindfulness practices and SEL (strengthening of self-awareness domain), incorporated in daily academic instruction in a pre-K classroom, would impact the inhibitory control in preschoolers. The comparative analysis of pre- and postimplementation questionnaires, surveys, the HTKS, as well as field notes and anecdotal notes demonstrated that mindfulness can be successfully used in the preschool environment in conjunction with SEL to increase inhibitory control, help control impulses, and use the short pause between the stimuli and reaction to take a breath and make the right choices.

Note: The researcher created several tools for assessing, including an observational rubric that assessed emotional identification (see Estner et al., 2019, for a sample rubric).

TRANSITIONING FROM PRESCHOOL, DAYCARE, OR HOME TO KINDERGARTEN IN THE UNITED STATES

READINESS ASSESSMENTS

Kindergarten programs began to receive state funding in the 1960s and 1970s. One of the more recent qualifiers for a child to enter kindergarten was to formally assess each child on their readiness. It wasn't until the late 1980s that children were beginning to be "formally" evaluated (assessed) on their readiness skills for kindergarten. While it is well-established now, it took until the first decade of the twenty-first century to adopt a formalized and universally accepted kindergarten program. Most recently, we have recognized the critical importance of early childhood education with the introduction of pre-K (preschool) and Transitional Kindergarten. Kindergarten classes have generally consisted of only five-year-olds, although enrollment requirements have varied throughout the United States. For example, in the State of California, the legislature approved the Kindergarten Readiness Act (SB 1381, 2010). Until then, children who were four years old on September 1 could still enroll in regular kindergarten as long as they turned five by December 2 of that year. But the new law changed that. Beginning in 2012, children in California had to be five by September 1 to enroll in kindergarten.

KINDERGARTEN READINESS ASSESSMENT

Across the United States, kindergarten readiness checklists or kindergarten entry assessments are not equally standardized. In their study of more than 230 educators, Harvey and Ohle (2018) reported "inconsistencies in the administration, implementation, perceptions, and use of the Alaska Developmental Profile (ADP). These inconsistencies were connected to an unclear understanding of the purpose of the ADP, a finding that most likely reflects the compliance model of those administering state-mandated assessments instead of educators seeing these tools as useful for instructional decision-making" (p. 1). Case in point, not all assessments are equal in how they evaluate readiness. There is not one standard tool for assessing kindergarten readiness.

Below is one version of a kindergarten readiness checklist. This general checklist can be used to determine how well a child is doing in acquiring the skills found on most kindergarten checklists.

SAMPLE KINDERGARTEN READINESS CHECKLIST

- ☐ Listens to stories without interrupting
- ☐ Recognizes rhyming sounds
- ☐ Pays attention for short periods of time to adult-directed tasks
- ☐ Understands that actions have both cause and effect
- ☐ Shows understanding of general times of day
- ☐ Cuts with scissors
- ☐ Uses words instead of being physical when angry
- ☐ Follows simple directions
- ☐ Expresses feelings and needs
- ☐ Waits their turn and shares
- ☐ Traces and recognizes basic shapes
- ☐ Starts to follow rules and routines
- ☐ Is able to recognize authority
- ☐ Manages bathroom needs
- ☐ Buttons, zips, and is able to manage clothing
- ☐ Begins to control oneself
- ☐ Separates from parents easily
- ☐ Speaks understandably
- ☐ Talks in complete sentences (five to six words)
- ☐ Looks at pictures and then tells stories
- ☐ Identifies the beginning sounds of some words
- ☐ Identifies some letters of the alphabet
- ☐ Sorts similar objects by color, size, and shape
- ☐ Recognizes groups of one, two, three, four, and five
- ☐ Bounces and catches a ball

(Continued)

Chapter 10 • Evidence-Based SEL Assessment 149

(Continued)

- ☐ Can identify six body parts
- ☐ Counts one to ten.
- ☐ Recognizes basic colors
- ☐ Tries to write their name
- ☐ Recognizes their written name

ELEMENTARY EDUCATION TOOLS AND ASSESSMENTS

Case Study 3—*Development of Social Awareness and Relationship Skills in Primary Elementary* (Watson, 2022)

Case Study 4—*Developing Emotional Vocabulary and Self-Regulation Through Morning Meetings* (Gerber, 2022)

Case Study 5—*Assessing SEL in Middle School, Supporting Those With Math Anxiety Through Social Emotional Learning Strategies* (Holden, 2021)

Case Study 6—*Building Inclusive Relationships Through a Peer Helper Program* (Hernandez, 2022)

CASE STUDY 3

Development of Social Awareness and Relationship Skills in Primary Elementary (Watson, 2022)

Overview: In today's society, classrooms are impacted by the underdeveloped abilities of social awareness and relationship-building skills in young children. Due to these factors, it is imperative that educators teach primary elementary students to become socially aware and build positive relationships with their peers, teachers, and family members. This study aimed to provide research evidence that storytelling through children's literature is an effective means to teach primary elementary students social awareness and relationship skills. Through selected stories and specially designed tools, the effectiveness of storytelling can be measured in this quasi-experimental action research.

Methods and Instruments: This research used a pre/postsurvey, a questionnaire, and an observational checklist of behaviors, actions, and words used by primary elementary second graders in Southern California.

Findings: The results of this action research study indicated that exposing second graders to appropriately selected children's literature related to SEL can have a positive impact on the development of social awareness and relationship skills.

CASE STUDY 4

Developing Emotional Vocabulary and Self-Regulation Through Morning Meetings (Gerber, 2022)

Overview: This action research study was conducted to help students build emotional vocabulary using evidence-based strategies to assist in identifying their emotions during morning meetings. As an experienced second-grade educator with a background in language development, this educator also applied other researched-based strategies grounded in the Frayer Model and Zones of Regulation that can be used to teach vocabulary. Another goal of the study apart from the social and emotional skill building was to improve students' understanding of terms and therefore further impact emotional literacy. By using these strategies, second graders would be better able to hold conversations to describe how they are feeling.

Methods and Instruments: Three instruments were used to collect data. The first was a pre/post self-assessment to determine how well students felt they could name feelings, understand why they feel that way, know strategies to regulate those feelings, and use the strategies before receiving instruction during class meetings. The second assessment was a biweekly Seesaw assignment where students identified which Zone of Regulation they were in and named the feeling they experienced as they entered the classroom each day. They also took a picture of themselves displaying that emotion. Finally, the researcher kept observational notes during class meetings, capturing the words students used to describe their emotions.

Findings: The findings show that not only did explicit vocabulary instruction help students name their emotions, but it also enabled them to better explain why they felt that emotion and then choose strategies to regulate their emotions as needed.

CASE STUDY 5

Assessing SEL in Middle School, Supporting Those With Math Anxiety Through Social Emotional Learning Strategies (Holden, 2021)

Overview: In order to support her middle school students in the sixth-grade math classroom, the researcher developed a teaching strategy that included a mastery-based grading policy and applied a student/teacher-developed assessment rubric along with daily emotional energy check-ins. Math anxiety is a predominant problem in this population and an impediment to success in mathematics. According to Richardson and Suinn (1972), math anxiety has been defined as "a feeling of tension and anxiety that interferes with the manipulation of numbers and the solving of mathematical problems in . . . ordinary life and academic situations." By empowering students to be in charge of their own learning in math, this study is a true example of student assessing through self-assessment and how the direct teaching of one weekly SEL lesson along with emotional identification helped her students to achieve their personal best in mathematics. (See Figure 10.2.)

FIGURE 10.2 • Educator Role: Identifying Math Anxiety

EDUCATOR ROLE: IDENTIFYING MATH ANXIETY

TALK IT OUT
Develop a relationship with students

SURVEY
Conduct student surveys to understand perspective

IT'S OK
It's okay to make mistakes

ENERGY
Check in on mindset

Source: Holden (2021). Used with permission.

FIGURE 10.3 • SEL Assessing in Middle School

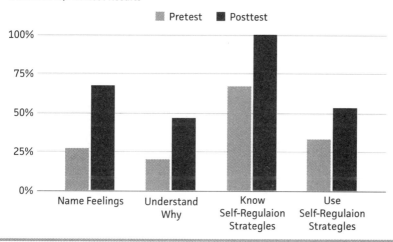

Source: Holden (2021). Used with permission.

Methods and Instruments: The researcher relied on daily emotional check-ins, pre/posttest surveys to determine perceptions of self, adaptation of growth mindset, and practice with i-Ready®.

Findings: Students in the research group all met 100 percent of their expected growth as reported on the i-Ready® diagnostic assessment and on posttest results. The students triangulated their scores and used a standards-based rubric as well as contributed written reflections. Students overall also reported a more positive math identity. This study deeply wove in daily emotional check-ins, making the connection to SEL and math instruction a critical component to learning math without anxiousness acting as a barrier. Overall, the atmosphere in the classroom changed considerably. The students who were most challenged with math voluntarily showed up to office hours while the students who were at a higher level of mastery developed habits of asking clarifying questions and were demonstrating a deeper level of engagement. Emotional identification in class moved from low energy/negative emotion to positive emotion with high energy and some with positive/low energy ratings. (See Figure 10.3)

CASE STUDY 6

Building Inclusive Relationships Through a Peer Helper Program (Hernandez, 2022)

Overview: This study explored the implementation effectiveness of a peer helper elective at a middle school to build and support a positive and inclusive classroom culture. Previous research has shown that there are crucial factors to consider in the implementation of a peer helper program—for example, meaningful time spent between students in general education and students receiving special needs services, staff collaboration, and the training of the peer helpers. This research applied previous findings for implementing a peer program and then assessed the effect the program has on peer helper students, as well as the perceptions of the program by the middle school staff.

Methods and Instruments: In order to facilitate an improved inclusive culture, four main elements were implemented in this peer helper program: (1) peer helpers and PALS (the name given to peer helpers) spent time together multiple times per week in high-interest activities, (2) peer helpers acquired knowledge through lessons, (3) peer helpers took an active participatory role in planning and leading activities, and (4) peer helpers regularly engaged in activities that involved reflection and teacher feedback.

Findings: Analysis of results from student and staff questionnaires and from teacher observation notes indicated that these elements had a positive impact on program participants. Thematic analysis of data also indicated that the main positive outcomes of the program included inclusivity of students with disabilities, relationship-building between the students, and personal student growth in social and emotional learning.

Overall, members in the study experienced improved social and emotional learning skills that included social awareness, relationship-building, and leadership skills. The implementation of the program has led to increased school enjoyment and a sense of belonging for the PALS group, along with an opportunity to practice these important SEL skills.

SUMMARY OF ACTION RESEARCH STRATEGIES, SEL SKILLS, AND COMPETENCIES ASSESSED

NAME OF RESEARCHER	TITLE	SEL SKILL OR COMPETENCY	SUMMARY OF FINDINGS
Sima, K. (2022, May)	*The Impact of Morning Meetings in an Early Childhood Classroom*	Self-Awareness Social Awareness Self-Management Relationship Skills Responsible Decision-Making	A daily morning meeting showed student growth in SEL throughout their school day. Students had a better grasp of self-management, relationship skills, social awareness skills, responsible decision-making skills, and self-awareness skills.
Movsisyan, H. (2022, April)	*Mindfulness as a Tool: Strengthening Inhibitory Control in Preschoolers Through Self-Awareness*	Self-Awareness Self-Management	Mindfulness can be successfully used in the preschool environment. SEL instruction increases inhibitory control, helps control impulses, and allows students to use the short pause between the stimuli and reaction to take a breath and make the right choices.
Watson, T. (2022, April)	*Development of Social Awareness and Relationship Skills in Primary Elementary*	Social Awareness Relationship Skills	Second graders who were exposed to appropriately selected children's literature related to SEL experienced a positive impact on their development of social awareness and relationship skills.
Gerber, J. (2022, May)	*Developing Emotional Vocabulary and Self-Regulation Through Morning Meetings*	Self-Awareness Self-Management Emotional Literacy	The findings show that not only did explicit vocabulary instruction help students name their emotions, but it also enabled them to better explain why they felt that emotion and then choose strategies to regulate their emotions as needed.
Holden, J. (2021, May)	*Assessing SEL in Middle School, Supporting Those With Math Anxiety Through Social Emotional Learning Strategies*	Self-Awareness Self-Identity Positive Math Identity Emotional Literacy	Students in the research group all met 100 percent of expected growth as reported on the i-Ready® diagnostic assessment and on post-test results. They also reported a more positive math identity. The students who were most challenged with math voluntarily showed up to office hours, while the students who were at a higher level of mastery developed habits of asking clarifying questions and were demonstrating a deeper level of engagement.

(Continued)

(Continued)

NAME OF RESEARCHER	TITLE	SEL SKILL OR COMPETENCY	SUMMARY OF FINDINGS
Hernandez, A. (2022, May)	*Building Inclusive Relationships Through a Peer Helper Program (PALS)*	Social Awareness Relationship Skills Leadership Skills	Overall, members in the study experienced improved social and emotional learning skills that included social awareness, relationship-building, and leadership skills. The implementation of the program has led to increased school enjoyment and a sense of belonging for the PALS group, along with an opportunity to practice these important SEL skills.

TEACHER ASSESSMENT AND TEACHER EFFECTIVENESS

As we close the circle of assessing, from assessing pre-K through middle school learners, we now move into teacher assessment and teacher effectiveness. Adults are regularly assessed in the workplace and are continuously self-assessing. Preservice and in-service educators/teachers are no exception.

EDTPA

The Educative Teacher Performance Assessment (edTPA) was developed by the Stanford Center for Assessment, Learning, and Equity (SCALE) and vetted by several agencies that had worked with developing performance-based assessments of teaching (National Board for Professional Teaching Standards, the InTASC Standards portfolio, and the Performance Assessment for California Teachers) (edTPA, 2009). By 2012, a division of Pearson was invited to assist with the national development and deployment of this assessment. In many states, Teacher Preparation Programs must have 70 percent of their candidates passing the edTPA on all three tasks to remain accredited. According to the edTPA website, the edTPA is a performance assessment for novice teachers to show they are ready to teach independently in a classroom environment. In 2013, the edTPA was released as a pilot and implemented in several states. The edTPA measured teacher effectiveness, including classroom observation, principal evaluation, performance review, presentation of instructional artifacts, teacher portfolio assessment, teacher self-report/reflection, student surveys, and other value-added models (Goe et al., 2008, pp. 16–19). We believe that when it comes to determining teacher effectiveness in implementing SEL programs, the criteria should be given thoughtful consideration. In our opinion, single measures are insufficient. A truly rich picture of teaching only emerges when multiple methods of data collection are combined.

High-stakes assessments in public education, specifically in teacher education, have long been debated at the local, state, and national levels. To what degree should uniform assessments, such as the edTPA, be used for teacher licensure? (Gitomer et al., 2021; Goe et al., 2008). In California, the CalTPA is administered for multiple subject credentials, single subject credentials, special education credentials, and administrative credentials. Recently an early childhood educator credential has been added.

TEACHER EFFECTIVENESS

Beyond preservice high-stakes assessment practices, the National Comprehensive Center for Teacher Quality provides some practical guidance on how best to evaluate teacher effectiveness. Their study includes (1) Tools for Measuring Teacher Effectiveness, (2) Technical Consideration in Assessing Teacher Effectiveness, (3) Outcomes of Interest in Teacher Evaluation, and (4) a Comprehensive List of Studies with Summaries.

ASSESSMENT LITERACY IN TEACHER EDUCATION PROGRAMS

This chapter included examples of assessing practices for readiness and for kindergarten. We also shared six action research studies from educators who are graduates of a MA SEL program. The overarching theme of assessment is knowing who to assess, where to assess, when to assess, and what to assess. There is, however, a glaring gap and an absence of "assessment literacy" in teacher education programs. Explicit integration of social and emotional learning skills and skills to support "assessment literacy" across the board, are not being addressed in most teacher education programs.

MULTIPLE MEASURES DONE RIGHT: THE 7 PRINCIPLES OF COHERENT ASSESSMENT SYSTEMS (CRONIN & HEGEDUS, 2016)

As defined by the National Task Force on Assessment Education for Teachers (see full PDF at QR code),

(Continued)

(Continued)

> Assessment is the process of gathering information about student learning to inform education-related decisions.... One becomes assessment literate by mastering basic principles of sound assessment practice, coming to believe strongly in their consistent, high-quality application in order to meet the diverse needs of all students, and acting assertively based on those values. (National Task Force on Assessment Education for Teachers, 2012, p. 135)

bit.ly/3Dg0j2T

Without a deep understanding of what constitutes a balanced approach to assessment, as well as what constitutes an assessment-literate educator, our teachers will remain ill-prepared.

Currently, preservice and in-service teachers are being told to use data to inform instructional decisions. They are not, for the most part, being given the support they need to do so effectively. Classroom teachers are also faced with an avalanche of data from a variety of tenuously connected sources, ranging from federally mandated high-stakes tests to state and district interim benchmarks to daily quizzes, observations, and performance assessments. The sheer volume of data is daunting. Teachers are not adequately equipped to access, sort, and apply assessment data to inform their own pedagogy, let alone to assist parents in understanding the bewildering array of evaluation tools.

It is time for teacher preparation programs to better prepare preservice (initial) and in-service (advanced) educators with the assessment literacy knowledge, skills, and expertise to maximize the use of robust data in furtherance of the ultimate goal of education—serving as a catalyst for social reform that improves the lives of every learner, and society as a whole (Rosebrough & Leverett, 2011).

> *It is time for teacher preparation programs to better prepare preservice (initial) and in-service (advanced) educators with the assessment literacy knowledge, skills, and expertise to maximize the use of robust data in furtherance of the ultimate goal of education—serving as a catalyst for social reform that improves the lives of every learner, and society as a whole (Rosebrough & Leverett, 2011).*

Assessment literacy intersects with social emotional learning when the assessments used to determine SEL competencies are analyzed, evaluated, and selected for use by states, districts, schools, and teachers. All too often those evaluating the SEL assessment instruments are not assessment-literate. The criteria for selecting programs and assessment tools do not align with the purposes and goals of SEL. One solution to this dilemma is to ensure that educators are assessment-literate during their professional preparation programs.

Practitioner "Wondering" Reflection

Time for Your SEL Reflection Journal

In your SEL journal, reflect on what you have learned in this chapter. Consider these prompts:

- Think about how you are assessed in your life, medically and professionally.
- In what ways have the MA SEL graduates applied assessment in their studies?
- What SEL skills were assessed?
- How does assessment literacy impact your life?

Takeaway to Practice

What is the one takeaway from this chapter you want to put into action? **Name it. Create your action plan.** Consider conducting your own action research study.

ADDENDUM OF EARLY CHILDHOOD ASSESSMENTS

The following assessments are used in early childhood settings and are commonly applied through observational checklists.

1. Assessment Evaluation and Programming System Interactive (AEPsi)
2. Child Observation Record (COR)
3. Creative Curriculum Developmental Continuum
4. Desired Results Developmental Profile (DRDP), DRDP-Preschool, and DRDP-K
5. Developing Skills Checklist (DSC)
6. Developmental Indicators for the Assessment of Learning (DIAL)
7. Devereux Early Childhood Assessment (DECA)
8. Early Learning Scale
9. Expressive One-Word Picture Vocabulary Test (EOWPVT)
10. Galileo
11. Language and Emergent Literacy Assessment (LELA)
12. Learning Accomplishment Profile
13. Peabody Picture Vocabulary Test (PPVT)
14. Phonological Awareness and Literacy Screenings (PALS)
15. PreLAS
16. State-developed assessments
17. Teaching Strategies GOLD (used in Sima, 2022)
18. Work Sampling System (WSS)

CHAPTER 11

SEL Intersections

Connecting to Content, Curriculum, Standards, and Frameworks

*Instead of a national curriculum for education, what is really needed is an **individual** curriculum for every child.*

—Charles Handy

> ### LEARNING OUTCOMES
> Colleagues on the assessing journey will be able to
>
> - Understand the function of frameworks and content standards
> - Explore national and state standards to discover the connections between subject-specific content and SEL
> - Examine the intersections of SEL to increase SEL competencies and embed SEL assessment practices
> - Recognize the intersections of SEL in the workplace

As humans, we make decisions that guide us to cross at the intersection of learning with self-reasoned beliefs. In this final chapter, we will examine the *many* intersections between social and emotional learning in the curriculum, standards, and in content-specific frameworks. Curriculum is a complex system that intersects with other systems, such as the needs of the students, the demands of society, the expectations of the educators, and the goals of the institution. We want to embrace these intersections and insert social and emotional practices at each crossroad. Rather than rushing through these intersections, we can combine the common tenets between them. Remember, all learning is social and emotional learning (Frey et al., 2019, p. 17). Rather than having separate goals, expectations, and outcomes, why not mesh them together and coalesce, strengthening lessons with intentionality through the lens of SEL?

Here in Chapter 11, we examine state, national, and subject-specific frameworks and connect and align them to the SEL competencies. We *unpack* history-social sciences (HSS), English language arts (ELA), science (Next Generation Science Standards or NGSS), health, physical education (PE), and career technical education (CTE) standards to address the overlap in skills and competencies. We discover that SEL intersects, is embedded in, and integrated into *all learning*. Social and emotional learning has the potential to be easily woven into the fabric of any school or learning organization. While some approach SEL as a separate curriculum, an intervention, or as a "one-shot" professional development strategy, we know that SEL cannot be separated from our daily interactions in school or in the workplace. We cannot leave our personal lives, feelings, and emotions at the door. We make decisions, react to people and situations, share ideas, and solve problems. This is all done with the ongoing undercurrent of SEL competencies. Our knowledge, skills, and dispositions are aligned with each of the SEL core competencies and help us to be more effective in our workplace roles. Let's further explore intersections and the many opportunities they present for SEL integration and growth.

WHAT IS A FRAMEWORK?

Let us begin with a firm definition of "frameworks" as cited in *An Integrative Perspective on SEL Frameworks* (Casillas et al., 2022): "One might define a framework in the social sciences as an organizing system, a blueprint, or even a roadmap that tells the user what they should be looking for" (p. 7). In another helpful analogy, Blythe and colleagues (2018) state,

> Frameworks are like maps, guidebooks, and other travel tools that help you think about where you want to go to set goals, communicate with others who have been there or are going on the journey with you, and figure out the best ways of getting from here to there [action]. (p. 1)

Simply put, frameworks are structures that organize, name, and divide competencies. They tell us what we are aiming for and what outcomes we should or can expect from a program, strategy, or practice. Furthermore, frameworks serve as a device or heuristic for communicating that information to stakeholders (researchers, practitioners, policymakers, and others).

FRAMEWORKS ARE DEVELOPMENTAL

Almost all frameworks are based on research and theories of human development, which identify typical patterns of growth and change across different domains of development, such as cognitive, emotional, social, and physical. Frameworks are developmental because they provide a way of understanding growth and change over time, and help to guide the process of learning, skill-building, and professional development in a structured and systematic way. An effective framework typically embodies several key features, such as delineating concrete intermediate and long-term outcomes. An effective framework is clear and transparent; it links to measurement and assessment. Finally, frameworks are developmental and contextual, highlighting what is salient (i.e., growing or emerging) at different developmental periods and linking their concepts and constructs to age-specific and context-relevant demands and opportunities.

FOUR PRIMARY PURPOSES OF FRAMEWORKS IN SEL

1. Summarize and advance theory and research

2. Support applied practice

3. Define key competencies and inform the development of standards

4. Inform assessment and measurement (Berg et al., 2017, pp. 33–36)

FRAMEWORKS ALL AROUND US

Below is a list of content standard frameworks that are applied by individual states or universally by most states.

- Common Core State Standards for English and Language Arts

- Common Core State Standards for Mathematics

- Next Generation Science Standards

- Social Science and History Framework

- Positive Student Behavior Support Framework

- Health, Wellness, and Physical Education Curriculum

- Positive Behavioral Interventions and Supports
- Coalition to Advance Future Student Success Framework
- Harvard Ecological Approaches to Social Emotional Learning Laboratory Non-SEL Framework Comparison Tool

COMMON CORE STATE STANDARDS

The Common Core State Standards Initiative, also known as Common Core, is an educational initiative from 2010 that details what K–12 students throughout the United States should know in ELA and mathematics at the conclusion of each school grade. According to the Council of Chief State School Officers (2010), the Common Core State Standards provide a "consistent, clear understanding of what students are expected to learn, so teachers and parents know what they need to do to help them. The standards are designed to be robust and relevant to the real world, reflecting the knowledge and skills that our young people need for success in college and careers."

CONTENT STANDARDS AND FRAMEWORKS

Let's begin this exercise by analyzing the intersections of SEL in a sample content standard (see Figure 11.1). We have selected standards from two states and pulled out SEL practices embedded into those standards. Beginning with the standards for early learning and kindergarten from one state, we identified the SEL practice of "sense of belonging." We then examined ELA standards from another state for grade level bands kindergarten through first grade, where we also found "sense of belonging." For example, if we were looking at the intersections of ELA and SEL, the practice of developing a sense of belonging in young children may be fostered by reading, writing, listening, speaking, role playing, movement, and many other learning activities. Although the descriptions are slightly different, they both outline what a sense of belonging looks like in children who are in educational learning environments. Key phrases for sense of belonging include (1) confidence in self and in skills, (2) goal setting and decision-making, (3) recognizing feelings and emotions, and (4) recognizing one's own unique abilities, characteristics, and interests. In each state's pre-K through first grade standards, a sense of belonging intersects with at least one SEL competency and supports both self-awareness (CASEL) and relationship building (CASEL).

FIGURE 11.1 ● Sample ELA Content Standards Intersections with Social and Emotional Learning

STATE #1 (KINDERGARTEN)	STATE #2 (K–1)
Sense of Belonging **Self-Awareness & Relationship Building (CASEL)**	
The child recognizes self as a unique individual having their own abilities, characteristics, emotions, and interests. The child expresses confidence in their own skills and positive feelings about themselves. The child has a sense of belonging to family, community, and other groups.	The child is capable of successfully making decisions, accomplishing tasks, and meeting goals.
Relationships with a Trusted Adult **Relationship Building (CASEL)**	
The child engages in and maintains positive relationships and interactions with a trusted adult. The child engages in prosocial and cooperative behavior with trusted adults.	Healthy relationships and interactions with adults and peers.
Relationships with Other Children **Relationship Building (CASEL)**	
The child engages in and maintains positive interactions and relationships with other children. The child engages in cooperative play with other children. The child uses basic problem-solving skills to resolve conflicts with other children.	The child forms positive interactions and relationships with other children. The child engages in cooperative play with other children.
Emotional Functioning **Self-Management (CASEL)**	
The child expresses a broad range of emotions and recognizes these emotions in self and others, expresses care and concern toward others, and manages emotions with increasing independence.	The child demonstrates a healthy range of emotional expression and learns positive alternatives to aggressive or isolating behaviors.

UNPACKING THE HISTORY–SOCIAL SCIENCE FRAMEWORK

The History-Social Science Framework was never "nationalized" as such, due to the need to customize history to each specific state. In addition, most states undergo rigorous adoption practices for this customized curriculum by textbook publishers. In Figure 11.2

Chapter 11 • SEL Intersections   **165**

FIGURE 11.2 ● California History–Social Science Framework Analysis, 2016

GRADE LEVEL	KEY CONCEPTS	INTERSECTIONS WITH SEL
Kindergarten	Students in kindergarten are introduced to basic spatial, temporal, and **causal relationships**, emphasizing the geographic and historical connections between the world today and the world long ago. The **stories of ordinary and extraordinary people** help describe the range and continuity of **human experience** and introduce the concepts of **courage, self-control, justice, heroism, leadership, deliberation, and individual responsibility**. Historical empathy for how people lived and worked long ago reinforces the concept of civic behavior: how we interact respectfully with each other, following rules, and respecting the rights of others.	Relationship Building Social Awareness Self-Management (Self-Control) Diversity Social Justice Empathy Respect Courage
Grade One	Students in grade one continue a more detailed treatment of the broad concepts of rights and responsibilities in the contemporary world. The classroom serves as a microcosm of society in which decisions are made with respect for individual responsibility, for other people, and for the rules by which we all must live, fair play, good sportsmanship, and respect for the rights and opinions of others. Students examine the geographic and economic aspects of life in their own neighborhoods and compare them to those of people long ago. Students explore the varied backgrounds of American citizens and learn about the symbols, icons, and songs that reflect our common heritage.	Responsible Decision-Making Relationship Building Social Awareness (Social Issues) Ethnic Identity Respect
Grade Two	Students in grade two explore the lives of actual people who make a difference in their everyday lives and learn the stories of extraordinary people from history whose achievements have touched them, directly or indirectly. The study of contemporary people who supply goods and services aids in understanding the complex interdependence in our free-market system.	Relationship Building Self-Awareness Diversity and Inclusion

GRADE LEVEL	KEY CONCEPTS	INTERSECTIONS WITH SEL
Grade Three	Students in grade three learn more about our connections to the past and the ways in which particularly local, but also regional and national, government and traditions have developed and left their marks on current society, providing common memories. Emphasis is on the physical and cultural landscape of California, including the study of American Indians, the subsequent arrival of immigrants, and the impact they have had in forming the character of our contemporary society.	Relationship Building Self-Awareness Cultural Identity Diversity Character
Grade Four	Students in grade four learn the story of their home state, unique in American history in terms of its vast and varied geography, its many waves of immigration beginning with pre-Columbian societies, its continuous diversity, economic energy, and rapid growth. In addition to the specific treatment of milestones in California history, students examine the state in the context of the rest of the nation, with an emphasis on the U.S. Constitution and the relationship between state and federal government.	Relationship Building Diverse Populations
Grade Five	Students in grade five study the development of the nation up to 1850, with an emphasis on the people who were already here, when and from where others arrived, and why they came. Students learn about the colonial government founded on Judeo-Christian principles, the ideals of the Enlightenment, and the English traditions of self-government. They recognize that ours is a nation that has a constitution that derives its **power from the people**, that has gone through a revolution, that once sanctioned slavery, that experienced **conflict** over land with the **original inhabitants**, and that experienced a westward movement that took its people across the continent. Studying the **cause, course, and consequences** of the early explorations through the War for **Independence** and western expansion is central to students' fundamental understanding of how the **principles** of the American republic form the basis of a **pluralistic society** in which **individual rights** are secured.	Relationship Building Pluralistic Society (Diversity, Equity, Inclusion) Conflict Acknowledgment

(Continued)

FIGURE 11.2 *(Continued)*

GRADE LEVEL	KEY CONCEPTS	INTERSECTIONS WITH SEL
Grade Six	Students in grade six expand their understanding of history by studying the people and events that ushered in the dawn of the major Western and non-Western ancient civilizations. Geography is of special significance in the development of the human story. Continued emphasis is placed on the **everyday lives, problems, and accomplishments of people, their role in developing social, economic, and political structures**, as well as in establishing and **spreading ideas** that helped transform the world forever. Students develop higher levels of critical thinking by considering why civilizations developed where and when they did, why they became dominant, and why they declined. Students analyze the interactions among the various cultures, emphasizing their enduring contributions and the link, despite time, between the contemporary and ancient worlds.	Plurality Ethnic Identity Religious Identity Relationship Building
Grade Seven	Students in grade seven study the **social, cultural,** and technological changes that occurred in Europe, Africa, and Asia in the years A.D. 500 to 1789. After reviewing the ancient world and the ways in which archaeologists and historians uncover the past, students study the history and geography of great civilizations that were developing concurrently throughout the world during medieval and early modern times. They examine the growing economic interaction among civilizations as well as the exchange of **ideas, beliefs,** technologies, and commodities. They learn about the resulting growth of Enlightenment philosophy and the new **examination of the concepts of reason and authority, the natural rights of human beings** and the divine right of kings, experimentalism in science, and the dogma of belief. Finally, students assess the political forces let loose by the Enlightenment, particularly the rise of **democratic ideas**, and they learn about the continuing influence of these ideas in the world today.	Recognizing Relationship Building Diversity of Religion and Languages Diversity of Thought

GRADE LEVEL	KEY CONCEPTS	INTERSECTIONS WITH SEL
Grade Eight	Students in grade eight study the **ideas, issues, and events** from the framing of the Constitution up to World War I, with an emphasis on America's role in the war. After reviewing the development of America's democratic institutions founded on the Judeo-Christian heritage and English parliamentary traditions, particularly the shaping of the Constitution, students trace the development of American politics, **society, culture**, and economy and relate them to the emergence of major regional differences. They learn about the challenges facing the new nation, with an emphasis on the causes, course, and consequences of the Civil War. They make connections between the rise of industrialization and contemporary social and economic conditions. Students confront the themes of **freedom, equality, and liberty**, and their changing definitions over time. Examine different motivations and expressions of manifest destiny, and encourage students to **collect multiple pieces of evidence** that explain the diverse motivations for western expansion.	Self-Awareness Social Awareness Cultural Awareness Diversity and Inclusion Freedom
Grade Nine	Choice of elective for HSS courses. Humanities, Psychology, Focus on Ethnic Studies. Explorations include: How have race and ethnicity been constructed in the United States, and how have they changed over time?	Relationship Skills Social Awareness Self-Awareness (Identity: Racial, Ethnic, Cultural)

(Continued)

Chapter 11 • SEL Intersections **169**

FIGURE 11.2 *(Continued)*

GRADE LEVEL	KEY CONCEPTS	INTERSECTIONS WITH SEL
Grade Ten	Students in grade ten study major turning points that shaped the modern world, from the late eighteenth century through the present, including the cause and course of the two world wars. They trace the rise of democratic ideas and develop an understanding of the historical roots of current world issues, especially as they pertain to international relations. They extrapolate from the American experience that **democratic ideals** are often achieved at a high price, remain vulnerable, and are not practiced everywhere in the world. Students **develop an understanding** of current world issues and **relate them to their historical, geographic, political, economic, and cultural contexts.** Students consider multiple accounts of events in order to understand international relations from a variety of **perspectives**.	Social Awareness Self-Awareness Critical Thinking and Decision-Making Social Justice, Equity, and Inclusion (Democratic Principles) Perspective Taking
Grade Eleven	Students in grade eleven study the major turning points in American history in the twentieth century. Following a review of the nation's beginnings and the impact of the Enlightenment on U.S. democratic ideals, students build upon the tenth-grade study of global industrialization to understand the emergence and impact of new technology and a corporate economy, including the **social and cultural effects**. They trace the change in the ethnic composition of American society; the movement **toward equal rights** for **racial minorities and women**; and the role of the United States as a major world power. An emphasis is placed on the expanding role of the federal government and federal courts as well as the continuing tension between the individual and the state. Students consider the major **social problems** of our time and trace their causes in historical events. They learn that the United States has served as a model for other nations and that the rights and freedoms we enjoy are not accidents, but the results of a defined set of political principles that are not always basic to citizens of other countries. Students understand that our rights under the U.S. Constitution are a precious inheritance that depends on an educated citizenry for their preservation and protection.	Self-Awareness (Identity: Racial, Ethnic, Cultural) Social Awareness Diversity, Equity, and Inclusion

GRADE LEVEL	KEY CONCEPTS	INTERSECTIONS WITH SEL
Grade Twelve	Students in grade twelve pursue a deeper **understanding of the institutions** of American government. They compare systems of government in the world today and **analyze the history and changing interpretations** of the Constitution, the Bill of Rights, and the current state of the legislative, executive, and judiciary branches of government. An emphasis is placed on analyzing the relationship among federal, state, and local governments, with particular attention paid to important historical documents such as the Federalist Papers. These standards represent the culmination of civic literacy as students prepare to vote, participate in community activities, and assume the responsibilities of citizenship.	Problem Solving Decision-Making Social Awareness Self-Awareness Perspective Taking

Source: California Department of Education (2016).

*Bolding added to represent key concepts connected to SEL.

we have presented the language of the California HSS Framework for kindergarten through twelfth grade, adopted by the California State Board of Education on July 14, 2016, and identified intersections with SEL (see also QR code).

EXAMINING THE SEL INTERSECTIONS IN NEXT GENERATION SCIENCE STANDARDS

bit.ly/3K1CNu1

In 2016, one additional national content framework, the NGSS, was added. In the NGSS, the most obvious intersection with SEL is experiencing the three dimensions of science. Experiential learning helps to build relationships between peers by developing and using elements of the three NGSS dimensions: (1) engineering practices (SEPs), (2) disciplinary core ideas, and (3) crosscutting concepts (CCCs). As a result, students collaboratively and purposefully explain phenomena or design solutions to problems. Science lessons and units aligned to the standards should be three dimensional; that is, they should allow students to actively engage with the practices and apply the crosscutting concepts to deepen their understanding of core ideas across science disciplines. In 2015, the National Research Council produced a guide that outlines new performance and implementation expectations for science (see Figure 11.3). Note the intersections with SEL competencies and key SEL tenets.

FIGURE 11.3 ● Performance and Implementation Expectations for Science

SCIENCE EDUCATION WILL INVOLVE MORE	INTERSECTIONS WITH SEL
Facts and terminology learned as needed while developing explanations and **designing solutions** supported by evidence-based arguments and reasoning.	Learning in context is a **culturally responsive teaching strategy.** ● Developing explanations ● Designing solutions ● Supported by evidence
Systems thinking and modeling to explain phenomena and to give a context for the ideas to be learned.	Learning in context is a **culturally responsive teaching strategy.** ● Context cues learning and thinking ● Decision-making and critical thinking applied to systems ● Students observe the relationships between the models and the phenomenon
Students conduct investigations, solve problems, and engage in discussions with teachers' guidance	Building relationships with peers through discussion. An investigation is a trial-by-error process that heightens personal awareness, self-awareness, self-management, and decision-making.
Students discuss open-ended questions that focus on the strength of the evidence used to generate claims.	Building relationships with peers through discussion. Open-ended questions produce qualitative responses.
Students read multiple sources, including science-related magazine and journal articles and web-based resources; students develop summaries of information.	Reading contemporary sources presumes learners are exposed to culturally relevant genres. The choice of media sources meets the individual's strengths in learning/modality (self-awareness).
Multiple investigations are driven by students' questions with a range of possible outcomes that collectively lead to a deep understanding of established core scientific ideas.	Student-centered investigations drive individualized learning, a form of authentic assessment. Inquiry-based learning.
Students write in journals, reports, posters, and media presentations that explain and argue.	Multiple means of representation provide Universal Design for Learning elements.
Provision of support so that all students can engage in sophisticated science and engineering practices.	Equity, inclusion, and access.

Source: Adapted from National Research Council (2015).

*Bolding added to represent key concepts connected to SEL.

> **Spotlight:** Take a look at one lesson exemplar for first grade that focuses on interpersonal communication (relationship building), "How Does Light Help Me See Things and Communicate with Others?" It can be found at the QR code.

bit.ly/44RppAX

HEALTH, WELLNESS, AND PHYSICAL EDUCATION CURRICULUM + SEL

Social and emotional learning competencies are embedded in numerous health and physical education national and state standards. Some states have included SEL competencies as a subset of health and wellness, while others have embedded SEL into physical education and health.

For example, let's begin by taking a look at the National Health Education Standards (NHES), a framework for health education in the United States. The NHES consists of the following seven standards:

1. Students will comprehend concepts related to health promotion and disease prevention to enhance health. (Self-Awareness)

2. Students will analyze the influence of family, peers, culture, media, technology, and other factors on health behaviors. (Relationship Skills)

3. Students will demonstrate the ability to access valid information, products, and services to enhance health. (Responsible Decision-Making)

4. Students will demonstrate the ability to use interpersonal communication skills to enhance health and avoid or reduce health risks. (Relationship Skills)

5. Students will demonstrate the ability to use decision-making skills to enhance health. (Responsible Decision-Making)

6. Students will demonstrate the ability to use goal-setting skills to enhance health. (Self-Management)

7. Students will demonstrate the ability to practice health-enhancing behaviors and avoid or reduce health risks. (Responsible Decision-Making)

These standards provide a comprehensive and holistic approach to health education and aim to equip students with the knowledge and skills necessary to make informed decisions about their health and well-being. When these health standards are assessed, there is great overlap with SEL.

HEALTH AND WELLNESS: CONNECTIONS TO SEL AND ACADEMICS

The Centers for Disease Control and Prevention (CDC) is a governmental agency that has set national standards and practices for creating healthy schools and recommending academics and programs to support health. According to the CDC website, "schools play an important role in promoting the health and safety of children and adolescents by helping them to establish lifelong health patterns." The connection between health, academics, and social and emotional learning is very apparent. Supported by numerous research studies, the CDC's website states, "Healthy students are better learners, and academic achievement bears a lifetime of benefits for health." The Youth Risk Behavior Surveillance System and subsequent studies conducted in 2021 indicate that higher academic grades are associated with more positive individual and cumulative health behaviors among high school students. Conversely, youth risk behaviors, such as physical inactivity, unhealthy dietary behaviors, tobacco use, alcohol use, and other drug use, are consistently linked to poor grades and test scores and lower educational attainment. Healthy students and those who practice social and emotional skills are better learners. As we previously shared in the book, the Whole School, Whole Community, Whole Child (WSCC) Model (through the CDC) is a student-centered model that emphasizes the role of the community in supporting the school, the connections between health and academic achievement, and the importance of evidence-based school policies and practices. The key to health success is to address the "whole" child by the "whole" community, not just school and not just home (Centers for Disease Control and Prevention, 2020).

There are several natural intersections between the WSCC Model and SEL competencies. Creating an SEL climate is done through heightened social and self-awareness resulting in building relationships in the school community and between home and school.

Several states and local school districts across the United States have included SEL in health or in the physical education curriculum and standards. In San Bernardino, California, for example, discussions about SEL are directed to the district's Student Health and Support Services Department. Several educators serve on this district committee.

In some states and local school districts, PE curriculum and programs also intersect with health and SEL, and in many states, the visual and performing arts curricula also include SEL competencies. Bailey (2021) outlines the important role physical activity plays in the overall physical, emotional, and academic well-being of students.

POSITIVE BEHAVIOR INTERVENTIONS AND SUPPORTS + SEL

Some district and state leaders have recommend embedding SEL competencies (SECs) within a prevention-focused, multitiered public health model because simply adopting a curriculum does not lead to adequate implementation or improved outcomes (Greenberg et al., 2017; Merrell & Gueldner, 2010). Positive Behavioral Interventions and Supports (PBIS) provide an ideal framework for promoting SECs to improve outcomes for the whole child. Can school personnel teach SECs within a PBIS framework? Advocates argue that in order to support systematic, schoolwide implementation through one system, the PBIS framework itself can improve student outcomes. Recommendations by Barrett and colleagues (2018) indicate how the PBIS framework can be adjusted to support instruction of SECs (p. 1).

COALITION TO ADVANCE FUTURE STUDENT SUCCESS (CAFS FRAMEWORK)

The CAFS is a collaborative of state and national nonprofit agencies that has driven educational policy to ensure that all federal funds provided to schools will be used equitably. In 2022, they developed a framework to provide support and consistent guidance across member organizations. While the components were primarily developed as a response to the 2020–2022 world pandemic, you will notice that there are many connections to SEL.

The framework consists of the following ten principles:

1. Continue to Keep Schools Safe for In-Person Learning (sense of belonging and building positive relationships)
2. Close the Digital Divide (equity and inclusion)
3. Provide Physical, Mental Health, and Well-Being Support (emotional literacy)
4. Address Attendance, Engagement, and Student Transitions (student self-management skills)

Chapter 11 • SEL Intersections 175

5. Ensure Students Stay on a Path to Postsecondary and Career Readiness (self-management, individual strengths, learner identity, and self-awareness with a positive growth mindset for the future)

6. Address COVID Learning Gaps for All Students (equity and personalized, individualized instruction)

7. Ensure High-Quality Curriculum and Instruction (curriculum that is free from bias and historical inaccuracies, and grounded in culturally responsive teaching practices that address all cultures and identities equally)

8. Recruit and Retain a Talented Educator Workforce (teacher self-care, adult SEL, and trained, culturally responsive teachers)

9. Create Balanced Assessment and Accountability Systems ("humanizing" assessment practices to include more learner-centered, authentic, and formative assessment practices that are not biased and are applied through the lens of SEL)

10. Explore and Implement New Education Delivery Models (apply UDL across all modalities)

BEHAVIORAL, EMOTIONAL, AND SOCIAL SKILLS INVENTORY (BESSI)

Because we are limited in our ability to compare and contrast all SEL frameworks, we encourage you to conduct more research on SEL frameworks, programs, and analyses on your own. (See Cipriano et al., 2010, 2023.) We do believe, however, that the BESSI is worth mentioning here. The BESSI is an integrative framework for conceptualizing and assessing social, emotional, and behavioral skills. Its creators (Soto et al., 2022) discovered that "many skill facets can be organized within five major domains representing Social Engagement, Cooperation, Self-Management, Emotional Resilience, and Innovation Skills" (p. 2). What is interesting is that these authors have applied a different lens of analysis and developed a novel categorization schema that does not exactly mirror the CASEL 5, but rather this unique organization leans toward many of the skills and attributes found in standards and frameworks for twenty-first-century learning, workforce development, and career technical education.

CAREER TECHNICAL EDUCATION

According to the Association for Career and Technical Education (ACTE), "social-emotional skills and attributes can be learned, taught, and modeled as well as dexterously interwoven and prioritized in career and technical education (CTE) programs," (Smith,

2020, p. 1). In fact, many states have embedded SEL into their CTE standards and competencies. The Coalition for Career Development Center and Civic Enterprises (known now as CIVIC) created a developmental framework in collaboration with eight states (Delaware, Kansas, Nevada, North Dakota, Ohio, Pennsylvania, Utah, and Wisconsin). These agencies and states have formed a Career and Workforce Development Community of Practice along with CASEL and the Collaborative States Initiative. Their developmental framework supports a multitude of career readiness skills and their Future Ready research has identified key college and career readiness skills, including life skills, twenty-first-century soft skills, noncognitive competencies, replacement behaviors, and habits of learning. The categorization is divided into four skill sets: self-awareness (directly aligned to the CASEL 5 framework), self-management (directly aligned to the CASEL 5 framework), social efficacy, and academic efficacy (All4Ed, n.d.; see also QR code).

bit.ly/3pQxyXh

Historically, school-to-career research has referred to "soft skills" and other interpersonal skills that are akin to SEL. In their study, Yoder and colleagues (2020) analyzed surveys of the skills that employers seek—and often have trouble finding—to identify the most in-demand skills, and they found that "80 percent of employers said these skills (SEL skills) are increasingly important to company success" (p. 5). From their report, they note that employers have consistently listed the following skills as critical to succeed in the world of work:

1. Communication Skills
2. Interpersonal Skills (CASEL, Relationship Building) (CASEL Competency)
3. Self-Management Skills (CASEL, Self-Management) (CASEL Competency)
4. Team Collaboration (CASEL, Relationship Building) (CASEL Competency)
5. Problem-Solving Skills
6. Integrity
7. Decision-Making Skills (CASEL, Decision-Making) (CASEL Competency)

According to Smith (2020), who writes about the connections between SEL and CTE, "Infusing SEL skills into the CTE curriculum helps support a solid foundation for a variety of career paths and gives students skills needed to thrive throughout life" (p. 3).

EXPLORING THE INTERCONNECTEDNESS OF FRAMEWORKS WITH EASEL

The Harvard Graduate School of Education has developed the Taxonomy Project at the Ecological Approaches to Social Emotional Learning (EASEL) Laboratory, which is an ongoing web-based initiative designed to create a scientifically grounded system for organizing, describing, and connecting frameworks and skills across the nonacademic domain. What is interesting about their website is how their web-based analysis tool can conduct side-by-side comparisons of non-SEL frameworks and can visually represent many of the intersections and interconnections (see also Figure 11.4). According to the EASEL website,

FIGURE 11.4 ● Bronfenbrenner's Ecological Model of Human Development

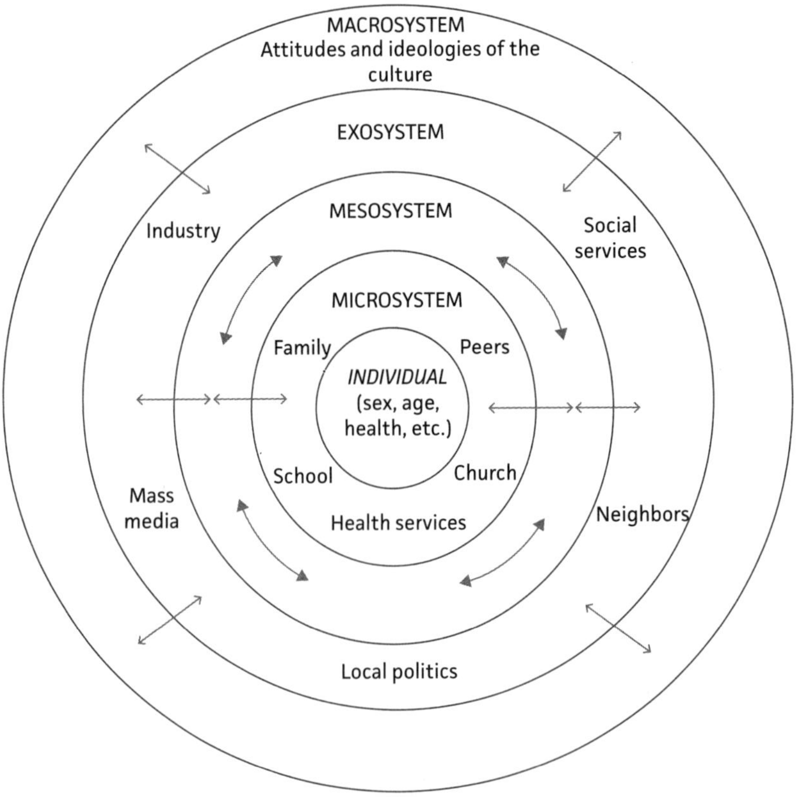

Source: Hchokr at English Wikipedia. https://creativecommons.org/licenses/by-sa/3.0/deed.en

Our lab's approach stems from Bronfenbrenner's bio-ecological model of human development, which situates individuals in the everyday contexts in which they live, learn, work and play. This means studying children and youth in their everyday settings: exploring interactions with peers, the quality of relationships with adults, the impact of broader influences such as culture, climate, and the policy landscape on children's experiences and development, and the impact of individual characteristics (e.g., temperament) and environmental factors (e.g., risk factors such as exposure to poverty, trauma or violence; and protective factors such as high-quality relationships with a caregiver) on developmental trajectories. (Ecological Approaches to Social Emotional Learning (EASEL) Laboratory, n.d.)

WHERE IS SEL IN THE EDUCATIONAL WORKPLACE?

As noted earlier, both authors teach in an MA SEL program. Our students come from K–12 public education, charter schools, and private institutions. We also draw students from a variety of organizations, ranging from private consulting businesses to social service agencies. To reveal where SEL can be found in the workplace, we will share evidence from some of our graduate students. You will also come to understand that SEL has the potential to increase self-awareness, self-management, responsible decision-making, relationship building, and more, in all workplaces. SEL is not just an educational phenomenon or imperative; the need for SEL is universal.

SEL is not just an educational phenomenon or imperative; the need for SEL is universal.

Case 1: Self-Awareness in a First-Grade Classroom

Elsa adapted a learning progressions approach for CASEL Competency #1 to assess the needs of her first-grade students. She states, "Assessment in SEL should serve as a tool to better meet the needs of our students in becoming successful in navigating the different aspects of their lives and implemented in a manner that will move the field in the right direction." She used the data from her action research project to inform her teaching practice and the SEL strategies that her students needed to learn.

Case 2: Dual Language Charter School SEL Implementation

This urban charter school prepares students from diverse populations to excel in higher education and to be leaders in creating a just, global society. SEL aligns with the mission of the charter school in which all students in K–8 were assessed to determine their SEL strengths and to inform planning for SEL direct instruction. All educators and staff received professional development on personal and professional SEL standards and competencies.

Case 3: Art Through the Lens of SEL

Tammy adapted a student learning progression approach to integrate and assess SEL in her art classes. She created a four-step process that included (1) selecting the SEL competency and art standard; (2) developing integrated strategies and an SEL assessing rubric and art grading rubric; (3) implementing the strategies and utilizing the rubrics for ongoing feedback and feed forward; and (4) collecting data as evidence of SEL and art growth and reflecting on the impact of the implementation. Tammy's art lessons are continually infused with SEL, and she has created a comprehensive process for formative ongoing assessing to inform both practice and learning.

Case 4: The Effects of Systematic Reflection on Teacher SEL Skills

Dana's research focuses on the acquisition of SEL competencies for adults. She states, "I believe that by engaging in their own social and emotional learning, teachers enhance their own efficacy and job satisfaction while creating models for students' SEL." Dana's study is one of the few focusing on the relationship between the level of adult SEL competencies and their ability to model and implement SEL knowledge, performances, and dispositions in the workplace. Dana adapted a student SEL progression approach for *adult* SEL learning progressions. She also created a systematic process for adult SEL competencies.

ASSESSMENT OF PROFESSIONAL ETHICS FOR TEACHING: THE INTERSTATE TEACHER ASSESSMENT AND SUPPORT CONSORTIUM

The Interstate Teacher Assessment and Support Consortium (InTASC) developed by the Council of Chief State School Officers with input from more than twenty seminal educational organizations, describes a vision of teaching for today's teachers and learners. It provides ten core teaching standards to support ongoing teacher development and inform decisions about both teaching practice and student learning. Four key assumptions in the standards include:

1. Learning and teaching are complex because they involve humans and relationships. The research tells us that the teacher/learner connection is the most critical factor in successful learning.

2. Teacher expertise can be learned, developed over time, and is not linear. InTASC has developed learning progressions to support this recursive process.

3. Growth in both teaching and learning can occur through reflection on experience and ongoing feedback, as well as a variety of learning opportunities.

4. Development depends on context and levels of support (Council of Chief State School Officers, 2013, p. 11).

SEL is embedded into each of the ten InTASC standards, which are then clustered around four themes: (1) The Learner and Learning, (2) Content, (3) Instructional Practices, and (4) Professional Responsibility. Within Theme 1 (The Learner and Learning), examples of SEL can be found in Critical Disposition: 2(m)—The teacher respects learners as individuals with differing personal and family backgrounds and various skills, abilities, perspectives, talents, and interests; and 2(n)—The teacher makes learners feel valued and helps them learn to value each other (p. 17). So, each of the ten standards is aligned with one of the four themes.

Standard 6, Assessment, is aligned to Theme 3 (Instructional Practices), and states, "The teacher understands and uses multiple methods of assessment to engage learners in their own growth, monitor learner progress, and guide the teacher's and learner's decision-making" (p. 30). This applies equally to academic and SEL growth.

Finally, Standard 9, Professional Learning and Ethical Practice, is aligned with Theme 4 (Professional Responsibility). Standard 9, which includes Performances, Essential Knowledge, and Critical Dispositions, describes a professional educator who engages in ongoing professional learning and uses evidence to evaluate and adjust teaching practices informed by data from student learning. Essential Knowledge 9 (i) states, "The teacher understands how personal identity, worldview, and prior experience affect perceptions and expectations and recognizes how they may bias behaviors and interactions with others" (p. 41).

This is a brief snapshot of the InTASC Model Core Teaching Standards and Learning Progressions for Teachers. While SEL is not separately called out in these standards, it is embedded and integrated into each of the ten standards. We urge you to explore this tool in greater depth. And, yes, it can be readily adapted beyond the intended educational application.

NATIONAL EDUCATION ASSOCIATION CODE OF ETHICS + SEL

Many states have a code of ethics for the teaching profession. The National Education Association (NEA) code of ethics has two major sections, I. Commitment to the Students and II. Commitment to the Profession. The preamble mentions key social and emotional principles, such as the dignity of human beings, pursuit of truth, equal opportunity, highest ethical standards, and respect and confidence of all (teachers, students, and parents):

> The educator, believing in the worth and dignity of each human being, recognizes the supreme importance of the pursuit of truth, devotion to excellence, and the nurture of democratic principles. Essential to these goals is the protection of freedom to learn and to teach and the guarantee of equal educational opportunity for all. The educator accepts the responsibility to adhere to the highest ethical standards.

> The educator recognizes the magnitude of the responsibility inherent in the teaching process. The desire for the respect and confidence of one's colleagues, of students, of parents, and of the members of the community provides the incentive to attain and maintain the highest possible degree of ethical conduct. The Code of Ethics of the Education Profession indicates the aspiration of all educators and provides standards by which to judge conduct. (NEA Representative Assembly, 1975)

SEL OUTSIDE OF THE EDUCATIONAL WORKPLACE

Many other caring professions have codes of ethics that include dozens of social and emotional tenets. Health care is an industry where professionals are expected to care for others in an ethical fashion. For example, physicians pledge to honor the Hippocratic oath, which has its roots in Greek medical texts. In its original form, it required new physicians to swear to uphold specific ethical standards in the name of several healing gods. Nowadays, this oath focuses on the idea of doing no harm and reads, in part, "I will practice medicine with integrity, humility, honesty, and compassion—working with my fellow doctors and other colleagues to meet the needs of my patients. I shall never intentionally do or administer anything to the overall harm of my patients."

Similarly in the practice of nursing, there are seven primary ethical principles: accountability, justice, nonmaleficence, autonomy, beneficence, fidelity, and veracity (see even more intersections with social and emotional practices in the six Cs of nursing: Care, Compassion, Competence, Communication, Courage, and Commitment). Likewise, mental health professionals are also bound by various legal acts, laws, and regulatory boards. For example, the US Congress recently enacted HR 7666— Restoring Hope for Mental Health and Well-Being Act of 2022, partly as a response to mental health–related issues incurred during the world pandemic, once again showing the primacy of SEL and related issues.

Several of our master's students have conducted research through the lens of SEL and have applied SEL strategies to mental health practices. For example, Crystal R. (2022, August), Case Study #5, works as an advocate for survivors of trauma. Her study, "The Effects of Stigma on the Post-Traumatic Growth of Trauma Survivors," focused on healing to build resilience in the aftermath of traumatic life experiences. Her action research was a qualitative study that included self-reports from trauma survivors. She explored the potential effects that stigma has had on the personal posttraumatic growth of these subjects. The survivors practiced self-assessment as a beginning step to their healing.

In a world impacted by unimaginable violence, rapid societal change, and traumatic events, SECs are needed more than ever. We are not talking about SEL only for children. Adults are challenged to display well-developed SEL knowledge, performances, and dispositions, even when they are faced with daunting decisions each day. Whether acknowledged or not, SEL is applicable to every workplace.

Social and emotional practices intersect all aspects of life. Some are even derived from practices in spirituality and through writings and sacred texts of ancient human cultures. Rules, laws, edicts, announcements, decrees, declarations, and proclamations contain language that is directly related to social, emotional, mental, and physical well-being. Social and emotional practices are human practices that are woven into every fiber of the human tapestry.

> Social and emotional tenets are also embedded in the First Amendment to the US Constitution: Congress shall make no law respecting an establishment of religion or prohibiting the **free exercise** thereof; or abridging the **freedom of speech**, or **of the press**; or the **right of the people peaceably to assemble**, and to petition the Government for a **redress** of **grievances**. Can you identify the SEL?

ASSESSING SEL

There are multiple approaches to addressing SEL needs in schools. Commercially prepared programs, school-developed materials, and individual teacher-created lessons are a few of the ways SEL is being taught. All have their place, with pros and cons for each.

We believe that all teaching and learning intersects with social emotional learning. "We are teaching SEL even if we don't think we are doing so" (Frey et al., 2019, p. 2). One authentic way to teach SEL competencies is by integrating SEL knowledge, performance, and dispositions into daily teaching, learning, and everyday assessing. When SEL is integrated, the message is clear—YOU, the student, and your SEL competencies are at the center of all learning. Here, we explain how to develop the parallel integration of SEL and academic content, which moves SEL from an "add-on" curriculum to a student-empowering belief system.

HOW TO GET STARTED

As with any curriculum development process, parallel integration follows a systemic process. There are four recursive steps to consider.

Step One: Select SEL and Content Standards and Competencies

Step Two: Develop Parallel Learning Activities and Assessment Strategies

Step Three: Implement Learning Sequence Using Rubrics

Step Four: Collect Data as Evidence of SEL and Academic Growth and Reflect

While this information may look familiar to you from other chapters, the parallel integration process that seamlessly integrates both academic and SEL standards and competencies requires a different perspective.

Practitioner "Wondering" Reflection

Time for Your Final SEL Reflection Journal

In your SEL journal, reflect on what you have learned in this chapter. Consider these prompts:

- Where can you uncover SEL practices in the content standards you teach every day?
- In which subject areas will you integrate an SEL approach to teaching, student learning, and assessing?

Takeaway to Practice

What is the one takeaway from this chapter you want to put into action? **Name it. Add it to your action plan.**

Appendix

Resources, Tools, Templates, and Ancillaries

This section provides you with supporting resources, tools, templates, and ancillaries for creating and developing your rich social emotional learning environment for assessment. It is organized by chapter for ease of alignment to the materials.

CHAPTER 1

SEL ASSESSMENT REFLECTION

Use this chart to reflect on the effective SEL assessing that is currently taking place in your workplace. What SEL assessment strategies may be creating unneeded stress or are inappropriate uses of SEL data? Remember, assessing is not something done to the learner to get data. Assessing is a partnership, a relationship builder that provides essential information for growth that is done *with* the learner.

EFFECTIVE SEL ASSESSING	INEFFECTIVE SEL ASSESSMENT STRATEGIES

 Available for download at **https://resources.corwin.com/AssessingThroughtheLensofSEL**

188 Assessing Through the Lens of Social and Emotional Learning

EXPLORING SEL COMPETENCIES
USING THE INTERACTIVE CASEL WHEEL

Directions: View the interactive CASEL wheel using the QR code and answer the following questions.

bit.ly/3NToc50

Activity Questions

1. What are the CASEL 5 competencies?

2. Describe the intersections that you see in your current curriculum.

3. What assessing activities might be aligned to each of the CASEL 5 competencies?

Available for download at https://resources.corwin.com/AssessingThroughtheLensofSEL

ONLINE RESOURCES AND TEMPLATES

EDGAR DALE'S CONE OF EXPERIENCE	GLORIA WILCOX'S FEELING WHEEL	MOOD METERS
bit.ly/44BZexN	bit.ly/3PVi0wh	bit.ly/3XITH6i

PLUTCHIK'S WHEEL OF EMOTION	VYGOTSKY'S ZONE OF PROXIMAL DEVELOPMENT	ZONES OF REGULATION
bit.ly/44AeWJS	tinyurl.com/ vygotskyzpdwiki	bit.ly/3PQ7N3R

ZONES OF REGULATION GLOSSARY	ASSESSMENT RESOURCES FROM CASEL
tinyurl.com/zonesglossary	bit.ly/3D9A7XE

CHAPTER 2

LIFE GOALS ACTIVITY

LIFE GOALS

For each of the categories below, write down things you are doing well and where you need improvement. Take the time to reflect on these, and write a goal for each category.

CATEGORY	WHAT I AM DOING WELL	WHERE I NEED IMPROVEMENT	GOAL SETTING
FAMILY			
FRIENDS			
WORK/ SCHOOL			
PHYSICAL HEALTH			
MENTAL HEALTH			
SPIRITUALITY			

 Available for download at **https://resources.corwin.com/ AssessingThroughtheLensofSEL**

CHAPTER 3

SEL SELF-PORTRAIT VISIONING ACTIVITY

Purpose: To ponder. To dream.

When: Find some uninterrupted quiet time. Put on your favorite "wondering" playlist.

Materials:
- Colored paper
- Scissors
- Crayons
- Markers
- Glue
- Pens
- Sketch paper
- Glue stick

Instructions: Jot down a few words or phrases that describe your ideal highly effective SEL environment, the teacher, and the students. Find some photos, pictures, and visuals that help you to create this portrait of SEL in action.

Reflection Questions:

1. What does the classroom feel like? Look like?

2. What is the teacher doing?

3. What are the students doing?

4. What knowledge, performances, and dispositions do the teacher and the students have?

5. How are they different from other teachers and students who may not possess their SEL knowing? Keep adding elements until you have a very clear portrait of this SEL environment.

6. Find a place to put this vision where it will remind you of your SEL portrait.

 Available for download at **https://resources.corwin.com/ AssessingThroughtheLensofSEL**

WRITING FRAMES TEMPLATE: RECALL-RECOUNTING

Name	
Date	
Title	

I thought I already knew…

I learned some new things. I learned that…

Another fact I learned…

The most interesting thing I learned…

 Available for download at **https://resources.corwin.com/ AssessingThroughtheLensofSEL**

Appendix 193

ONLINE RESOURCES AND TEMPLATES

STRUCTURED STUDENT OBSERVATION CHECKLIST	WRITING FRAMES TEMPLATES
bit.ly/3D6DEWB	bit.ly/3JRyPEx

CHAPTER 4

WHO AM I? WORD CLOUD TEMPLATE

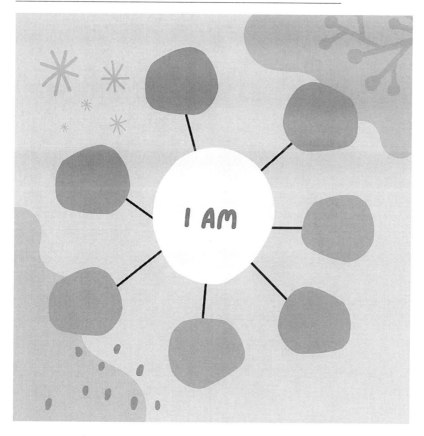

 Available for download at **https://resources.corwin.com/ AssessingThroughtheLensofSEL**

ONLINE RESOURCES AND TEMPLATES

CULTURALLY RESPONSIVE TEACHING CHECKLIST	CULTURALLY RESPONSIVE CURRICULUM SCORECARD
bit.ly/3D7qOaw	bit.ly/3JPfvaR

CHAPTER 5

DESIGNING AND PLANNING FOR TEACHING AND LEARNING IMPROVEMENT

Developing a theory of action will assist educators in planning a new unit of instruction, which will integrate SEL skills, competencies, and practices. In the plan for instructional action, three areas will be identified and targeted:

1. Key performance targets
2. Process target (the teaching strategy, strategies, or techniques)
3. Program target (the relationship or context where teaching and learning will take place and the evidence that will be identified in advance)

For more on how to develop a *theory of action*, visit the University of Washington Center for Educational Leadership via the QR code. The document was adapted from Meredith I. Honig's *Creating Your Theory of Action for Districtwide Teaching and Learning Improvement* (2014), commissioned by the Wallace Foundation.

bit.ly/3NFsQ6G

Appendix 197

THEORY OF ACTION PLAN

Step One: What the teacher does (What will happen and why?)

Step Two: What the student does (performance)

Step Three: What the teacher does (teacher teaching strategies or techniques)

Step Four: What occurs at various levels (class, school, organization)

> **Note:** *Many researchers as well as graduate students in masters' programs who focus on social and emotional learning will use this process as part of developing action research for classroom application.*

SAMPLE

PERFORMANCE TARGET	PROCESS TARGET	EVIDENCE OF PROGRAM TARGET
Students: Improve personal narratives through the use of emotional vocabulary	*Teacher: Model emotional vocabulary using read aloud, responding to writing prompts through shared writing*	*In-class writing assignments will use a rubric to evaluate the use of emotional vocabulary*
Class: Increase participation in classroom discussions	*Teacher: Develop a system to improve student performance*	*Track and monitor student engagement with use of participation involvement feedback tool*

198 ● Assessing Through the Lens of Social and Emotional Learning

TEMPLATE

Stated Theory of Action: What will happen if a specific SEL performance is targeted during a unit of instruction?

PERFORMANCE TARGET	PROCESS TARGET	EVIDENCE OF PROGRAM TARGET

online resources

Available for download at https://resources.corwin.com/AssessingThroughtheLensofSEL

Appendix ● **199**

CHAPTER 6

APPLYING SMART GOALS TEMPLATE

Today's Date:
Start Date:
Target Date:
Date Achieved:
Goal (write your goal):
Verify that your goal is SMART. • Specific: What exactly will you accomplish? • Measurable: How will you know when you have reached this goal? • Achievable: Is achieving this goal realistic with effort and commitment? Do you have the resources to achieve this goal? If not, how will you get them? • Relevant: Why is this goal significant to your life? • Timely: When will this goal be achieved?
This goal is important because:
The benefit(s) of achieving this goal will be:
Who are the people you will ask to help you?
Specific action steps:
List the steps in the order you will take. Having a specific plan with these steps increases your success.
Potential obstacles:
Potential solutions:
Expected completion date completed:

 Available for download at https://resources.corwin.com/AssessingThroughtheLensofSEL

PEER REVIEW WRITING TEMPLATE

NAME OF REVIEWER	WHAT I LIKED BEST ABOUT YOUR WRITING IS ...	YOU CAN ENHANCE YOUR WRITING BY ...

Note: *For students in grades 9–12, complete the below as well.*

Paraphrase the author's main topic.	
What were some supporting facts that the author used to make their claim? Use specific quotes from the paper.	
What are some suggestions to improve specific parts of the essay?	
Is the essay clear? Does it flow well? Do you understand the introduction and conclusion? How can the organization be better?	

online resources ► Available for download at https://resources.corwin.com/AssessingThroughtheLensofSEL

Appendix ● 201

PEER FEEDBACK CHOICE BOARD FOR PROMOTING UDL

Select **TWO** prompts from the peer feedback choice board to provide your classmate with specific, meaningful, and kind feedback. Capture your feedback in the space below the choice board!

Greatest Strength	**Tiny Tweaks**	**Celebrate Surprises**
Identify the strongest aspect of the draft. What specifically was strong? Why do you think this element was particularly powerful or well done? How did this element positively impact the overall quality of the draft?	Identify one aspect of the draft that would benefit from a minor adjustment, modification, or tweak. What would you suggest the student rework or reimagine in this draft? How would reworking this element of their draft impact the overall quality? Do you have specific recommendations for how they might improve this aspect of their draft?	As you reviewed the draft, what surprised you about this student's work? Was there an aspect of their work that was unexpected, original, outside-the-box, engaging, or particularly thought-provoking? Describe why you liked this aspect of their work.
Hungry for More	**Mind Blown**	**Clarifying Confusion**
Identify a part of the draft that needs further development. What would you have enjoyed knowing more about or having more information on? Where could more detail and development have strengthened this draft? Can you identify the specific places in the draft where the student/peer should spend time digging deeper?	Identify something in this draft that you loved and had not considered as you completed your draft. Is there a great idea or approach that this student used to complete this draft that you would like to incorporate into your work? Why did you like this element of their draft? How can you incorporate this idea or approach into your revision?	As you reviewed this draft, was there anything unclear, confusing, or that left you wondering? Is there an aspect of this draft that you would like clarity on or more specifics about? Were any of the steps or statements unclear? Can you identify specific elements of this draft that would benefit from clearer language and/or more explanation?

Choice Board Selection	Write your feedback below. Please be specific and kind.
Title of Feedback Prompt 1:	
Title of Feedback Prompt 2:	

Source: Adapted from Dr. Catlin Tucker.

online resources ⟍ Available for download at **https://resources.corwin.com/AssessingThroughtheLensofSEL**

FISHBOWL CONVERSATIONS PROTOCOL

Arrange chairs in a concentric configuration with outer layers looking in (see image below). The center five chairs are key speakers, otherwise known as the fishbowl. Anyone can occupy the center chairs. A moderator is designated as a facilitator.

Used to engage large groups of people in dialogue, the advantage of a fishbowl conversation is its participatory nature.

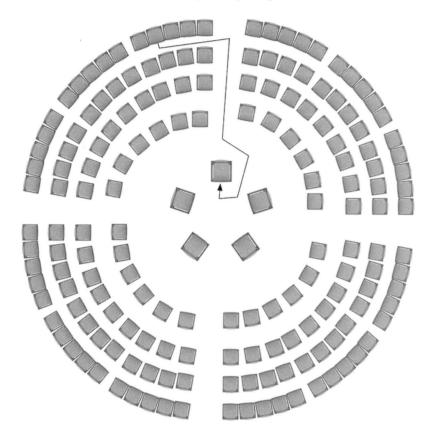

Available for download at **https://resources.corwin.com/AssessingThroughtheLensofSEL**

Appendix   203

GALLERY WALK PROTOCOL

A Gallery Walk is a classroom-based, active learning strategy where peers and adults are encouraged to build on their prior knowledge of a topic, engage in higher order thinking, interact with peers, and build a sense of community and trust in a shared environment. Typically, all move through stations (exhibits) where different media/content and questions are posted.

I NOTICE...	I WONDER...	QUESTIONS

online resources — Available for download at **https://resources.corwin.com/AssessingThroughtheLensofSEL**

SOCRATIC CIRCLES PROTOCOL

Similar to a fishbowl, the Socratic Seminar uses the same concentric seating, but the outer circle or circles are attentive listeners. These roles can switch. The Socratic Circle (Seminar) is driven by questions where participants can probe, clarify, agree, or disagree. The seminar is entirely student led, only moderated by the instructor. Formative assessment is conducted through student discussion and student reflection.

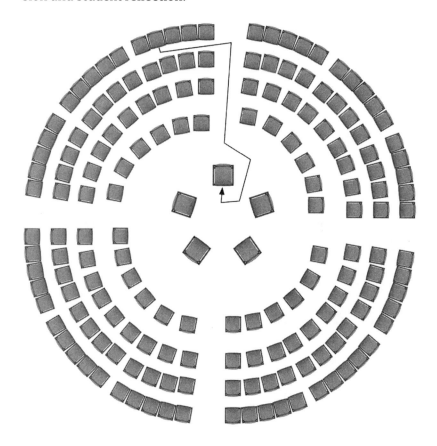

Available for download at **https://resources.corwin.com/AssessingThroughtheLensofSEL**

WORLD CAFÉ PROTOCOL

A World Café is a structured conversation and an opportunity for people to share knowledge. This knowledge sharing occurs in groups where participants discuss topics at small tables like those in a café. Groups are typically smaller (five to six people) but the numbers can be increased. All participants seated at the table are invited to speak. The café works best when each table is focused on a universal topic with predefined questions used as prompts, but the outcomes or solutions are not provided. The group decides together how to answer the question(s).

Use the QR code and link to visit *Café to Go*, a guidebook on how to conduct a World Café.

http://bit.ly/worldcafeguide

Image source: iStock.com/IconicBestiary

 Available for download at **https://resources.corwin.com/AssessingThroughtheLensofSEL**

MOTIONS ON SUNNY STICKS (PRE-K–2) ACTIVITY

INSTRUCTIONS:

1. Cut out the sun and attach it to a popsicle stick with tape on the back.
2. Use this shape to write a word in the center circle that describes an emotion (student or teacher can write the word).
3. Students can hold up the sunny emotion stick when giving a compliment to someone in the class.
4. Create many sunny emotion sticks for classroom use.
5. Write an emotion on each spoke of the sun.
6. Draw faces in the circle that show emotion.

Image source: istock.com/Elena Brovko

 Available for download at **https://resources.corwin.com/ AssessingThroughtheLensofSEL**

GROW A GARDEN OF EMOTIONS (PRE-K–2) ACTIVITY

INSTRUCTIONS:

1. Students can hold up the flower emotion stick when giving a compliment to someone in the class.
2. Use this shape to write a word in the center circle that describes an emotion (student or teacher can write the word).
3. Create a flower garden of emotion sticks for classroom use.
4. Write an emotion on each petal.
5. Draw faces in the circle that show emotion.
6. Color and label the emotion word on the flower and add it to a bulletin board with the child's name.

Image source: istock.com/JDawnInk

 Available for download at **https://resources.corwin.com/ AssessingThroughtheLensofSEL**

208 Assessing Through the Lens of Social and Emotional Learning

CHAPTER 7

INFOGRAPHICS

Infographics are visual representations of information, data, or knowledge that are designed to present complex ideas or concepts in a clear and concise manner. They typically combine text, graphics, and images to convey information in an engaging and visually appealing way.

When it comes to assessment, infographics can be used in various ways to enhance the evaluation process. Here are a few examples:

- **Summarizing results:** Infographics can be used to summarize assessment results, providing a visual overview of key findings or statistics. This can help stakeholders quickly grasp the main insights without having to analyze lengthy reports.

- **Data visualization:** Infographics excel at representing data in a visually appealing manner. By converting raw data into charts, graphs, or diagrams, infographics make it easier to identify trends, patterns, or correlations, which can aid in the assessment of performance or progress.

- **Comparative analysis:** Infographics can be used to compare different sets of data or assess multiple variables simultaneously. By presenting information side by side or using elements like bar graphs or pie charts, infographics enable easy comparison and analysis of various factors or benchmarks.

- **Process explanation:** Assessments often involve complex processes or procedures. Infographics can be used to break down these processes into simpler, step-by-step visual representations, helping learners or participants understand the assessment workflow more effectively.

- **Knowledge mapping:** Infographics can be employed to create visual knowledge maps that illustrate the relationships between different concepts or ideas. This can be particularly useful in assessing understanding or knowledge gaps, as well as identifying areas that require further exploration or clarification.

- **Storytelling:** Infographics can tell a story using visuals and minimal text. This storytelling approach can be used to present assessment narratives, highlight achievements, or showcase progress over time. It helps engage stakeholders and facilitates communication of assessment outcomes.

Appendix 209

Overall, infographics offer a powerful tool for assessment by transforming complex information into visually appealing and easily digestible formats. They enhance comprehension, aid in decision-making, and provide a concise representation of assessment findings.

Since the point of an infographic is to transfer knowledge and information quickly, the infographic should be informative, simple, engaging, and design friendly.

INFOGRAPHIC RUBRIC: ASSESSING AN INFOGRAPHIC

DEFINITIONS OF RATINGS

Highly developed: Provides convincing evidence that demonstrates depth and knowledge of content and explains connections made to real-world situations. Goes beyond the expectations.

Developed: Provides evidence that demonstrates understanding of the content that meets the criteria but lacks the depth of knowledge and makes general connections without explanations. All components required are met.

Emerging: Provides partial evidence that demonstrates the required depth in all criteria of the assignment. Response may be unsupported, flawed, or missing elements.

Initial: Lacks the evidence required in all criteria of the assignment. Evidence presented may be minimal, unsupported, inadequate, or missing.

CRITERIA	HIGHLY DEVELOPED	DEVELOPED	EMERGING	INITIAL
Process Representation	The infographic is highly developed and demonstrates an in-depth understanding of a concept or process. Clear and specific connections of the process are provided, as applicable.	The infographic is developed and generally represents a concept or process. Appropriate examples are provided, as applicable.	The infographic is emerging and demonstrates a partial representation of a concept or process. Appropriate examples are provided, as applicable.	The infographic demonstrates an initial understanding of a concept or process, but certain explanations are missing or unsupported. Examples, when applicable, are not provided.
Design	The infographic incorporates principles of design that are highly developed and includes evidence of alignment, balance, consistency, contrast, directional flow, proportion, whitespace, and color.	The infographic incorporates principles of design that are developed and include visual attention to alignment, balance, consistency, contrast, directional flow, proportion, whitespace, and color.	The infographic incorporates principles of design that are emerging and demonstrates some attention to alignment, balance, consistency, contrast, directional flow, proportion, whitespace, and color.	The infographic incorporates principles of design that are initial and certain elements may be missing or are not represented, including alignment, balance, consistency, contrast, directional flow, proportion, whitespace, and color.
Research, Data, and Citations	The infographic is highly developed and includes a comprehensive synthesis of research data into a coherent visual narrative, with excellent cohesion. The infographic is highly organized with a logical flow of ideas for maximum narrative impact. All sources are accurately and properly cited.	The infographic is developed and includes a synthesis of research data into a coherent visual narrative. The infographic is organized with a logical flow of ideas. All sources are accurately and properly cited.	The infographic is emerging. It includes a synthesis of research data. The infographic is somewhat organized with a flow of ideas. One or more sources are not accurately and properly cited.	The infographic is initially developed. It includes some research data. The infographic is lacking a logical flow of ideas and sources are not accurately and properly cited.

 Available for download at https://resources.corwin.com/AssessingThroughtheLensofSEL

ONLINE RESOURCES AND TEMPLATES

TIPS FOR GETTING STARTED

Part of the challenge (the fun) is deciding what to design. Is there a procedure that you need to explain again and again that a visual diagram could help solve? Can students use the infographic as a way to present knowledge?

As you plan out your design, ask and answer questions like:

- Which information, facts, and data are essential to include? Which aren't?
- What colors and layout work best in sharing the information?
- What graphs and graphics best convey information and data to the viewer?
- What is the order, or flow, of information?

EXPLOITING INFOGRAPHICS EBOOK BY NIK PEACHY	WHAT IS AN INFOGRAPHIC?	KATHY SCHROCK'S GUIDE TO INFOGRAPHICS
bit.ly/44iSzZA	bit.ly/44C8xxJ	bit.ly/3rmbOTI

CANVA	CHARTLE	EASEL.LY
bit.ly/3PTnLKH	https://www.chartle.com/	https://www.easel.ly/

Appendix 213

HOW TO ACTIVATE GOOGLE DRAW IN A GOOGLE DRIVE	INKSCAPE	MIRO
bit.ly/43elz3D	https://inkscape.org/	https://miro.com/

PICSART	PIKTOCHART	PIXLR
https://picsart.com/	https://piktochart.com/	https://pixlr.com/

SKETCHPAD	SPLASHUP LIGHT	VENNGAGE
bit.ly/3Ogkvbc	bit.ly/44Lp0Qm	https://venngage.com/

VISME
https://www.visme.co/

214 Assessing Through the Lens of Social and Emotional Learning

CHAPTER 8

Cambridge University's Centre for Teaching and Learning has designed and shared several evaluation tools for teaching:

1. Curriculum design
2. Assessment and feedback
3. Teaching practices
4. Learning environments
5. Staff and student engagement

All tools can be downloaded from the QR code that follows.

SELF-EVALUATION RATING SCALE

You are encouraged to self-evaluate your progress against each prompt using the following **Self-Evaluation Rating Scale** provided on the Centre for Teaching and Learning site.

CHAPTER 9

WHY STUDENT SOCIAL EMOTIONAL LEARNING PROGRESSIONS?

In working with graduate students in a master's degree program in social emotional learning, one essential concept became clear— SEL growth is a lifelong process. One does not have a finite end to becoming self-aware or developing responsible decision-making skills. As we discussed this thinking, the need for understanding what a progression of learning might look like for students became apparent. Educators asked for guidance to determine developmental awareness of social emotional learning progress across the continuum. As I considered how to present a model for educator use, the Student Social Emotional Learning Progressions model took form. These progressions are now part of the course that focuses on assessing social and emotional learning competencies.

The progressions were derived from examining both SEL and assessment standards, competencies, essential knowledge, skills, and dispositions from multiple sources. The model utilizes a structure presented in the InTASC Model Core Teaching Standards and Learning Progressions for Teachers 2.0; SEL competency frameworks from the Collaborative for Academic, Social, and Emotional Learning (CASEL); assessment literacy standards developed by the Michigan Assessment Consortium; and *An Examination of K–12 SEL Learning Competencies/Standards in 18 States* authored by Linda Dusenbery, Nick Yoder, Caitlin Dermody, and Roger Weissberg.

The resulting Student SEL Progressions were developed with one intention: to give educators and those working in education-related environments with a process for providing meaningful ongoing formative feedback to increase essential skills, performances, and dispositions. The Student SEL Progressions model is *not* intended to create more summative assessing. And these progressions are models. It is assumed that you will adapt these to the needs of your own classroom, grade level, school, etc.

STUDENT SEL PROGRESSIONS

STANDARD 1: SELF-AWARENESS

Self-Awareness—The conscious knowledge of one's own feelings, desires, and motives.   **Standard 1: Develop self-awareness knowledge, performances, and dispositions to achieve academic and life success.**
Sub-Competencies
(S1) S.A. C-1. Identifying emotions and each student's specifically
(S1) S.A. C-2. Knowing how to express emotions constructively
(S1) S.A. C-3. Identifying personal abilities and strengths
(S1) S.A. C-4. Creating goals for self-awareness improvement
(S1) S.A. C-5. Knowing when to ask for help
(S1) S.A. C-6. Monitoring progress in increasing self-awareness knowledge, skills, and performance
Student Learning Progressions
Sub-Competency 1
Competency 1 – (S1) S.A. C-1. Identifying emotions and each student's specifically
Essential Knowledge
(S1) S.A. C-1. Identifying emotions and each student's specifically
Emerging: The student can clearly identify and describe emotions, such as happy, surprised, proud, excited, bored, distracted, sad, afraid, confused, etc.   Developing: The student can identify, describe, and explain their own emotions in the context of the situation.
Performances
(S1) S.A. C-1. Identifying emotions and each student's specifically
Emerging: The student names a range of emotions from positive to negative and identifies the emotions that they feel and express.   Developing: The student identifies, describes, and explains a continuum of emotions in the context of their own situations and when these emotions can be categorized as negative or positive.
Critical Dispositions
(S1) S.A. C-1. Identifying emotions and each student's specifically
Emerging: The student is committed to learning about emotions and wants to understand their own and why they have them.   Developing: The student seeks to understand their emotions and how and why they vary in different situations.

Appendix   217

Sub-Competency 2
Competency 2 – (S1) S.A. C-2. Knowing how to express emotions constructively
Essential Knowledge
(S1) S.A. C-2. Knowing how to express emotions constructively
Emerging: Identifies the emotions characters have in a story and categorizes the emotion(s) as positive or negative. Describes a time when the student had the same or similar emotion and why. Developing: Describes the emotions the student is feeling in a given situation and why. Accurately categorizes the emotion as appropriate or inappropriate.
Performances
(S1) S.A. C-2. Knowing how to express emotions constructively
Emerging: Explains whether the emotions of a character in a story are helpful or harmful to the character. Can suggest a more helpful emotion for a better outcome. Describes a time when the student had a negative emotion and how that emotion could have been changed to a more positive one. Developing: Gains constructive strategies to better control inappropriate emotions. Articulates the reasons for making better emotional choices.
Critical Dispositions
(S1) S.A. C-2. Knowing how to express emotions constructively
Emerging: The student has a growth mindset concerning how emotions can be appropriate or inappropriate and desires to change inappropriate feelings. Developing: The student has a growth mindset and knows they have the ability to control inappropriate emotions.
Sub-Competency 3
(S1) S.A. C-3. Identifying personal abilities and strengths
Essential Knowledge
(S1) S.A. C-3. Identifying personal abilities and strengths
Emerging: Clearly articulates what they like to do and why. Describes things they do well and why. Developing: Identifies what they enjoy doing, what they do well, a special skill or talent, and how that connects to being confident.
Performances
(S1) S.A. C-3. Identifying personal abilities and strengths
Emerging: Demonstrates skills and strengths willingly and tries new things knowing they take practice. Developing: Participates in activities they do well to build self-confidence, has the self-confidence to try new activities knowing they take effort, and demonstrates special skills and talents.

218 ● Assessing Through the Lens of Social and Emotional Learning

Critical Dispositions
(S1) S.A. C-3. Identifying personal abilities and strengths
Emerging: Is willing to try new things and knows they need to practice to get better. Developing: Has a growth mindset knowing that effort is a critical part of gaining new skills.
Sub-Competency 4
(S1) S.A. C-4. Creating goals for self-awareness improvement
Essential Knowledge
(S1) S.A. C-4. Creating goals for self-awareness improvement
Emerging: Identifies a behavior that they want to change. Describes one or more steps to take toward changing the behavior. Developing: Explains a personal goal they want to achieve and why.
Performances
(S1) S.A. C-4. Creating goals for self-awareness improvement
Emerging: Keeps track of the times they improved on the identified behavior. Developing: Tracks the progress toward the personal goal and reflects on growth.
Critical Dispositions
(S1) S.A. C-4. Creating goals for self-awareness improvement
Emerging: Acknowledges need for self-awareness improvement. Wants to change behavior. Developing: Takes responsibility for progress toward improvement.
Sub-Competency 5
(S1) S.A. C-5. Knowing when to ask for help
Essential Knowledge
(S1) S.A. C-5. Knowing when to ask for help
Emerging: Knows when to ask a responsible adult for help. Developing: Can identify appropriate adults to assist in various situations and describe instances when the assistance of an adult would be desirable.
Performances
(S1) S.A. C-5. Knowing when to ask for help
Emerging: Asks for help when needed. Developing: Maintains a list of adults to contact in time of need with updated information.

Appendix 219

Critical Dispositions
(S1) S.A. C-5. Knowing when to ask for help
Emerging: Is willing to request help when needed. Developing: Understands that adult assistance is part of a healthy support system.
Sub-Competency 6
(S1) S.A. C-6. Monitoring progress in increasing self-awareness knowledge, skills, and performance
Essential Knowledge
(S1) S.A. C-6. Monitoring progress in increasing self-awareness knowledge, skills, and performance
Emerging: Understands that improving knowledge and skills is a process and takes time. Developing: Knows that improvement and growth is a life-long learning process and takes commitment.
Performances
(S1) S.A. C-6. Monitoring progress in increasing self-awareness knowledge, skills, and performance
Emerging: Identifies an area of need and tracks improvement. Developing: Sets both short-term and long-term goals, monitors and tracks progress, and reflects on changes.
Critical Dispositions
(S1) S.A. C-6. Monitoring progress in increasing self-awareness knowledge, skills, and performance
Emerging: Understands that improvement can be achieved and wants to work toward changing. Developing: Knows that improvement is an ongoing process and is willing to do the long-term work to make it happen.

 Available for download at https://resources.corwin.com/AssessingThroughtheLensofSEL

CHAPTER 10

DAILY OBSERVATION FOR PRESCHOOL: ASSESSMENT OF INHIBITORY CONTROL

Teacher Name:

Student Name:

CATEGORY	DEVELOPED (3 POINTS)	DEVELOPING (2 POINTS)	NOT DEVELOPED (0 POINTS)
Happiness	Names the emotion without identifying themselves with the emotion, "I feel..."	Names the emotion with identifying themselves, "I am..."	Does not name the emotion
Sadness	Names the emotion without identifying themselves with the emotion, "I feel..."	Names the emotion with identifying themselves, "I am..."	Does not name the emotion
Fear	Names the emotion without identifying themselves with the emotion, "I feel..."	Names the emotion with identifying themselves, "I am..."	Does not name the emotion
Anger	Names the emotion without identifying themselves with the emotion, "I feel..."	Names the emotion with identifying themselves, "I am..."	Does not name the emotion
Surprise	Names the emotion without identifying themselves with the emotion, "I feel..."	Names the emotion with identifying themselves, "I am..."	Does not name the emotion
Frustration	Names the emotion without identifying themselves with the emotion, "I feel..."	Names the emotion with identifying themselves, "I am..."	Does not name the emotion

Source: Movsisyan (2022). Used with permission.

CHAPTER 11

TARGETING CONTENT STANDARDS/ PLANNING AND ALIGNING

> **Note:** Each standard needs to
> 1. Describe the expectations associated with the specific content area.
> 2. State what students need to know (Knowledge) and be able to demonstrate (Application).
> 3. Apply to specific performance standards.
> 4. Align with the targeted big idea.

Goal Statement:

Standard	Description	Rationale for SEL Skill or Competency

 Available for download at **https://resources.corwin.com/ AssessingThroughtheLensofSEL**

ADDITIONAL RESOURCES: ALTERNATIVE ASSESSMENT TOOLS AND STRATEGIES

THINK TAC TOE PROTOCOL

Create a timeline of the critical events that happened in the story or in the time period.	Design a poster for a campaign to _____. Make sure your poster includes a powerful graphic and a meaningful message.	Write a letter from _____ perspective describing what they are seeing and feeling.
Write an obituary, a wanted poster, or a job description for one of the characters or historical figures from the text.	Write a paragraph taking a position.	Create two collages of images to represent content.
Create a Venn diagram comparing and contrasting ____.	Identify fifteen vocabulary words from the informational text or the piece of literature that are new to you. Then illustrate what each one means, either through pictures, drawings, definitions, or examples.	Design and illustrate a comic strip about _____.

online resources ⟋ Available for download at **https://resources.corwin.com/AssessingThroughtheLensofSEL**

Appendix ● **223**

FRAYER MODEL

The Frayer Model is a graphic organizer used to help students unpack and better understand complex vocabulary terms and concepts. The Frayer Model asks students to write a definition, important characteristics of the term, and provide examples and nonexamples of a single word.

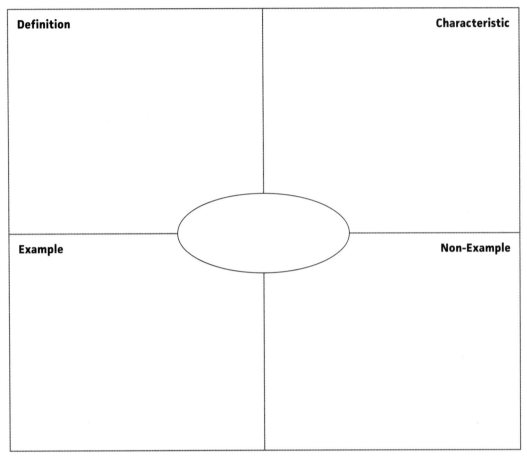

Available for download at **https://resources.corwin.com/AssessingThroughtheLensofSEL**

Glossary of Terms

assessment: The process of evaluating or measuring a person's knowledge, skills, abilities, or performance. There are various types of assessment that are used for different purposes.

authentic assessment: This type of assessment measures students' performance in real-life situations and contexts.

CASEL (The Collaborative for Academic, Social, and Emotional Learning): A prominent organization promoting SEL research and practice.

character development: The development of conscience, moral concepts, religious values, and social attitudes.

child development: The biological, psychological, and emotional changes that occur in human beings between birth and the conclusion of adolescence. The three main stages of life include early childhood, middle childhood, and adolescence.

communication skills: The transmission of a message that involves the shared understanding between the contexts in which the communication takes place. Communication skills involve listening, speaking, reading, and writing.

compassion: Recognizing the physical, mental, or emotional pains of another and self. Compassion is often regarded as having sensitivity.

competencies: Standards broken down into more granular chunks of learning.

confidence: A belief in oneself to meet life's challenges and to succeed with the willingness to act accordingly. Being confident requires a realistic sense of one's capabilities and feeling secure in that knowledge.

criterion-referenced assessment: This type of assessment measures students' performance against specific learning objectives or criteria.

data-driven decision-making: Using assessment data to inform instructional and policy decisions.

DESSA (Devereux Student Strengths Assessment): A widely used SEL assessment tool.

diagnostic assessment: This type of assessment is used to identify students' strengths and weaknesses to determine their instructional needs.

diversity: The attributes of human differences, unique to individuals or groups of individuals, that include demographic factors such as race, gender, sexual orientation, age, social class, physical attributes, religious or ethical values, national origin, cultural norms, and political beliefs.

emotional intelligence: A term popularized by American psychologists Peter Salovey and John D. Mayer (1990) that became widespread by Daniel Goleman (1995). EQ, for short, is the ability to recognize, understand, manage, and express one's own emotions and empathize with the emotions of others.

emotional literacy: The ability to understand your emotions, listen to others, empathize with their emotions, and express emotions productively. Persons who are emotionally literate handle emotions in a way that improves personal power and the quality of life around them.

empathy: The capacity to understand or feel what another person is experiencing and place oneself in another's position. Empathy is *not* the same as sympathy.

formative assessment: This type of assessment is used to monitor students' progress and provide feedback to improve their learning. Formative assessments give in-process, real-time feedback about what students are learning or not learning so that instructional approaches, teaching materials, and academic support can be modified accordingly. Formative assessments are usually not scored or graded, and they may take a variety of forms, from more formal quizzes and assignments to informal questioning techniques and in-class discussions with students.

growth mindset: The belief that abilities and intelligence can be developed through effort and learning.

high-stakes assessment: Standardized tests used for the purposes of accountability—i.e., any attempt by federal, state, or local government agencies to ensure that students are enrolled in effective schools and are being taught by effective teachers.

interpersonal skills: Interactions with people through effective listening and communication.

intrapersonal skills: Internal abilities and behaviors that help manage emotions, cope with challenges, and learn new information.

learning progressions: Explanations of how a learner moves from novice to greater sophistication as the learner gains knowledge and skills.

longitudinal data: Data collected over an extended period to track growth and change.

mental health: The emotional, psychological, and social well-being of individuals.

mindset: A set of assumptions, methods, or notions. People who hold a growth learning mindset are more motivated to take on challenging work, persist in the face of setbacks, and achieve at higher levels.

morals: A person's standards of behavior, beliefs, and personal ethics. Morality is shaped by a combination of factors: cultural, religious, philosophical, and personal beliefs, as well as societal norms and values.

norm-referenced assessment: This type of assessment compares students' performance to that of a larger group, often standardized, to determine their rank or percentile.

peer assessment: This type of assessment involves students evaluating their peers' work.

performance-based assessment: Performance-based assessment requires students to complete a complex task, such as a writing assignment, science experiment, speech, presentation, performance, or long-term project. This type of assessment evaluates students' skills and knowledge through hands-on tasks or projects.

portfolio assessment: This type of assessment is used to evaluate students' work over a period and can include a collection of various types of assessment.

purpose: A clarification of the beliefs, vision, and mission held by members of the school community about what the school can do for students with respect to knowledge, skills, and understanding through the school program.

reflection: The process of critically examining and assessing one's own thoughts, feelings, and actions in relation to their learning experiences. It involves introspection and thoughtful analysis to gain insights into one's strengths, weaknesses, and areas for growth. Learners can deepen their understanding of themselves as learners, identify their learning needs, set goals, and make necessary adjustments to improve their academic performance and personal development. It encourages self-awareness, metacognition, and a proactive approach to learning.

relationship skills: Establishing and maintaining healthy and rewarding relationships with diverse individuals and groups. Such skills include communicating clearly, listening actively, cooperating, resisting inappropriate social pressure, negotiating conflict, and seeking and offering help when needed.

responsible decision-making: The ability to make constructive and respectful choices about personal behavior and social interactions based on consideration of ethical standards, safety concerns, social norms, the realistic evaluation of consequences of various actions, and the well-being of self and others.

rubric: An evaluation tool or set of guidelines/criteria used to promote the consistent application of learning expectations and learning objectives/standards, and measure attainment against a consistent set of criteria. Rubrics clearly define academic expectations and ensure consistency in the evaluation of academic work. Analytic rubrics break down the criteria, holistic rubrics have a single score, and single-point rubrics focus on a single set of criteria, checklists, and numeric rubrics.

school community: This community includes (1) local business and industry, educational institutions, agencies, and service organizations; (2) parents, students, and school board; and (3) all employees.

schoolwide action plan: Improvement strategies that are reviewed and refined regularly based on progress and impact on student learning.

schoolwide learner outcome: What each student should know, understand and be able to do after exit (e.g., graduation) from the school, or by the time the student completes the planned program, to be globally competent. These learner outcomes are collaboratively developed and represent the focus of the entire school community based on current and future learning needs of the students. These global outcomes must be assessed as they complement the school's vision, mission, and academic standards.

SE SEL: Student empowered social and emotional learning where the student is the focus of all learning activities and assessments.

SEL assessing: The process of gathering information about the acquisition of social emotional learning knowledge, skills, and performances to monitor and track student growth for learning.

SEL 5 core competencies: The five core areas of social emotional learning defined by CASEL.

self-assessment: This type of assessment requires students to reflect on their learning and evaluate their own performance.

self-awareness: The ability to recognize one's emotions and thoughts and their influence on personal behavior; the awareness of one's strengths and limitations, a grounded sense of confidence, and optimism.

self-efficacy: An individual's belief in their capacity to execute behaviors necessary to produce specific performance attainments.

self-management: The effective regulation of one's emotions, thoughts, and behaviors in different situations, including managing stress, controlling impulses, motivating oneself, and setting and working toward achieving personal and academic goals.

social and emotional learning: The process through which individuals learn and apply a set of social, emotional, and related skills, attitudes, behaviors, and values that help direct their thoughts, feelings, and actions in ways that enable them to succeed in school, work, and life (cited from https://drc.casel.org/what-is-sel/).

social awareness: The ability to recognize and understand the emotions, needs, and perspectives of others, as well as broader social and interpersonal dynamics between persons.

social justice: Addresses and rectifies disparities and inequities that may exist in an educational system based on race, socioeconomic status, gender, ability, and other identity-related characteristics. Key focus areas include equal access, equity, diversity and inclusion, culturally responsive teaching, antibias, antiracism, curriculum inclusivity, advocacy, policy, and empowerment.

Glossary of Terms   227

special needs student: Students who need additional physical and/or mental support services to reach their maximum potential, including individualized education plans (IEPs) or other accommodations to meet their "special need."

stakeholders: A general term referring to all members of a school community: administrators or leadership, governing board, teachers, support staff, students, parents, etc.

standards: Statements that explain the expected end results of what a student needs to know or do.

standards-based system: Curriculum, instruction, assessment, and reporting to parents, students, and the public designed to improve educational clarity, transparency, and alignment.

student learning outcomes: Statements of what the student will be able to do at the end of the learning time/activity.

summative assessment: Used to evaluate students' learning at the end of a unit, course, or program. Examples include midterms, final examinations, a project, or a paper.

sympathy: The perception, understanding, and reaction to the distress or need of another person.

wellness: Dimensions of physical, mental, and social well-being that extend beyond the traditional definition of health. This includes choices and activities aimed at achieving physical vitality, mental readiness, social satisfaction, a sense of accomplishment, and personal fulfillment.

whole-child education: Policies, practices, and relationships that engage all stakeholders and ensure each child, in each school, in each community, is healthy, safe, engaged, supported, and challenged.

Note: For more detailed information on assessment terms and definitions, navigate to the *Glossary of Education Reform*, created by Great Schools Partnership. Permission to copy granted. Visit https://www.edglossary.org/assessment/ for more definitions.

References and Further Readings

FOREWORD

AIR. (2019, October 1). *Are you ready to assess social and emotional learning and development?* AIR (American Institutes for Research). https://www.air.org/resource/are-you-ready-assess-social-and-emotional-learning-and-development-second-edition

Yoder, N. (2021, December 21). *Instructional practices that integrate equity-centered social, emotional, and academic learning.* AIR (American Institutes for Research). https://www.air.org/resource/brief/instructional-practices-integrate-equity-centered-social-emotional-and-academic

INTRODUCTION

Salzburg Global Seminar. (2018, December). *The Salzburg statement for social and emotional learning.* https://www.salzburgglobal.org/fileadmin/user_upload/Documents/2010-2019/2018/Session_603/SalzburgGlobal_Statement_SEL_01.pdf

CHAPTER 1

Beaty, J. (2018). History of social and emotional learning. *International Arab Journal of English for Specific Purposes, 1*(2), 67–72.

Brown, L. M., Biddle, C., & Tappan, M. (2022). *Trauma-responsive schooling: Centering student voice and healing.* Harvard Education Press.

CDC Healthy Schools. (2023). *Whole school, whole community, whole child framework.* Centers for Disease Control and Prevention. https://www.cdc.gov/healthyschools/wscc/index.htm

Comer, J. (1980). School power: Implications of an intervention project. Free Press.

Dewey, J. (1966). *The middle works of John Dewey, 9, 1899–1924: Democracy and education 1916* (J. A. Boydston, Ed.). Southern Illinois University Press.

Durlak, J. A., Weissberg, R. P., Dymnicki, A. B., Taylor, R. D., & Schellinger, K. B. (2011). The impact of enhancing students' social and emotional learning: A meta-analysis of school-based universal interventions. *Child Development, 82*(1), 405–432. https://doi.org/10.1111/j.1467-8624.2010.01564.x

Frey, N., Fisher, D., & Smith, D. (2019). *All learning is social and emotional: Helping students develop essential skills for the classroom and beyond.* ASCD.

Goleman, D. (1996). *Emotional intelligence: Why it can matter more than IQ.* Bloomsbury Publishing.

Hawkins, J. D., Smith, B. H., & Catalano, R. F. (2004). Social development and social and emotional earning. In J. E. Zins, R. P. Weissberg, M. C. Wang, & H. J. Walberg (Eds.), *Building academic success on social and emotional learning. What does the research say?* (pp. 135–150). Teachers College Press.

Mayer, J. D., Salovey, P., & Caruso, D. R. (2002). *Mayer-Salovey-Caruso emotional intelligence test (MSCEIT) item booklet.* UNH Personality Lab. https://scholars.unh.edu/personality_lab/26

Muhammad, G. (2020). *Cultivating genius: An equity framework for culturally and historically responsive literacy*. Scholastic.

Salovey, P., & Mayer, J. D. (1990). Emotional intelligence. *Imagination, Cognition and Personality, 9*(3), 185–211. https://doi.org/10.2190/DUGG-P24E-52WK-6CDG

Salovey, P., Woolery, A., & Mayer, J. D. (2001). Emotional intelligence: Conceptualization and measurement. In G. J. O. Fletcher & M. S. Clark (Eds.), *Blackwell handbook of social psychology: Interpersonal processes* (pp. 279–307). Wiley.

Steiner, C., & Perry, P. (1997). *Achieving emotional literacy*. Simon & Schuster.

Stiggins, R. (2014). *Revolutionize assessment*. Corwin.

Stiggins, R. (2017). The perfect assessment system. ASCD.

Terada, Y. (2021, January 29). A *fuller picture of what a "good" school is*. Edutopia. https://www.edutopia.org/article/fuller-picture-what-good-school

Tudor, K. (2020). Claude Michel Steiner: An annotated bibliography. In K. Tudor (Ed.), *Claude Steiner, emotional activist* (pp. 27–54). Routledge.

Vygotsky, L. (1978). *Mind in society: The development of higher psychological processes* (M. Cole, V. John-Steiner, S. Scribner, & E. Souberman, Eds. & Trans.). Harvard University Press.

CHAPTER 2

CASEL. (2023, March 3). *What does the research say?* https://casel.org/fundamentals-of-sel/what-does-the-research-say/

Collaborative for Academic, Social, and Emotional Learning (CASEL). https://www.casel.org

Council of Chief State School Officers. (2013). *InTASC model core teaching standards and learning progressions for teachers*. https://ccsso.org/resource-library/intasc-model-core-teaching-standards-and-learning-progressions-teachers-10

Denham, S. A. (2018). *Keeping SEL developmental: The importance of a developmental lens for fostering and assessing SEL competencies*. CASEL.

Frey, N., & Fisher, D. (2011). *The formative assessment action plan: Practical steps to more successful teaching and learning*. ASCD.

Frey, N., Fisher, D., & Smith, D. (2019). *All learning is social and emotional: Helping students develop essential skills for the classroom and beyond*. ASCD.

Hahn, J. S. (2016, October 12). *National task force on assessment education introduces assessment literacy definition for states and districts creating new assessment systems*. NWEA. https://www.prweb.com/releases/national_task_force_on_assessment_education_introduces_assessment_literacy_definition_for_states_and_districts_creating_new_assessment_systems/prweb13757961.htm

Michigan Assessment Consortium. *Assessment literacy standards*. (n.d.). https://www.michiganassessmentconsortium.org/assessment-literacy-standards/

NWEA. (2016, October 12). *National task force releases assessment literacy definition* [Press release]. https://www.nwea.org/news-center/press-releases/8776/

Stiggins, R. (2017). *The perfect assessment system*. ASCD.

CHAPTER 3

Brown, L. M., Biddle, C., & Tappan, M. (2022b, November 1). *Letting student voice lead the way*. ASCD. https://www.ascd.org/el/articles/student-led-sel

Caldera, A. (2020). The power of formative assessments: Using classroom assessment techniques (CATs) to promote learning. In A. M. Quinzio-Zafran & E. A. Wilkins, *The new teacher's guide to overcoming common challenges: Curated advice from award-winning teachers*. Routledge.

CASEL. https://www.casel.org

CASEL. (2019). *SEL 3 signature practices playbook*. https://schoolguide.casel.org/resource/three-signature-sel-practices-for-adult-learning/

Frey, N., & Fisher, D. (2011). *The formative assessment action plan: Practical steps* to more successful teaching and learning. ASCD.

Hammond, Z. (2014). *Culturally responsive teaching and the brain: Promoting authentic engagement and rigor among culturally and linguistically diverse students.* Corwin.

Popham, W. J. (2001). Uses and misuses of standardized tests. *NASSP Bulletin, 85*(622), 24–31.

Stiggins, R. (2014). *Revolutionize assessment.* Corwin.

Stiggins, R. (2017). *The perfect assessment system.* ASCD.

CHAPTER 4

Alber, R. (2017, January 27). Gender equity in the classroom. *Edutopia.*

American Federation of Teachers, National Council on Measurement in Education, and the National Education Association. (1990). *Standards for teacher competence in educational assessment of students.* BUROS. https://buros.org/standards-teacher-competence-educational-assessment-students

Blaisdell, B. (2016). Schools as racial spaces: Understanding and resisting structural racism. *International Journal of Qualitative Studies in Education, 29*(2), 248–272.

Boudreau, E. (2020). What makes effective anti-bias training? *Harvard Graduate School of Education.* https://www.gse.harvard.edu/news/uk/20/03/what-makes-effective-anti-bias-training

Capital Region BOCES. (2021). *Style guide for inclusive communications.* https://www.boces.org/style-guide-for-inclusive-communications/

Danielewicz, J., & Elbow, P. (2009). A unilateral grading contract to improve learning and teaching. *College Composition and Communication, 61*(2), 244–268.

Datnow, A., & Park, V. (2018). Opening or closing doors for students? Equity and data use in schools. *Journal of Educational Change, 19*(2), 131–152.

Feldman, J. (2018). *Grading for equity: What it is, why it matters, and how it can transform schools and classrooms.* Corwin.

Freedle, R. (2003). Correcting the SAT's ethnic and social-class bias: A method for re-estimating SAT scores. *Harvard Educational Review, 73*(1), 1–43.

Geiser, S. (2015, October). *The growing correlation between race and SAT scores: New findings from California.* Center for Studies in Higher Education.

Graham, J. (2022). Explaining the racial school climate gap: Evidence from Georgia. *AERA Open, 8,* 23328584221131529.

Krasnoff, B. (2016). *Culturally responsive teaching: A guide to evidence-based practices for teaching all students equitably.* Region X Equity Assistance Center (EAC) at Education Northwest.

Mahfouz, J., & Anthony-Stevens, V. (2020). Why trouble SEL? The need for cultural relevance in SEL. *Occasional Paper Series, 43,* 6. https://doi.org/10.58295/2375-3668.1354

Montenegro, E., & Jankowski, N. A. (2017). *Equity and assessment: Moving towards culturally responsive assessment.* National Institute for Learning Outcomes Assessment.

Natanson, H., & Meckler, L. (2020, December 6). A lost generation, a surge of research reveals students sliding backward, most vulnerable most affected. *Washington Post.*

Ogletree, C., Smith, R. J., & Wald, J. (2012). Criminal law—Coloring punishment: Implicit social cognition and criminal justice. In J. D. Levinson & R. J. Smith (Eds.), *Implicit racial bias across the law.* Cambridge University Press.

Poe, M., Inoue, A. B., & Elliot, N. (Eds.). (2018). *Writing assessment, social justice, and the advancement of opportunity.* WAC Clearinghouse.

Potapchuk, M. (2021). *Transforming organizational culture assessment tool.* http://www.mpassociates.us/uploads/3/7/1/0/37103967/transformingorganizationalcultureassessmenttool_mpassociates__final_4.21.pdf

Poulsen, J., & Hewson, K. (n.d.). *Standardized testing: Fair or not?* University of Lethbridge. https://www.ulethbridge.ca/teachingcentre/standardized-testing-fair-or-not

Quinn, D. M. (2021). How to reduce racial bias in grading: New research supports a simple, low-cost teaching tool. *Education Next*, 21(1), 72–78.

Randazzo, S. (2023, April 26). Schools are ditching homework, deadlines favor "equitable grading": Approach aims to measure mastery and accounts for hardships at home. *Wall Street Journal*.

Reibel, A. R. (2021, March 11). Uncovering implicit bias in assessment, feedback, and grading. *All Things Assessment*. https://allthingsassessment.info/2021/03/11/uncovering-implicit-bias-in-assessment-feedback-and-grading/

Rosales, J., & Walker, T. (2021). *The racist beginnings of standardized testing*. NEA. https://www.nea.org/advocating-for-change/new-from-nea/racist-beginnings-standardized-testing

Sadker, D., & Zittleman, K. R. (2009). *Still failing at fairness: How gender bias cheats girls and boys in school and what we can do about it*. Simon & Schuster.

Schneider, J., & Hutt, E. (2014). Making the grade: A history of the A–F marking scheme. *Journal of Curriculum Studies*, 46(2), 201–224.

Schwartz, S. (2019, May 14). Next step in diversity training: Teachers learn to face their unconscious biases. *EdWeek*. https://www.edweek.org/leadership/next-step-in-diversity-training-teachers-learn-to-face-their-unconscious-biases/2019/05

Staats, C. (2014). Implicit racial bias and school discipline disparities: Exploring the connection. *Anti-Racism Digital Library*. https://sacred.omeka.net/items/show/93

Staats, C., Capatosto, K., Tenney, L., & Mamo, S. (2017). *State of the science: Implicit bias review*. Kirwan Institute.

Staats, R. (2014). Using First Nations children's literature in the classroom [Portfolio of learning, Brock University], pp. 12–35.

TNTP. (2018). *The opportunity myth: What students can show us about how school is letting them down—and how to fix it*. https://tntp.org/assets/documents/TNTP_The-Opportunity-Myth_Web.pdf

Voight, A., Hanson, T., O'Malley, M., & Adekanye, L. (2015). The racial school climate gap: Within-school disparities in students' experiences of safety, support, and connectedness. *American Journal of Community Psychology*, 56, 252–267.

Wilcox, J., & Townsley, M. (2022). Debunking myths of standards-based grading. *The Science Teacher*, 90(1), 28–33.

ADDITIONAL RESOURCES AND REFERENCES

Abawi, Z. E. (2018). *Troubling the teacher diversity gap: The perpetuation of whiteness through practices of bias free hiring in Ontario school boards* [dissertation]. University of Toronto. https://tspace.library.utoronto.ca/bitstream/1807/82960/3/Abawi_Zuhra_E_201803_EdD_thesis.pdf

Alexander, M. (2020). *The new Jim Crow: Mass incarceration in the age of colorblindness*. New Press.

Alliance to Reclaim Our Schools. (2018). *Confronting the education debt: We owe billions to Black, Brown, and low-income students and their schools*. http://educationdebt.reclaimourschools.org/wp-content/uploads/2018/08/Confronting-the-Education-Debt_FullReport.pdf

Ames Community School District. (2017). *Tackling the racial disparity gap: Step one*. www.ames.k12.ia.us/2017/09/tackling-racial-disparity-gap-step-one

Ames Community School District. (2021). *Black Lives Matter at school week of action*. https://amescsd.org/2021/01/black-lives-matter-at-school-week-of-action-february-1-5-2021/

Anzaldúa, G. (1987). *Borderlands/La frontera: The new mestiza*. Aunt Lute Books.

Avila-Salmon, K. (Host). (2020). Why awareness is not enough with Barbara Furlow-Smiles & Sherice Torres [Audio podcast episode]. In *From Woke to Work: The Anti-Racist Journey*. StudioPod Media.

Bailey, J. M., & Guskey, T. R. (2000). *Implementing student-led conferences*. Corwin.

Bambrick-Santoyo, P. (2010). *Driven by data: A practical guide to improve instruction.* Jossey-Bass.

Barnum, M. (2015). *Fact-check: Just how many tenured teachers are fired each year anyway? (Hint: Not many).* The 74. www.the74million.org/article/fact-check-just-how-many-tenured-teachers-are-fired-each-year-anyway-hint-not-many

Barnum, M. (2016). Eleven things you might not know about teacher retention and turnover—but should. *The 74 Million.* www.the74million.org/article/eleven-things-you-might-not-know-about-teacher-retention-and-turnover-but-should

Barshay, J. (2020, November 12). PROOF POINTS: *White and female teachers show racial bias in evaluating second grade writing.* Hechinger Report. https://hechingerreport.org/white-and-female-teachers-show-racial-bias-in-evaluating-second-grade-writing/

Bell, D. (2018). *Faces at the bottom of the well: The permanence of racism.* Basic Books.

Bell, J., Traynor, S., Stidham, L., Schubert, J., Kohrman, E., Hoots, C., & Cheney, G. (2004). *Comparative similarities and differences between action research, participative research, and participatory action research.* https://arlecchino.org/ildottore/mwsd/group2final-comparison.html

Bennett, L. (2019). *Women amplified: 20 years of insights from trailblazing leaders from the stage of the Texas Conference for Women.* Greenleaf Book Group.

Biss, E. (2015, December 6). White debt. *New York Times.* www.nytimes.com/2015/12/06/magazine/white-debt.html

Blaisdell, B. (2016). Schools as racial spaces: Understanding and resisting structural racism. *International Journal of Qualitative Studies in Education, 29*(2), 248–272.

Bruner, J. S. (1987). *Actual minds, possible worlds.* Harvard University Press.

Carver-Thomas, D. (2018). *Diversifying the teaching profession: How to recruit and retain teachers of color.* Learning Policy Institute.

Carver-Thomas, D., & Darling-Hammond, L. (2019). The trouble with teacher turnover: How teacher attrition affects students and schools. *Education Policy Analysis Archives, 27,* 36.

Centers for Disease Control and Prevention. (2020). *About the CDC-Kaiser Ace study.* Author. www.cdc.gov/violenceprevention/aces/about.html

Coates, T. (2014). The case for reparations. *The Atlantic.* www.theatlantic.com/magazine/archive/2014/06/the-case-for-reparations/361631/

Crenshaw, K. (1989). Demarginalizing the intersection of race and sex: A Black feminist critique of antidiscrimination doctrine, feminist theory and antiracist politics. *University of Chicago Legal Forum, 1989*(1), 8.

Creswell, J. W., & Poth, C. N. (2018). *Qualitative inquiry and research design: Choosing among five approaches.* Sage.

Delgado, R., & Stefancic, J. (2017). *Critical race theory: An introduction* (3rd ed.). New York University Press.

Digest of Education Statistics. (2021). *Table 209.20. Number, highest degree, and years of teaching experience of teachers in public and private elementary and secondary schools, by selected teacher characteristics: Selected years, 1999–2000 through 2017–18.* National Center for Education Statistics. https://nces.ed.gov/programs/digest/d20/tables/dt20_209.20.asp

Dixon, R. D., Griffin, A. R., & Teoh, M. B. (2019). *If you listen, we will stay: Why teachers of color leave and how to disrupt teacher turnover.* Education Trust & Teach Plus.

Domina, T., Lewis, R., Agarwal, P., & Hanselman, P. (2015). Professional sensemakers. *Educational Researcher, 44*(6), 359–364.

Downey, D. B., & Condron, D. J. (2016). Fifty years since the Coleman report. *Sociology of Education, 89*(3), 207–220.

DuFour, R., & Eaker, R. (1998). *Professional learning communities at work: Best practices for enhancing student achievement.* Solution Tree.

Durm, M. W. (1993, September). An A is not an A is not an A: A history of grading. In

The educational forum (Vol. 57, No. 3, pp. 294–297). Taylor & Francis Group.

EdBuild. (n.d.). Nonwhite school districts get $23 billion less than white districts despite serving the same number of students. *EdBuild*. https://edbuild.org/content/23-billion

The Education Justice Research and Organizing Collaborative. *Culturally responsive curriculum scorecard*. New York University. https://steinhardt.nyu.edu/metrocenter/ejroc/services/culturally-responsive-curriculum-scorecards

Escobedo, J., & Liou, T. (2021, March 31). 3 Carrollton-Farmers Branch teachers placed on leave after racist language about Asian Americans used on test, district says. *WFAA*. https://www.wfaa.com/article/news/local/carrollton-farmers-branch-isd-test-inappropriate-language-about-asian-americans/287-1ee817d6-8d10-4d4e-9cf7-e77c1ad98de5

Ewing, E. L. (2020, July 2). I'm a black scholar who studies race: Here's why I capitalize "White." *Medium*. https://zora.medium.com/im-a-black-scholar-who-studies-race-here-s-why-i-capitalize-white-f94883aa2dd3

Falk, B., & Blumenreich, M. (2005). *The power of questions: A guide to teacher and student research*. Heinemann.

Feagin, J. (2013). *The white racial frame: Centuries of racial framing and counter-framing*. Routledge.

Fincke, K., Morrison, D., Bergsman, K., & Bell, P. (2021). Formative assessment for equitable learning. *The Science Teacher*, 89(2), 32–36. https://www.proquest.com/scholarly-journals/formative-assessment-equitable-learning/docview/2668445919/se-2

Freire, P. (1970). *Pedagogy of the oppressed*. (M. B. Ramos, Trans.). Seabury Press.

Freire, P. (2005). *Teachers as cultural workers: Letters to those who dare teach*. Routledge.

Freire, P. (2014). *Pedagogy of the oppressed* (30th anniversary ed.). Bloomsbury Academic & Professional.

Ginwright, S. (2018). The future of healing: Shifting from trauma informed care to healing centered engagement. *Medium*. https://ginwright.medium.com/the-future-of-healing-shifting-from-trauma-informed-care-to-healing-centered-engagement-634f557ce69c

Goldhaber, D. (2016). In schools, teacher quality matters most. *Education Next*, 16(2), 56–62.

Green, M. C., & Brock, T. C. (2000). The role of transportation in the persuasiveness of public narratives. *Journal of Personality and Social Psychology*, 79(5), 701–721.

Green, T. L. (2016). Community-based equity audits. *Educational Administration Quarterly*, 53(1), 3–39.

Greig, J. (2018). Linking unconditional positive regard and teacher wellbeing. *Berry Street*. www.berrystreet.org.au/news/linking-unconditional-positive-regard-and-teacher-wellbeing

Griffin, A., & Tackie, H. (2016). *Through our eyes: Perspectives and reflections from Black teachers*. Education Trust.

Harro, B. (2000). The cycle of liberation. In M. Adams, W. J. Blumenfeld, H. W. Hackman, M. L. Peters, X. Zúñiga, & C. Castaneda (Eds.), *Readings for diversity and social justice* (pp. 463–469). Routledge.

Hersey, T. (2021). *How will you be useless to capitalism today?* The Nap Ministry. https://thenapministry.wordpress.com/2021/08/03/how-will-you-be-useless-to-capitalism-today

Hooks, B. (1994). *Outlaw culture: Resisting representations*. Taylor & Francis.

Hubbard, R. S., & Power, B. M. (2003). *The art of classroom inquiry: A handbook for teacher-researchers*. Heinemann.

Hussar, B., Zhang, J., Hein, S., Wang, K., Roberts, A., Cui, J., Smith, M., Bullock Mann, F., Barmer, A., & Dilig, R. (2020). *The condition of education 2020 (NCES 2020-144)*. US Department of Education, National Center for Education Statistics.

Hutchins, C. L. (1996). *Systemic thinking: Solving complex problems*. Professional Development Systems.

Johnson, S. K., Hekman, D. R., & Chan, E. T. (2016). If there's only one woman in your candidate pool, there's statistically no chance she'll be hired. *Harvard Business Review*. https://hbr.org/2016/04/if-theres-only-one-woman-in-your-candidate-pool-theres-statistically-no-chance-shell-be-hired

Kegan, R., & Lahey, L. (2001). The real reason people won't change. *Harvard Business Review*. https://hbr.org/2001/11/the-real-reason-people-wont-change

Kendi, I. X. (2019). *How to be an antiracist*. One World.

Knips, A., Lopez, S., Savoy, M., & LaParo, K. (2022). *Equity in data: A framework for what counts in schools*. ASCD.

Kuypers, L. M. (2019). *The zones of regulation: A curriculum designed to foster self-regulation and emotional control*. Langara College.

Lorde, A. (1984). *Sister outsider: Essays and speeches*. Crossing Press.

McDonald, J. P., Mohr, N., Dichter, A., & McDonald, E. C. (2013). *The power of protocols: An educator's guide to better practice*. Hawker Brownlow.

Montenegro, E., & Jankowski, N. A. (2017). *Equity and assessment: Moving towards culturally responsive assessment*. National Institute for Learning Outcomes Assessment.

Motamedi, J. G., & Stevens, D. (2018). *Human resources practices for recruiting, selecting, and retaining teachers of color*. Regional Educational Laboratory at Education Northwest. https://ies.ed.gov/ncee/edlabs/regions/northwest/pdf/human-resources-practices.pdf

Muhammad, G. (2020). *Cultivating genius: An equity framework for culturally and historically responsive literacy*. Scholastic Incorporated.

Office of Civil Rights. (2016). *2015–16 state and national estimations*. US Department of Education. https://ocrdata.ed.gov/estimations/2015-2016

Reardon, S. F., & Fahle, E. M. (2017). *State of the union: 2017*. Stanford Center on Poverty & Inequality. https://inequality.stanford.edu/publications/media/details/state-union-2017-education

Ryan, R. (2020). Black lives matter! Time employers update their interview questions. *Forbes*. www.forbes.com/sites/robinryan/2020/08/11/black-lives-matter-time-employers-update-their-interview-questions/?sh=44618fcc5567

Singleton, I. (2021, February 24). *Flipping the script on grading alternative*. City University of New York. https://transform.commons.gc.cuny.edu/2021/02/24/flipping-the-script-on-grading-alternative-anti-racist-grading-practices-event-recap/

HELPFUL WEBSITES AND NEWSPAPER ARTICLES

California Department of Justice. (2020, August 25). *Attorney General Becerra secures settlements with Barstow and Oroville school districts to address discriminatory treatment of students based on race and disability status* [Press release]. https://oag.ca.gov/news/press-releases/attorney-general-becerra-secures-settlements-barstow-and-oroville-school

Dinin, A., & Hill, J. (2021). *Discussing a framework towards anti-racist assessment*. Office of Assessment, Trinity College, Duke University. https://assessment.trinity.duke.edu/sites/assessment.trinity.duke.edu/files/documents/SACS%20COC%20Annual%20Meeting_Duke_Trinity%20College_Anti-racism%20in%20assessment%20practice.pdf

Facilitated Resolution Between the Parties (FRBP) Agreement Concerned African American Parents (CAAP) v. Upper Dublin School District #03-16-1054. (2019). Public Interest Law Center. https://pubintlaw.org/wp-content/uploads/2019/10/19.10.28-Fully-Executed-Settlement-Agreement-pubintlaw.pdf

Hope, M. (2020, September 1). *The only "F" that matters*. ASCD. https://www.ascd.org/el/articles/the-only-f-that-matters

McKibben, S. (2020). *Turn and talk: Identifying pernicious grading practices and pernicious pedagogy to develop more equitable grading*. ASCD. https://www.ascd.org/el/articles/turn-and-talk-antiracist-grading-starts-with-you

Natanson, H. (2020, November 19). Virginia chemistry teacher asked students to insert "neon ... neck" to describe how George Floyd died. *Washington Post*.

https://www.washingtonpost.com/local/education/george-floyd-chemistry-quiz-virginia/2020/11/19/295b0d42-2a88-11eb-92b7-6ef17b3fe3b4_story.html

NYC Coalition for Educational Justice. http://www.nyccej.org/

Pillay, J. (2004). Experiences of learners from informal settlements. *South African Journal of Education, 24*(1). https://journals.co.za/doi/abs/10.10520/EJC31980

Quinn, D. M. (2021). *How to reduce racial bias in grading. Education Next, 21*(1), 72–78. https://www.educationnext.org/how-to-reduce-racial-bias-in-grading-research/

Razi, N. (2021). *Interactive phase theory* [Infographic]. https://create.piktochart.com/output/52899431-my-visual

Singleton, M. (2016, June 2). Shockingly racist math quiz puts middle school teacher on leave. *WRBL.* https://www.wrbl.com/news/alabama-news/shockingly-racist-math-quiz-puts-middle-school-teacher-on-leave/

CHAPTER 5

Berger, R., Rugen, L., & Woodfin, L. (2014). *Leaders of their own learning: Transforming schools through student-engaged assessment.* John Wiley & Sons.

Black, P., & William, D. (1998). Inside the black box: Raising standards through classroom assessment. *Phi Delta Kappan, 80*(2), 139–148.

CAST. (2018). *Universal design for learning guidelines version 2.2.* http://udlguidelines.cast.org

Center for K–12 Assessment and Performance Standards (2012, April). *Coming together to raise achievement: New assessments for the Common Core State Standards.* Educational Testing Service. https://www.cgcs.org/cms/lib/DC00001581/Centricity/Domain/25/Guide%20to%205%20Assessment%20Consortia%20April%202012.pdf

Common Core State Standards. https://corestandards.org/

Davidson, K. L., & Frohbieter, G. (2011). *District adoption and implementation*

of interim and benchmark assessments (CRESST Report 806). National Center for Research on Evaluation, Standards, and Student Testing (CRESST).

Dorn, S. (2010). The political dilemmas of formative assessment. *Exceptional Children, 76*(3), 325–337.

Madison-Harris, R., & Muoneke, A. (2012, January). *Using formative assessment to improve student achievement in the core content areas.* Southeast Comprehensive Center.

Rao, K., & Meo, G. J. (2016). Using universal design for learning to design standards-based lessons. *Sage Open, 6*(4), 1–12. https://doi.org/10.1177/2158244016680688

Salvia, J., Ysseldyke, J. E., & Bolt, S. (2009). *Assessment in special and inclusive education* (11th ed.). Wadsworth.

Thompson, S. J., Johnstone, C. J., & Thurlow, M. L. (2002). *Universal design applied to large scale assessments* (Synthesis Report 44). University of Minnesota, National Center on Educational Outcomes. http://education.umn.edu/NCEO/OnlinePubs/Synthesis44.html

CHAPTER 6

Allport, G. W. (1942). The use of personal documents in psychological science. *Social Science Research Council Bulletin.*

Andersen, K. (2023, February). *What impact does nature journaling have on 6th grade students' emotional presence and self-awareness?* (Action Research Study). Master of Arts in Social and Emotional Learning, National University.

Angelo, T. A., & Cross, K. P. (1993). Minute paper. In Angelo & Cross (Eds.), *Classroom assessment techniques: A handbook for college teachers* (2nd ed., pp. 148–153). Wiley.

Bandura, A. (1989). Regulation of cognitive processes through perceived self-efficacy. *Developmental Psychology, 25*(5), 729–735. https://doi.org/10.1037/0012-1649.25.5.729

Baughcum, C. (2019). Sketchnote graphic. In K. Schwartz, Why teachers are so excited about the power of sketchnoting. KQED. https://www.kqed.org/mindshift/54655/why-teachers-are-so-excited-about-the-power-of-sketchnoting

Block, N. C. (2019). Evaluating the efficacy of using sentence frames for learning new vocabulary in science. *Journal of Research in Science Teaching, 57*(3), 454–478. https://doi.org/10.1002/tea.21602

Brackett, M. A., Bailey, C. S., Hoffmann, J. D., & Simmons, D. N. (2019). RULER: A theory-driven, systemic approach to social, emotional, and academic learning. *Educational Psychologist, 54*(3), 144–161.

Brackett, M. A., & Rivers, S. E. (2014). Transforming students' lives with social and emotional learning. In R. Pekrun & L. Linnenbrink-Garcia (Eds.), *International handbook of emotions in education* (pp. 368–388). Routledge.

Brackett, M. A., Rivers, S. E., & Salovey, P. (2011). Emotional intelligence: Implications for personal, social, academic, and workplace success. *Social and Personality Compass, 5*, 88–103. https://doi.org/10.1111/j.1751-9004.2010.00334.x

Bromley, K. (2007). Best practices in teaching writing. *Best Practices in Literacy Instruction, 3*, 243–263.

Bromley, K., & Powell, P. (1999). Interest journals motivate student writers. *The Reading Teacher, 53*(2), 111.

Brown, G. T., & Harris, L. R. (2014). The future of self-assessment in classroom practice: Reframing self-assessment as a core competency. *Frontline Learning Research, 2*(1), 22–30.

Caldera, A. (2020). The power of formative assessments: Using classroom assessment techniques (CATs) to promote learning. In A. M. Quinzio-Zafran & E. A. Wilkins (Eds.), *The new teacher's guide to overcoming common challenges: Curated advice from award-winning teachers.* Routledge.

CASEL. (2019). 3 signature practices playbook: A tool that supports systemic SEL. Author. https://casel.org/casel_sel-3-signature-practices-playbook-v3/

Chancer, J., & Rester-Zodrow, G. (1997). *Moon journals: Writing, art, and inquiry through focused nature study.* Heinemann.

Chick, N. (2013). *Metacognition.* Vanderbilt University Center for Teaching. https://cft.vanderbilt.edu/guides-sub-pages/metacognition/

Cross, K. P., & Angelo, T. A. (1993). *Classroom assessment techniques: A handbook for college teachers.* National Center for Research to Improve Postsecondary Teaching and Learning.

Cultivating Literacy. (2020). Sentence stems. https://www.cultivatingliteracy.org/our-blog/2020/11/25/sentence-stems

Devaney, E., O'Brien, M. U., Resnik, H., Keister, S., & Weissberg, R. P. (2006). *Sustainable schoolwide social and emotional learning (SEL): Implementation guide and toolkit.* Collaborative for Academic, Social, and Emotional Learning.

Dewey, J. (1910/1966). *The middle works of John Dewey, 9, 1899–1924: Democracy and education (1916)* (J. A. Boydston, Ed.). Southern Illinois University Press.

Dillon, L. H. (2009, November 29–December 3). *Gifted young adolescents and email: Developing a personal language of self* [Conference presentation]. AARE 2009 Conference, Canberra, Australia.

Dillon, L. (2010). Listening for voices of self-digital journaling among gifted young adolescents. *Qualitative Research Journal, 10*(1), 13–27.

Dillon, L. (2011). Writing the self: The emergence of a dialogic space. *Narrative Inquiry, 21*(2), 213–237.

Dweck, C. S. (2006). *Mindset: The new psychology of success.* Random House.

Feldman, J. (2018). *Grading for equity: What it is, why it matters, and how it can transform schools and classrooms.* Corwin.

Fowler, K., Windschitl, M., & Richards, J. (2019). Exit tickets. *The Science Teacher, 86*(8), 18–26.

Guthrie Yarwood, M. (2022). *Psychology of human emotion: An open access textbook.* Pressbooks. https://psu.pb.unizin.org/psych425/

Hammond, Z. (2014). *Culturally responsive teaching and the brain: Promoting authentic engagement and rigor among* culturally and linguistically diverse students. Corwin.

Hammond, Z. (2021). Looking at SoLD through an equity lens: Will the science of learning and development be used to advance critical pedagogy or will it be used to maintain inequity by design? In P. Cantor & D. Osher (Eds.), *The science of learning and development* (pp. 185–197). Routledge.

Hoffmann, J. D., Brackett, M. A., Bailey, C. S., & Willner, C. J. (2020). Teaching emotion regulation in schools: Translating research into practice with the RULER approach to social and emotional learning. *Emotion*, 20(1), 105.

Holden, J. (2021, May). *Assessing SEL in middle school, supporting those with math anxiety through social emotional learning strategies* (Action Research Report). Master of Arts in Social and Emotional Learning, National University.

Hunter, R. (2004). *Madeline Hunter's mastery teaching: Increasing instructional effectiveness in elementary and secondary schools.* Corwin.

Jorn Barger. (2023, September 6). In *Wikipedia.* https://en.wikipedia.org/wiki/Jorn_Barger

Kamil, M. L., Borman, G. D., Dole, J., Kral, C. C., Salinger, T., & Torgesen, J. (2008). *Improving adolescent literacy: Effective classroom and intervention practices.* IES Practice Guide. NCEE 2008-4027. National Center for Education Evaluation and Regional Assistance.

Keltner, D., & Haidt, J. (1999). Social functions of emotions at four levels of analysis. *Cognition & Emotion*, 13(5), 505–521.

Lew, M. D., & Schmidt, H. G. (2011). Self-reflection and academic performance: Is there a relationship? *Advances in Health Sciences Education*, 16(4), 529–545.

Lewis, M., & Wray, D. (1996). *Writing frames.* Reading and Language Information.

Lewis, M., & Wray, D. (2002). *Writing frames: Scaffolding children's non-fiction writing in a range of genres.* National Centre for Language and Literacy, University of Reading.

Littlepythagoras. (2012, March 8). *Audri's Rube Goldberg monster trap* [Video]. YouTube. https://youtu.be/0uDDEEHDf1Y

Locke, E. A., & Latham, G. P. (2013). *Goal setting theory, 1990.* In E. A. Locke & G. P. Latham (Eds.), *New developments in goal setting and task performance* (pp. 3–15). Routledge/Taylor & Francis Group.

Luttenberger, S., Wimmer, S., & Paechter, M. (2018). Spotlight on math anxiety. *Psychology Research and Behavior Management*, 11, 311–322.

McEwan, E. K. (2004). *Seven strategies of highly effective readers: Using cognitive research to boost K–8 achievement.* Corwin.

McMillan, J. H., & Hearn, J. (2008). Student self-assessment: The key to stronger student motivation and higher achievement. *Educational Horizons*, 87(1), 40–49.

McTighe, J. (2021, January). *8 quick checks for understanding.* Edutopia. https://www.edutopia.org/article/8-quick-checks-understanding/

Moore, K. (2022, December). *The impact of closing routine protocols on engagement and sense of belonging among 8th grade students* (Action Research Report). Master of Arts in Social and Emotional Learning, National University.

Muhammad, G. (2020). *Cultivating genius: An equity framework for culturally and historically responsive literacy.* Scholastic.

Ogle, D. (1986). K-W-L: A teaching model that develops active reading of expository text. *The Reading Teacher*, 39, 564–570.

Organisation for Economic Co-operation and Development (OECD). (2013). *PISA 2012 results: Ready to learn (Volume III): Students' engagement, drive and self-beliefs.* OECD Publishing.

Perry, K., Weimar, H., & Bell, M. A. (2017). *Sketchnoting in school: Discover the benefits (and fun) of visual note taking.* Rowman & Littlefield.

Pressley, M., El-Dinary, P. B., Gaskins, I., Schuder, T., Bergman, J. L., Almasi, J., & Brown, R. (1992). Beyond direct explanation: Transactional instruction of reading comprehension strategies. *The Elementary School Journal*, 92(5), 513–555.

Price, R., & Stern, L. (1953/2008). *Best of Mad Libs: World's greatest word game.* Penguin.

Quinzio-Zafran, A. M., & Wilkins, E. A. (2020). *The new teacher's guide to overcoming common challenges: Curated advice from award-winning teachers.* Routledge.

Ramlal, A., & Augustin, D. S. (2020). Engaging students in reflective writing: An action research project. *Educational Action Research, 28*(3), 518–533. https://doi.org/10.1080/09650792.2019.1595079

Rivers, S. E., & Brackett, M. A. (2011). Achieving standards in the English language arts (and more) using the RULER Approach to social and emotional learning. *Reading & Writing Quarterly, 27*(1–2), 75–100. https://doi.org/10.1080/10573569.2011.532715

Robertson, S. (2022, July). *The foundation of an effective social and emotional learning classroom* (Action Research Report). National University, Master of Arts in Social and Emotional Learning.

Roe, C. (2014). Teaching difficult text: Using close reading for text success. *The Reading Teacher, 68*(4), 266.

Russell, J. A. (1980). A circumplex model of affect. University of Vermont Press.

Russell, J. A., & Barrett, L. F. (1999). Core affect, prototypical emotional episodes, and other things called *emotion*: Dissecting the elephant. *Journal of Personality and Social Psychology, 76*(5), 805–819. https://doi.org/10.1037/0022-3514.76.5.805

Schwartz, K. (2019, November 3). Why teachers are so excited about the power of sketchnoting. *KQED.* https://www.kqed.org/mindshift/54655/why-teachers-are-so-excited-about-the-power-of-sketchnoting

Statista.com. (2022). 31 million blogs. https://www.statista.com/

Tan, K. (2007). Conceptions of self-assessment: What is needed for long-term learning? In D. Boud & N. Falchikov (Eds.), *Rethinking assessment in higher education* (pp. 124–137). Routledge.

Thomas-Brown, E. K. (2022). *The impact of social emotional learning interventions on student behavior and achievement* [Dissertation]. Wilmington University.

https://www.proquest.com/openview/24e23fcf944a431b395b8265d02544a7/1?pq-origsite=gscholar&cbl=18750&diss=y

Vygotsky, L. S., & Cole, M. (1978). *Mind in society: Development of higher psychological processes.* Harvard University Press.

Westby, C. (2013). Sentence frames for developing academic syntax. *Word of Mouth, 25*(2), 13–14. https://doi.org/10.1177/1048395013503808d

Yoder, N. (2014, February). *Self-assessing social and emotional instruction and competencies.* American Institutes for Research. https://www.air.org/resource/self-assessing-social-and-emotional-instruction-and-competencies-tool-teachers

CHAPTER 7

Almaki, S. H., Gunda, M. A., Idris, K., Hashim, A. T. M., & Ali, S. R. (2023). A systematic review of the use of simulation games in K–12 education. *Interactive Learning Environments*, 1–25.

Brown, T., Mann, B., Ryder, N., Subbiah, M., Kaplan, J. D., Dhariwal, P., Neelakantan, A., Shyam, P., Sastry, G., Askell, A., Agarwal, S., Herbert-Voss, A., Krueger, G., Henighan, T., Child, R., Ramesh, A., Ziegler, D., Wu, J., Winter, C., . . . , & Amodei, D. (2020). Language models are few-shot learners. *Advances in Neural Information Processing Systems, 33,* 1877–1901. https://arxiv.org/pdf/2005.14165.pdf

Bunderson, C. V., Inouye, D. K., & Olsen, J. B. (1998). *The four generations of computerized educational measurement.* Educational Testing Services.

Dana, N. F., & Yendol-Hoppey, D. (2008). *The reflective educator's guide to professional development: Coaching inquiry-oriented learning communities.* Corwin.

DeLuca, C., & Volante, L. (2016). Assessment for learning in teacher education programs: Navigating the juxtaposition of theory and praxis. *Journal of the International Society for Teacher Education, 20*(1), 19–31.

DeLuca, D., & Klinger, D. A. (2010). Assessment literacy development: Identifying gaps in teacher candidates' learning. *Assessment in Education: Principles, Policy & Practice, 17*(4), 419–438. https://doi.org/10.1080/0969594X.2010.516643

Dewey, J. (1966). *The middle works of John Dewey, 9, 1899–1924: Democracy and education (1916)* (J. A. Boydston, Ed.). Southern Illinois University Press.

Dowker, A., Sarkar, A., & Looi, C. Y. (2016). Mathematics anxiety: What have we learned in 60 years? *Frontiers in Psychology, 7*, 508. https://doi.org/10.3389/fpsyg.2016.00508

DuFour, R., & Reeves, D. (2016). The futility of PLC Lite. *Phi Delta Kappan, 97*(6), 69–71. https://doi.org/10.1177/0031721716636878

Dyer, C. (2022, January 18). 27 easy formative assessment strategies for gathering evidence of student learning. *NWEA Blog.* https://www.nwea.org/blog/2022/27-easy-formative-assessment-strategies-for-gathering-evidence-of-student-learning/

Elliott, E. S., & Dweck, C. S. (1988). Goals: An approach to motivation and achievement. *Journal of Personality and Social Psychology, 54*, 5–12. https://doi.org/10.1037/0022-3514.54.1.5

Epstein, A. S., Schweinhart, L. J., DeBruin-Parecki, A., & Robin, K. B. (2004). *Preschool assessment: A guide to developing a balanced approach* (NIEER Preschool for Policy Brief, Issue 7). National Institute for Early Education Research.

Farrell, T. S. C. (2003). *Reflective practice in action: 80 reflection breaks for busy teachers.* Sage.

Koster, M. A., & Soffler, M. (2021). Navigate the challenges of simulation for assessment: A faculty development workshop. *MedEdPORTAL, 17*, 11114.

Landriscina, F. (2013). *Simulation and learning: A model-centered approach.* Springer. https://doi.org/10.1007/978-1-4614-1954-9

Learning for Justice. (n.d.). *Social justice standards: Unpacking identity, professional development.* https://www.learningforjustice.org/professional-development/social-justice-standards-unpacking-identity

Moradkhani, S., Raygan, A., & Moein, M. S. (2017). Iranian EFL teachers' reflective practices and self-efficacy: Exploring possible relationships. *System, 65*, 1–14. https://doi.org/10.1016/j.system.2016.12.011

Nordengren, C., Mabry, B., Underwood, S., Beard, E., Wells, L., & McCoy, V. (2021). *Making it work: How formative assessment can supercharge your practice.* NWEA. https://www.nwea.org/resource-center/ebook/47433/Making-it-work-How-formative-assessment-can-supercharge-your-practice_NWEA_ebook-1.pdf/

Olson, L. (2019). *The new testing landscape: How state assessments are changing under the federal Every Student Succeeds Act.* FutureEd.

PhET Interactive Simulations. (n.d.). https://phet.colorado.edu/

Schrock, K. (n.d.). *Kathy Schrock's guide to everything: Assessments and rubrics.* https://www.schrockguide.net/

SimSchool. (n.d.). https://simschool.org/home/simschool

Steinaker, N., & Bell, M. R. (1979). *Experiential taxonomy: A new approach to teaching and learning.* Academic Press Inc.

Suppes, P., & Macken, E. (1978). The historical path from research and development to the operational use of CAI. *Educational Technology, 18*(4), 9–12.

Thorpe, K. (2004). Reflective learning journals: From concept to practice. *Reflective Practice, 5*(3), 327–343. https://doi.org/10.1080/1462394042000270655

Victoria State Government. (n.d.). *Teacher self-reflection and approaches to peer observations.* https://www.education.vic.gov.au/school/teachers/classrooms/Pages/approachesppnpeerobstip.aspx

von Davier, A. A., Mislevy, R. J., & Hao, J. (Eds). (2021). *Computational psychometrics: New methodologies for a new generation of digital learning and assessment. methodology of educational measurement and assessment.* Springer.

CHAPTER 8

Dana, N. F., & Yendol-Hoppey, D. (2008). *The reflective educator's guide to professional* development: *Coaching inquiry-oriented learning communities*. Corwin.

Dewey, J. (1933). *How we think*. D. C. Heath and Company.

Dewey, J. (1958). *Experience and nature*. Dover Publications.

Dewey, J. (1966). *The middle works of John Dewey, 9, 1899–1924: Democracy and education (1916)* (J. A. Boydston, Ed.). Southern Illinois University Press.

DuFour, R., & Eaker, R. (1998). *Professional learning communities at work: Best practices for enhancing student achievement*. Solution Tree.

Farrell, T. S. C. (2003). *Reflective practice in action: 80 reflection breaks for busy teachers*. Sage.

Farrell, T. S. C. (2016). Teacher researchers in action. *ELT Journal, 70*(3), 352–355. https://doi.org/10.1093/elt/ccw034

Januszka, D. (2022, October). *The effects of systematic reflection on teacher SEL skills* (Action Research Report). Master of Arts in Social and Emotional Learning, National University.

Korthagen, F. A. J. (1993, June). Two modes of reflection. *Teaching and Teacher Education 9*(3), 317–326. https://doi.org/10.1016/0742-051X(93)90046-J

Malone, K. (2020, September 2). Strategies for teaching metacognition in the classroom. *Graduate Programs for Educators*. https://www.graduateprogram.org/2020/09/strategies-for-teaching-metacognition-in-the-classroom/#:~:text=Teachers%20can%20facilitate%20metacognition%20by,building%20these%20skills%20in%20students

Mlinac, M. E., & Feng, M. C. (2016). Assessment of activities of daily living, self-care, and independence. *Archives of Clinical Neuropsychology, 31*(6), 506–516.

Nordengren, C., Mabry, B., Underwood, S., Beard, E., Wells, L., & McCoy, V. (2021). *Making it work: How formative assessment can supercharge your practice*. NWEA. https://www.nwea.org/resource-center/ebook/47433/Making-it-work-How-formative-assessment-can-supercharge-your-practice_NWEA_ebook-1.pdf/

Olson, L. (2019). *The new testing landscape: How state assessments are changing under* the federal Every Student Succeeds Act. FutureEd.

Restifo, D. (2021, April 21). *Best free formative assessment tools*. Tech & Learning. https://www.techlearning.com/how-to/formative-assessment-tools-and-apps

Robertson, S. (2022, July). *The foundation of an effective social and emotional learning classroom* (Action Research Report). Master of Arts in Social and Emotional Learning, National University.

Suppes, P., & Macken, E. (1978). The historical path from research and development to the operational use of CAI. *Educational Technology, 18*(4), 9–12.

Thomas, L. (2019, April 26). *7 smart, fast ways to do formative assessment*. Edutopia. https://www.edutopia.org/article/7-smart-fast-ways-do-formative-assessment?gclid=CjwKCAiAwomeBhBWEiwAM43YIAL3oi-0RhtPap12Pcwer8PyP5vsjiPbdvGvpWH5bp22Lpfp2ia2YhoC9s4QAvD_BwE

Thorpe, K. (2004). Reflective learning journals: From concept to practice. *Reflective Practice, 5*(3), 327–343. https://doi.org/10.1080/1462394042000270655

US Department of Education. (2018). Partnership for Assessment of Readiness for College and Careers. https://files.eric.ed.gov/fulltext/ED599198.pdf

Van Diggelen, M., den Brok, P., & Beijaard, D. (2013). Teachers' use of a self-assessment procedure: The role of criteria, standards, feedback and reflection. *Teachers and Teaching, 19*(2), 115–134. https://doi.org/10.1080/13540602.2013.741834

CHAPTER 9

American Institutes for Research (AIR). (2019). *Are you ready to assess social and emotional learning and development?* https://www.air.org/resource/are-you-ready-assess-social-and-emotional-learning-and-development-second-edition

Bronfenbrenner, U. (1979). *The ecology of human development: Experiments by nature and design*. Harvard University Press.

CASEL. https://www.casel.org

CASEL. (n.d.). *CASEL assessment guide: A sample of tools that assess SEL in educational settings, assessment work group, collaborative for academic, social, and emotional learning.* https://casel.org/state-resource-center/assessment-tools/

Center for Child & Family Well-Being. (n.d.). *Bronfenbrenner's bioecological model of human development.* University of Washington. https://ccfwb.uw.edu/about-us/the-bioecological-model/#:~:text=The%20bioecological%20model%20is%20based,%2C%20cultural%2C%20and%20policy%20conditions

Council of Chief State School Officers. (2013). *InTASC model core teaching standards and learning progressions for teachers.* https://ccsso.org/resource-library/intasc-model-core-teaching-standards-and-learning-progressions-teachers-10

Ecological Approaches to Social Emotional Learning (EASEL) Laboratory. https://easel.gse.harvard.edu/

Ecological Approaches to Social Emotional Learning (EASEL) Laboratory. (n.d.). *About.* https://easel.gse.harvard.edu/about

Grant, C. A., & Gillette, M. D. (2006). *Learning to teach everyone's children: Equity, empowerment, and education that is multicultural* (pp. 76–79). Thompson Wadsworth.

McKown, C. (2018, October 4). *6 steps to effective SEL assessment.* ASCD. https://www.ascd.org/el/articles/six-steps-to-effective-sel-assessment

RAND. (n.d.). *RAND education assessment finder.* https://www.rand.org/education-and-labor/projects/assessments.html

xSEL Labs. https://xsel-labs.com/

CHAPTER 10

Bradbury-Huang, H. (2010). What is good action research? *Action Research, 8*(1), 93–109.

Carr, W., & Kemmis, S. (1986). *Becoming critical: Education, knowledge, and action research.* Falmer Press.

Cronin, J., & Hegedus, A. (2016). *Multiple measures done right: The seven principles of a coherent assessment system.* NWEA.

Curriculum Associates. (2011). *I-Ready diagnostic assessments.* https://www.curriculumassociates.com/programs/i-ready-assessment/diagnostic

Dana, N. F., & Yendol-Hoppey, D. (2008). *The reflective educator's guide to professional development: Coaching inquiry-oriented learning communities.* Corwin.

Dwyer, C. A. & Jackson, A. (2007). The National Comprehensive Center for Teacher Quality: A resource for systemic improvement in the equitable distribution of teachers. In C. Dwyer (Ed.), *America's challenge: Effective teachers for at-risk schools and students* (pp. 105–107). National Comprehensive Center for Teacher Quality.

edTPA. https://www.edtpa.com/Home.aspx

Elliott, E. S., & Dweck, C. S. (1988). Goals: An approach to motivation and achievement. *Journal of Personality and Social Psychology, 54*, 5–12. https://doi.org/10.1037/0022-3514.54.1.5

Estner, H., Fox, K., & McLean, E. (2018). *Social and emotional learning observation rubric.* https://www.lrs.org/wp-content/uploads/2019/02/SEL_Rubric_Estner_Fox_McLean-1.pdf?lrspdfmetric=no

Gerber, J. (2022, May). *Developing emotional vocabulary and self-regulation through morning meetings* (Action Research Report). Master of Arts in Social and Emotional Learning, National University.

Gitomer, D. H., Martínez, J. F., Battey, D., & Hyland, N. E. (2021). Assessing the assessment: Evidence of reliability and validity in the edTPA. *American Educational Research Journal, 58*(1), 3–31.

Goe, L., Bell, C., & Little, O. (2008). *Approaches to evaluating teacher effectiveness: A research synthesis.* National Comprehensive Center for Teacher Quality.

Harvey, H., & Ohle, K. (2018). What's the purpose? Educators' perceptions and use of a state-mandated kindergarten entry assessment. *Education Policy Analysis Archives, 26*(142), n142.

Hernandez, A. (2022, May). *Building inclusiveness and relationships through a peer helper program* (Action Research Report). Master of Arts in Social and Emotional Learning, National University.

Holden, J. (2021, May). *Assessing SEL in middle school, supporting those with math anxiety through social emotional learning strategies* (Action Research Report). Master of Arts in Social and Emotional Learning, National University.

Movsisyan, H. (2022, April). *Mindfulness as a tool: Strengthening inhibitory control in preschoolers through self-awareness* (Action Research Report). Master of Arts in Social and Emotional Learning, National University.

National Task Force on Assessment in Education for Teachers. (2012). *Definition of assessment literacy.* https://www.nwea.org/news-center/press-releases/8776/

Peer Assistance and Leadership (PAL). http://palusa.org

Ponitz, C. C., McClelland, M. M., Matthews, J. S., & Morrison, F. J. (2009). A structured observation of behavioral self-regulation and its contribution to kindergarten outcomes. *Developmental Psychology, 45*(3), 605.

Richardson, F. C., & Suinn, R. M. (1972). The mathematics anxiety rating scale: Psychometric data. *Journal of Counseling Psychology, 19*(6), 551.

Rosebrough, T. R., & Leverett, R. G. (2011). *Transformational teaching in the information age: Making why and how we teach relevant to students.* ASCD.

Sagor, R., & Williams, C. (2017). *The action research guidebook.* Corwin.

SB 1381, 2009–2010 Reg. Sess. (Calif. 2010). http://www.leginfo.ca.gov/pub/09-10/bill/sen/sb_1351-1400/sb_1381_bill_20100930_chaptered.pdf

Sima, K. (2022, May). *The impact of morning meetings in an early childhood classroom* (Action Research Report). Master of Arts in Social and Emotional Learning, National University.

Watson, T. (2022, April). *Development of social awareness and relationship skills in primary elementary* (Action Research Report). Master of Arts in Social and Emotional Learning, National University.

CHAPTER 11

All4Ed. (n.d.). *Future ready framework.* https://futureready.org/ourwork/future-ready-frameworks/

Bailey, K. (2021). *Moving forward with purpose: Increasing physical activity for school wellness.* Repository [Dissertation]. University of Pennsylvania.

Barrett, S., Eber, L., McIntosh, K., Perales, K., & Romer, N. (2018). *Teaching social-emotional competencies within a PBIS framework.* OSEP Technical Assistance Center on Positive Behavioral Interventions and Supports.

Berg, J., Osher, D., Same, M. R., Nolan, E., Benson, D., & Jacobs, N. (2017, December). *Identifying, defining, and measuring social and emotional competencies: Final Report* (pp. 33–36). American Institutes for Research.

Blythe, D. A., Jones, S. M., & Borowski, T. (2018). *SEL frameworks—What are they and why are they important?* CASEL. https://measuringsel.casel.org/wp-content/uploads/2018/09/Frameworks--A.1.pdf

California Department of Education. (2016). *History-social science framework.* https://www.cde.ca.gov/ci/hs/cf/hssframework.asp

Casillas, A., Roberts, B., Jones, S. (2022). *Assessing competencies for social and emotional learning: Conceptualization, development, and applications.* Routledge.

Cipriano, C., Strambler, M. J., Naples, L. H., Ha, C., Kirk, M., Wood, M., . . . & Durlak, J. (2023). The state of evidence for social and emotional learning: A contemporary meta-analysis of universal school-based SEL interventions. *Child Development, 94*(5), 1181–1204.

Council of Chief State School Officers. (2010). National Governors Association Center for Best Practices, Council of Chief State School Officers.

Council of Chief State School Officers. (2013). *Interstate Teacher Assessment and Support Consortium (InTASC) model core teaching standards and learning progressions for teachers 1.0: A resource for ongoing teacher development.* Author. https://ccsso.org/sites/default/files/2017-12/2013_INTASC_Learning_Progressions_for_Teachers.pdf

Denham, S. A. (2018). *Keeping SEL developmental: The importance of a developmental lens for fostering and assessing SEL competencies.* Measuring SEL.

Division of Population Health. (2020). *Whole school, whole community, whole child model.* Centers for Disease Control and Prevention. https://www.cdc.gov/NCCDPHP/dph

Durlak, J. A., Weissberg, R. P., Dymnicki, A. B., Taylor, R. D., & Schellinger, K. B. (2011). The impact of enhancing students' social and emotional learning: A meta-analysis of school-based universal interventions. *Child Development, 82*(1), 405–432.

Ecological Approaches to Social Emotional Learning (EASEL) Laboratory. (n.d.). *About.* https://easel.gse.harvard.edu/about

Frey, N., Fisher, D., & Smith, D. (2019). *All learning is social and emotional: Helping students develop essential skills for the classroom and beyond.* ASCD.

Greenberg, M. T., Domitrovich, C. E., Weissberg, R. P., & Durlak, J. A. (2017). Social and emotional learning as a public health approach to education. *The Future of Children, 27*(1), 13–32.

Merrell, K. W., & Gueldner, B. A. (2010). Preventive interventions for students with internalizing disorders: Effective strategies for promoting mental health in schools. In H. M. Walker & M. R. Shinn (Eds.), *Interventions for achievement and behavior problems in a three-tier model including RTI* (pp. 799–824). National Academies Guide to Implementing.

National Research Council. (2015). *Guide to implementing the Next Generation Science Standards* (pp. 8–9). National Academies Press.

Next Generation Science Storylines (NGSS). (n.d.) *How does light help me see things and communicate with others? (v2.0) Grade 1.* https://www.nextgenstorylines.org/how-does-light-help-me-see-and-communicate

Sidorowicz, K., & Yang, A. (2021). Strengthening college and career readiness with social and emotional learning: Integrating explicit SEL in CTE. In T. Madden-Dent & D. Oliver, *Leading schools with social, emotional, and academic development (SEAD)* (pp. 247–272). IGI Global.

Smith, A. (2020). *Connecting social-emotional learning (SEL) to career success.* Association for Career and Technical Education.

Soto, C. J., Napolitano, C. M., Sewell, M. N., Yoon, H. J., & Roberts, B. W. (2022). An integrative framework for conceptualizing and assessing social, emotional, and behavioral skills: The BESSI. *Journal of Personality and Social Psychology, 123,* 192–222.

Yoder, N., Atwell, M. N., Godek, D., Dusenbury, L., Bridgeland, J. M., & Weissberg, R. (2020). *Preparing youth for the workforce of tomorrow: Cultivating the social and emotional skills employers demand. SEL for workforce development.* CASEL.

APPENDIX

All the Feelz. (n.d.). *The feelings wheel.* https://allthefeelz.app/feeling-wheel/#recommended_uses

CASEL. https://www.casel.org

Council of Chief State School Officers. (2013, April). *Interstate teacher assessment and support consortium (InTASC) model core teaching standards and learning progressions for teachers 1.0: A resource for ongoing teacher development.* Author.

Dusenbury, L., Yoder, N., Dermody, C., & Weissberg, R. (2020, March). *Framework briefs: An examination of K–12 SEL learning competencies/standards in 18 states.* CASEL.

Honig, M. I. (2013). *Creating your theory of action for districtwide teaching and learning improvement.* University of Washington Center for Educational Leadership.

Movsisyan, H. (2022, April). *Mindfulness as a tool: Strengthening inhibitory control in preschoolers through self-awareness* (Action Research Report). Master of Arts in Social and Emotional Learning, National University.

Willcox, G. (1982). The feelings wheel. *Transactional Analysis Journal, 12*(4), 274–276. https://doi.org/10.1177/036215378201200411

Index

ACTE (Association for Career and Technical Education), 176
Action research, 112, 116, 142–44, 147, 155, 183
  embedding teacher, 144
  ongoing teacher, 141
  studies, 83, 141, 145, 151, 157, 159
ADP (Alaska Developmental Profile), 148
Alaska Developmental Profile (ADP), 148
Almaki, S. H., 104–5
Association for Career and Technical Education (ACTE), 176

Belonging, 36, 83, 141, 154, 156, 164–65, 175
Bias, 39, 41–42, 50–51, 53–56, 62, 176
  gender, 43
  implicit, 52, 54, 58–59
  role of, 41
BrainPOP, 103, 107
Brains, 10, 35, 74, 79, 82, 93, 113

CAI (computer-aided instruction), 97
Cards, 65, 67–68
Careers, 1, 162, 164, 176–77
  readiness skills, 177
  technical education. See CTE
CASEL (Collaborative for Academic, Social, and Emotional Learning), 10–11, 13, 20, 24, 82, 121, 138, 164–65, 176–77, 189–90, 216
  Competencies, 132, 177, 179
Case studies, 144–46, 150–52, 154, 183
CAST, 61–62
CBT (computer-based tests), 97–98
CFU, 65–68
ChatGPT, 108–9
Check-ins, 75–76, 79, 94
  emotional, 76, 79, 94, 153
Child Observation Record (COR), 160
ClassFlow, 101, 107
cognitive growth, 20, 130
Collaborative for Academic, Social, and Emotional Learning. See CASEL
Common Core State Standards, 98, 163–64

Community, sense of, 109, 204
Competencies
  emotional, 7, 19, 119, 130
  first student-focused, 132
  impact student learning, 24
  and learning progressions, 126
  student SEL, 24, 138
Computer-aided instruction (CAI), 97
Computer-based tests (CBT), 97–98
Confidence, 109, 136, 164–65, 182
Content areas, 81, 88, 98, 102–3, 184, 222
Content standards, 57–58, 161, 164, 184–85, 222
Conversations, 22, 32–34, 37, 108, 121, 123, 128, 137, 151
COR (Child Observation Record), 160
CTE (career technical education), 162, 176–77

DECA (Devereux Early Childhood Assessment), 160
Desired Results Developmental Profile (DRDP), 160
Developing Skills Checklist (DSC), 160
Development
  emotional, 12–13, 55
  human, 28, 136, 139, 163, 178–79
Devereux Early Childhood Assessment (DECA), 160
Dewey, J., 90, 115, 117
Digital tools, 2, 69, 84, 96–110
Disabilities, 63, 154
Diversity, 52, 56–57, 59, 62–63, 166–67, 169–70
DRDP (Desired Results Developmental Profile), 160
DSC (Developing Skills Checklist), 160

EASEL (Ecological Approaches to Social Emotional Learning), 138–39, 164, 178–79
Ecological Approaches to Social Emotional Learning. See EASEL

245

Elementary and Secondary Education Act (ESEA), 64
emotions
  continuum of, 132, 217
  experience, 82, 92
  identifying, 79, 131–32, 217
  inappropriate, 218
  practice navigating, 79
  skills, 9, 58, 81, 145, 174
  social functions of, 81
English learners, 63, 85
Environment, simulated, 104–6, 108
EQ, 8, 10
ESEA (Elementary and Secondary Education Act), 64
ESSA (Every Student Succeeds Act), 98
Ethics, 9, 110, 180, 182
Everyday SEL Practice, 17, 19, 21, 23, 25
Every Student Succeeds Act (ESSA), 98
Exit tickets, 76, 82–84, 91, 94

Failure, 6, 71–74, 90
Families, 9, 20, 22, 31, 127, 130, 165, 173, 178
Feldman, J., 58–59, 73
Flow, 131, 201, 212–13
Fowler, K., 76, 82
Frameworks, 12, 20, 34, 61, 85, 130, 161–64, 173, 175–78
  developmental, 177
  effective, 163
  rigor, 34–35
Frayer Model, 151, 224
Freedom, 169–70, 182, 184

Gaslighting, 55
Gender, 42–44, 109
  bias, unconscious, 43
Generations, 97–98
Goal setting, 17, 62, 75, 77–78, 93, 118–19, 164
GoClass, 101, 107
Grading, 17, 23, 40–44, 50–52, 59, 70, 73, 126
  equitable, 52, 59
  practices, 40–41, 44, 46–48, 51
  systems, traditional, 45
Graduate students, 72, 143–44, 179, 198, 216

Head-Toes-Knees-Shoulders (HTKS), 147
Health, 12, 103, 162–63, 173–75, 178
  education, 13, 106, 173
History, 40, 52, 73, 96, 98, 165–66, 168, 171
  history-social sciences (HSS), 162, 165

Holden, J., 71, 150, 152–53, 155
HSS (history-social sciences), 162, 165
HTKS (Head-Toes-Knees-Shoulders), 147

Impulses, controlling, 147–48, 155
Information Processing, 34–35
Inhibitory control, 146–48, 155, 221
Instruments, 123, 133, 146, 150–51, 153–54
InTASC (Interstate Teacher Assessment and Support Consortium), 139, 180–81
Intelligence, 40, 72, 74–75
  artificial, 97, 99, 104–5, 108
  emotional, 8, 10, 79
  intelligent tutoring systems, 100, 108
Internet, 97, 99, 108
Interstate New Teacher Assessment and Support Consortium, 139
Interstate Teacher Assessment and Support Consortium (InTASC), 139, 180–81
Interventions, 139
i-Ready, 103, 107, 153, 155

Januszka, D., 116, 118–19
Journals, 15, 23, 77, 84, 88, 90–92, 94, 114, 172

Key concepts, 92, 166–72
Kindergarten, 148, 157, 164–66, 171
Knowledge
  building, 100
  creation, 142
  essential, 9, 21, 117, 131–33, 181, 216–20
  gaining, 22–23
  individual, 134

Lack, 14, 46, 55, 57–58, 104, 130
Language
  racist, 40, 54
  Language and Emergent Literacy Assessment (LELA), 160
LGBTQ+ students, 43
Lifelong learning, 111, 113
Literacy
  assessment, 75, 135, 157–58
  emotional, 8–10, 64, 80, 84, 151, 175

Machine learning, 97, 110
Mastery, 2, 45–48, 57, 153, 155
  learning, 52, 72–73, 94
Mathematics, 71, 85, 105, 152, 163–64
  math anxiety, 71, 150, 152, 155

Metacognition, 24, 77, 90, 113
Metaverse, 97, 106–8
Mindfulness, 90, 144, 146–47, 155
Mindsets
    fixed, 74, 136
    growth, 14, 71–72, 74–75, 136, 153, 218–19
Morning Meetings, 1, 144–45, 150–51, 155
    impact of, 144–45
Motivation, 17, 26, 70, 75, 78, 88, 136, 169

National Center on Educational Outcomes (NCEO), 63
National Education Association (NEA), 49, 182
National Health Education Standards (NHES), 173

Observations, 31, 120–21, 133, 135, 147, 158
OECD (Organisation for Economic Co-operation and Development), 71
OLE (online learning environment), 109

Padlets, 102, 107
PALS (Phonological Awareness and Literacy Screenings), 154, 156, 160
PARCC (Partnership for Assessment of Readiness for College and Careers), 64, 99
Partnership for Assessment of Readiness for College and Careers (PARCC), 64, 99
PBIS (Positive Behavioral Interventions and Supports), 164, 175
PE. *See* physical education
PEE (prototypical emotion episodes), 80
Peers
    helper programs, 150, 154, 156
    observation, 120, 123
    review, 56, 79, 120
Phonological Awareness and Literacy Screenings (PALS), 154, 156, 160
Physical education (PE), 13, 162–63, 173–74
Planning, 19, 77, 112, 117, 126, 135, 154, 197, 222
PLCs (professional learning community), 120
Plutchik's Wheel of Emotion, 80, 190
Polls, 96, 100–103, 107
Positive Behavioral Interventions and Supports (PBIS), 164, 175
Posters, 36, 172, 223
Preschool, 116, 144–48, 155, 221
Principles of design, 212

Procedural Genre Frames, 86–87
Professional learning community (PLCs), 120
Programs, 14, 83, 108, 129, 142–43, 154, 156, 162, 174–76, 198
    teacher education, 105, 142, 156–58
Progress
    monitoring, 131, 217, 220
    student, 32, 52
Progressions, 33, 72, 128, 130, 216
Prototypical emotion episodes (PEE), 80

Questions, open-ended, 101, 172
Quizlet, 102, 107
Quizzes, 39, 46, 48, 65, 87, 96, 101–3, 107

Race, 35, 40–42, 56, 64, 109, 169
Racism, 39–40, 53–54, 58
    racist language, 40, 54
Reality, virtual, 97, 104–5, 108
Reflection, Five Rs of, 115–16
Reflective practice, 90, 94, 114–15, 117–18, 123
Relationships
    building, 7, 154, 156, 164–68, 172–74, 177, 179
    skills, 20, 30, 127, 145, 150–51, 155–56, 169, 173
    student-teacher, 55, 145
Researchers, 10, 146–48, 151–53, 155–56
Responsible Decision-Making, 76, 173
Rights, 157, 166, 170–71
Rigor Framework, 34–35

SBAC (SMARTER Balanced Assessment Consortium), 64
Scenarios, 23, 53–54, 56, 108
Self-regulation, 7, 77, 88–89, 150–51, 153, 155
Sentences, 68, 85
    frames, 75–76, 84–85
    starters, 68, 85–86
Simulations, 104–7, 110
    SGs (simulation games), 104
    simSchool, 105, 107
SMARTER Balanced Assessment Consortium (SBAC), 64
SMART Goals, 76, 78, 94
Social awareness, 7, 10, 19–20, 30, 58, 127, 150–51, 154–56, 166, 169–71
    and relationship skills, 145, 150, 155
Social justice, 8, 166, 170

Index   247

Social media, 54, 102
Social reform, 158
Social sciences, 105, 142, 162–63
Social services, 11, 13, 31, 127
Social skills, 10–11, 176
Social studies, 85, 103
Solutions, 19, 40, 53–56, 73, 106, 159, 206
SSA. *See* student self-assessment
Standardized tests, 40–41, 45, 97–98
Standards-based grading, 45, 48, 176
Stereotypes, 56–58
Stiggins, R., 22, 27, 32–33
Stories, 1, 23, 68, 87, 149, 166–67, 209, 218, 223
Strengths, identifying, 117–18
Student self-assessment (SSA), 30, 77, 88, 90, 94, 127
Student voices, 17, 27, 29, 34–37
    community building and inclusion of, 34
Subcompetencies, 131–32, 217–20
Summative assessments, 62–65, 73, 99

Teacher action research, 114, 116, 141, 143–44
    impact of, 141
    inquiry for, 114
Technology, 1, 65, 69, 97, 103, 106, 168, 173
Templates, 2, 75, 86–87, 101, 123, 187, 190, 194, 196, 199, 213
Theory of action, 197, 199

TK (transitional K), 20, 142, 148
Training, 57, 106, 154
Transitional K (TK), 20, 142, 148
Tutors, intelligent, 97, 108

UDL (Universal Design for Learning), 18, 60–62, 69, 172, 176, 202

Virtual reality (VR), 97, 104–8
Virtual worlds, 104, 106, 108, 110
Vocabulary, 74, 85, 87, 198
    emotional, 81, 151
    student emotional, 146
VR. *See* virtual reality
Vygotsky, L., 9, 72

Weaknesses, 33, 45, 47, 109, 114, 117–18, 135
Wellness, 45, 163, 173–74
Whole School, Whole Community, Whole Child (WSCC), 9–12, 80, 174–75
    Model, 12–13, 174
Work Sampling System (WSS), 160
WSS (Work Sampling System), 160

YMCA (Young Men's Christian Association), 8–9

Zone of Proximal Development (ZPD), 72, 76, 80, 100, 151, 190

Solutions YOU WANT | Experts YOU TRUST | Results YOU NEED

INSTITUTES
Corwin Institutes provide regional and virtual events where educators collaborate with peers and learn from industry experts. Prepare to be recharged and motivated!

corwin.com/institutes

ON-SITE PROFESSIONAL LEARNING
Corwin on-site PD is delivered through high-energy keynotes, practical workshops, and custom coaching services designed to support knowledge development and implementation.

www.corwin.com/pd

VIRTUAL PROFESSIONAL LEARNING
Our virtual PD combines live expert facilitation with the flexibility of anytime, anywhere professional learning. See the power of intentionally designed virtual PD.

www.corwin.com/virtualworkshops

CORWIN ONLINE
Online learning designed to engage, inform, challenge, and inspire. Our courses offer practical, classroom-focused instruction that will meet your continuing education needs and enhance your practice.

www.corwinonline.com

Visit www.corwin.com

Helping educators make the greatest impact

CORWIN HAS ONE MISSION: to enhance education through intentional professional learning.

We build long-term relationships with our authors, educators, clients, and associations who partner with us to develop and continuously improve the best evidence-based practices that establish and support lifelong learning.